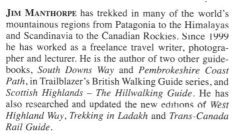

JIM MANTHORPE has trekked in many of the world's mountainous regions from Patagonia to the Himalayas and Scandinavia to the Canadian Rockies. Since 1999 he has worked as a freelance travel writer, photographer and lecturer. He is the author of two other guidebooks, *South Downs Way* and *Pembrokeshire Coast Path*, in Trailblazer's British Walking Guide series, and *Scottish Highlands – The Hillwalking Guide*. He has also researched and updated the new editions of *West Highland Way*, *Trekking in Ladakh* and *Trans-Canada Rail Guide*.

Following stints working at Stanfords travel bookshop in London and on *The Scotsman* newspaper in Edinburgh he is now living on the far side of the waves in Knoydart on the west coast of Scotland where, when not writing, he works as a ranger.

You can contact him at www.jimmanthorpe.com.

HENRY STEDMAN researched and wrote the first edition of this book. He's been writing guidebooks for over ten years and walking for a lot longer and is the author or co-author of half a dozen titles including Trailblazer's guides to *Kilimanjaro*, *Hadrian's Wall Path* and *Trekking in the Dolomites*, *The Bradt Guide to Palestine* and the *Rough Guides* to *Indonesia* and *Southeast Asia*.

When not trekking or travelling, Henry lives in Hastings, editing other people's guidebooks and putting on weight.

Coast to Coast
First edition 2004; this second edition: 2006

Publisher
Trailblazer Publications
The Old Manse, Tower Rd, Hindhead, Surrey, GU26 6SU, UK
Fax (+44) 01428-607571, info@trailblazer-guides.com
www.trailblazer-guides.com

British Library Cataloguing in Publication Data
A catalogue record for this book is available from the British Library

ISBN 1-873756-92-5
EAN 978-1873756-928

© **Trailblazer 2004, 2006**
Text and maps

Editor: Anna Jacomb-Hood
Series editor: Anna Jacomb-Hood
Additional research: Jenny Hill
Layout: Anna Jacomb-Hood and Bryn Thomas
Proof-reading: Jim Manthorpe and Henry Stedman
Illustrations: pp62-4: Nick Hill, p66: Rev CA Johns
Photographs (flora): C1 Row 3 left and centre, C2 Row 2 centre,
C3 Row 1 centre and right, © Charlie Loram; all others © Bryn Thomas
Cartography: Nick Hill
Index: Jane Thomas

The maps in this guide were prepared from out-of-Crown-
copyright Ordnance Survey maps amended and updated by Trailblazer.

Warning: hill walking can be dangerous
Please read the notes on when to go (pp24-5) and on outdoor safety (pp52-4).
Every effort has been made by the author and publisher to ensure that the information
contained herein is as accurate and up to date as possible. However, they are unable
to accept responsibility for any inconvenience, loss, or injury sustained by anyone
as a result of the advice and information given in this guide.

Printed on chlorine-free paper from farmed forests by
D2Print (☎ +65-6295 5598), Singapore

COAST
TO
COAST
PATH

ST BEES TO ROBIN HOOD'S BAY
planning, places to stay, places to eat
includes 109 large-scale walking maps

HENRY STEDMAN

SECOND EDITION RESEARCHED AND UPDATED BY
JIM MANTHORPE

TRAILBLAZER PUBLICATIONS

Acknowledgements

From Jim Manthorpe: A big thank you to everyone at Trailblazer, particularly Henry Stedman, whose conscientious research for the first edition made my job a lot easier, and of course to the rest of the team: Bryn Thomas, Anna Jacomb-Hood and Nick Hill.

I am also very grateful to a number of fellow walkers, the likes of whom make the Coast to Coast such a wonderful trek. Firstly to Rex (UK) for his indefatigable spirit and overwhelming generosity, to Gaby (Germany), Peter (UK), John and Penny (Australia), Tony and Shirley (UK) and all the others, whose names I have forgotten, including 'The Americans'. Thank you all for your company and your help.

Thank you to all the readers who sent in their contributions and comments, notably: Gary Wiswell, Margaret Fee, Steve Lazrove, Andrew Murphy, Jason, Sue V, Ian Wallis, Josephine Collinson, David Pitt, Terry Carr, Ken Pearson, Jim Nolan, Kath and Neil Stocks, Nicola Stavrinides; particular thanks go to Paul Gurn and Eileen Synnott of the USA.

From Henry Stedman: Thanks, firstly, to Charlie for all the work he did before I even put pen to paper or foot to path. Also at Trailblazer I'm grateful to John King, Nick Hill and Jane Thomas.

Thanks also to Trish and John Pain, Bob 'Bertie Walker', Roger Edwards, Nigel Barrett, Colin and Jillian Brown, Hazel Massey and Jane, Pauline and Jimmy Bray, David Wall, Diane and Bill Riddell, all of whom provided both advice and company during the research of this book; and last, but very far from least, Rachel, Lesley and Jo, for adding a much-needed sprinkling of glamour to the trail. Huge thanks also to Dan Martin for rescuing me at the end of the first trek; to Kim Pasley – for thinking about coming; to Louise Payne – for not coming at all; and as ever to Bryn, for keeping me in work.

A request

The author and publisher have tried to ensure that this guide is as accurate and up to date as possible. Nevertheless things change. If you notice any changes or omissions that should be included in the next edition of this book, please write to Trailblazer (address on p2) or email us at info@trailblazer-guides.com. A free copy of the next edition will be sent to persons making a significant contribution.

Updated information will shortly be available on the Internet at
www.trailblazer-guides.com

Front cover: The precarious Striding Edge, as viewed from near the top of Helvellyn, England's third highest peak (see p109). © Henry Stedman

CONTENTS

INTRODUCTION

The Coast to Coast path runs between St Bees on the Irish Sea coast and Robin Hood's Bay on England's north-eastern shore. It was devised in the early 1970s by the legendary fell walker, guidebook writer and illustrator, Alfred Wainwright. At first glance it doesn't appear to be anything special. At 191½ miles (307km) it is not the longest path in the country and certainly doesn't, as some people mistakenly think, span England at its widest point. It makes no claim to being technically demanding or especially tough either – though we can safely predict that those who attempt it will find it sufficiently challenging. Nor does it, unlike the long-distance paths that run alongside Hadrian's Wall or Offa's Dyke, follow any ancient construction or border. In fact, it's not even an official National Trail.

In truth, the Coast to Coast is but one route out of an infinite number that could be devised by joining the various footpaths and byways to form a single, unbroken route across England. It's just a testing, long-distance path from one side of northern England to another that provides those who complete it with a quick snapshot of the country.

But what a snapshot that is! Around two-thirds of the walk are spent in the national parks of the Lake District, the Yorkshire Dales and the North Yorkshire Moors. These parks encompass some of the most dramatic scenery in the country, from its highest fells to its largest lakes, its most beautiful woods and its bleakest, barest moors. The walk also passes through areas alive with some of Britain's rarest wildlife, including red squirrels, pine martens and otters, and even skirts around the eyrie of England's only breeding pair of golden eagles.

Furthermore, where man has settled on the trail he has, on the whole, worked in perfect harmony with nature to produce some of England's finest villages, from elegant Grasmere to exquisite, refined Egton Bridge. The trail itself is a further example of the harmony between man and nature. The paths and bridleways that make up the trail have existed for centuries and as such, though man-made, do not feel or look like an imposition on the landscape but are very much part of it. It is a subtle distinction, and an important one.

While these paths and villages continue to thrive, in other places where man once lived and worked, nature has been allowed to reclaim the upper hand yet again: the poignant, overgrown ruins of mills and mines, of ancient Iron Age villages and mysterious stone circles are all silent witnesses to a bygone age. They punctuate the path and provide absorbing highlights along the way.

All this, and all within a trail that takes around a fortnight to complete. It's true that the Coast to Coast may not be the longest, most difficult or most recognized of long-distance trails in England. But few, if any, can match it for beauty or splendour.

About this book

This guidebook contains all the information you need. The hard work has been done for you so you can plan your trip from home without the usual pile of books, maps, guides and tourist brochures. It includes:

● All standards of accommodation from campsites to B&Bs and luxurious hotels
● Walking companies if you want an organized tour and baggage carriers if you just want your luggage carried
● Itineraries for all types of walkers
● Answers to all your questions: when to go, degree of difficulty, what to pack, and how much the whole walking holiday will cost

When you're all packed and ready to go, there's comprehensive public transport information to get you to and from the Coast to Coast path and 109 detailed maps and town plans to help you find your way along it. The route guide section includes:

● Walking times
● Reviews of campsites, bunkhouses, hostels, B&Bs, guesthouses and hotels
● Cafés, pubs, tearooms, takeaways, restaurants and shops for buying supplies
● Rail, bus and taxi information for all the villages and towns along the path
● Street plans of the main towns: St Bees, Grasmere, Shap, Orton, Kirkby Stephen, Reeth, Richmond and Robin Hood's Bay
● Historical, cultural and geographical background information

PART 1: PLANNING

About the Coast to Coast path

HISTORY

The Coast to Coast path owes its existence to one man: Alfred Wainwright. It was in 1972 that Wainwright, already renowned for his exquisitely illustrated guides to walking in the Lake District, trekked across England on a path of his own devising. It was an idea that he had been kicking around for a time: to cross his native land on a route that, as far as he was aware, would 'commit no offence against privacy nor trample on the sensitive corns of landowners and tenants'. The result of his walk, a guidebook, was originally printed by his long-time publishers *The Westmoreland Gazette* the following year. It proved hugely successful. Indeed, a full twenty years after the book was first published a spin-off television series of the trail was also made in which Wainwright himself starred, allowing a wider public to witness firsthand his wry, abrupt, earthy charm.

Wainwright reminds people in his book that his is just one of many such trails across England that could be devised, and since Wainwright's book other Coast to Coast walks have indeed been established. Yet it is still *his* trail that is by far and away the most popular, and in order to distinguish it from the others, it is now commonly known as Wainwright's Coast to Coast path.

The route has been amended slightly since 1973 mostly because, though careful to try to use only public rights of way, in a few places Wainwright's original trail actually intruded upon private land. Indeed, even today the trail does in places cross private territory, and it is only due to the largesse of the landowners that the path has remained near-enough unchanged throughout its 191$^{1}/_{2}$ miles.

Though the trail passes through three national parks, crosses the Pennine Way and at times joins with both the Lyke Wake Walk and the Cleveland Way, it is not itself one of the 15 national trails in the UK, though there are some who are campaigning for it to be included in order that it may enjoy greater protection and maintenance than it has received heretofore. Whether that ever arises remains to be seen. What is certain is that the path is one of the most popular of Britain's long-distance trails, with around 9500 people attempting it every year.

HOW DIFFICULT IS THE COAST TO COAST PATH?

The Coast to Coast path is just a long walk and there's no need for crampons, ropes or any other climbing paraphernalia. So, despite the presence of some fairly steep ascents and descents, all of them are 'walkable', and no mountaineering or climbing skills are necessary. All you need is some suitable clothing, a bit of money, a rucksack full of determination and a half-decent pair of calf muscles.

❏ Mr Coast to Coast – Alfred Wainwright

The popular perception of the man who devised the Coast to Coast path is that of a gruff, anti-social curmudgeon with little time for his fellow men, though one who admittedly knew what he was doing when it came to producing guidebooks. It's an unflattering portrait, but one that the man himself did little to destroy. Indeed, many say that he deliberately cultivated such a reputation in order to make himself unapproachable, thus allowing him to continue enjoying his beloved solitary walks without interruptions from the cagoule-clad masses who trudged the fells in his wake.

Yet this unflattering and rather dull two-dimensional description disguises a very complex man: artist, father, divorcé, pipe smoker, accountant, part-time curator at Kendal Museum, TV personality, romantic and cat-lover.

Alfred Wainwright was born in Blackburn on 17 January 1907, to a hardworking, impoverished mother and an alcoholic father. Bright and conscientious, his early years gave little clue to the talents that would later make him famous, though his neat handwriting – a feature of his guidebooks – was frequently praised by his teachers. Leaving school to work in accounts at the Borough Engineer's Office in Blackburn Town Hall, he regularly drew cartoons to entertain his colleagues. When, in December 1931, he married Ruth Holden, it seemed that Wainwright's life was set upon a course of happy – if humdrum – conformity.

Wainwright, however, never saw it like that. In particular, he quickly realized that his marriage had been a mistake and felt stifled and bored with his home life; feelings that not even the arrival of a son, Peter, could erase. His wife, though loyal, good and obedient, left Wainwright unfulfilled and any trace of romantic love that had been in the marriage at the beginning quickly drained away.

To escape the misery at home, Wainwright threw himself into his new-found hobby, fellwalking. He first visited the Lakes in 1930 and soon after was making detailed notes and drawings on the walks he made. Initially, these visits were few and far between, but a move to Kendal ten years later to take up a position as an accounting assistant allowed Wainwright to visit the Lakes virtually every weekend. Yet it wasn't until the early 1950s that Wainwright struck upon the idea of shaping his copious notes and drawings into a series of walking guides.

The idea wasn't a new one: guides to the Lakes had existed since at least the late 18th century and previous authors had included such literary luminaries as William Wordsworth. Where Wainwright's guides differed, however, was in their detail and the unique charm of their production.

For Wainwright was a publisher's dream: his writing was concise and laced with a wry humour, his ink sketches were delightful, and every page was designed and laid down by the author himself, with the text justified on both sides (and without hyphens!) around the drawings. As a result, all the publisher really needed to do was crank up the printing press, load in the paper, and hey presto! They had another bestseller on their hands.

His first seven books, a series of guides to the Lakeland fells, took fourteen years to produce and by the end had built up quite a following amongst both walkers and those who simply loved the books' beauty. Further titles followed, including one on the Pennine Way (a walk that he seemed to have enjoyed rather less than the others, possibly because at one point he had needed to be rescued by a warden after falling in a bog). As an incentive to walkers, however, he offered to buy every reader who completed the entire walk a pint, telling them to put it on his bill at the Border Hotel at the end of the Pennine Way. *(continued on p11)*

❏ Mr Coast to Coast – Alfred Wainwright

(continued from p10) The Coast to Coast was the follow-up to the Pennine Way, with the research starting in 1971 and the book published in 1973. It was a project that Wainwright seemed to have derived much greater enjoyment from (though, unfortunately, there was no offer of a free drink this time!).

While all this was going on, however, Wainwright's private life was in turmoil. Though his homelife with Ruth remained as cold as ever, Wainwright had found the love of his life in Betty McNally, who had visited him in his office on official matters sometime in 1957. For Wainwright, it was love at first sight, and he began courting Betty soon after. They married eventually in 1970, and by all accounts this union provided Wainwright with the contentment and happiness he had so signally failed to find in his first marriage. She also accompanied Wainwright on his forays into television, where his gruff, no-nonsense charm proved a big hit.

At the time of their marriage Wainwright, already 63, promised Betty ten happy years. In the event, he was able to provide her with 21, passing away on Sunday, January 20, 1991. His last wish, fulfilled two months later by Betty and his long-time friend Percy Duff, was to have his ashes scattered on Hay Stacks. At the end of his autobiography, *Ex-Fellwanderer*, he sums his life up thus:

I have had a long and wonderful innings and enjoyed a remarkable immunity from unpleasant and unwelcome incidents. ... I never had to go to be a soldier, which I would have hated. I never had to wear a uniform, which I also would have hated. ... I was never called upon to make speeches in public nor forced into the limelight; my role was that of a backroom boy, which suited me fine. I never went bald, which would have driven me into hiding. ... So, all told, I have enjoyed a charmed life, I have been well favoured. The gods smiled on me since the cradle. I have had more blessings than I could ever count.

It is, however, quite a lengthy trek. The Ramblers' Association of Great Britain officially describe the walk as 'challenging' and they're not wrong. The Lake District in particular contains many up-and-down sections that will test you to the limit; however, usually there is also plenty of accommodation and tearooms on the way in this section should you decide to take a break. The topography of the eastern section, on the other hand, is less dramatic, though the number of places with accommodation drops too, and for a couple of days you may find yourself walking 15 miles or more in order to reach a town or village on the trail that has somewhere to stay.

Regarding safety, there are few places on the regular trail where it would be possible to fall from a great height, save perhaps for the cliff walks that book-end the walk (though I've never heard of it happening before, particularly as there's a fence or wall between you and the cliffs for most of the way now). On some of the high-level alternatives (see p90 and p109), however, there is a slightly greater chance of being blown off a precipice, though again it's highly unlikely.

The greatest danger to trekkers is, perhaps, the chance of becoming lost or disorientated, particularly in the Lake District, where there is a distinct lack of signposting, and especially in bad weather. A compass is thus pretty vital, as is dressing for inclement weather, or at least carrying a spare set of clothes with you. Not pushing yourself too hard is important too, as this will lead only to exhaustion and all its inherent dangers. In case all this deters you from the walk because it sounds too difficult or dangerous bear in mind that a seven-year-old girl completed the walk with her father in 13 days!

Route finding

Waymarking varies along the path. Once over the Pennines and into Yorkshire the trail is fairly well signposted and finding your way shouldn't be a problem. In the Lakes, on the other hand, there are no Coast-to-Coast signposts and you may have to rely on the maps and descriptions in this book to find your way. For much of the time the path is well-trodden and obvious, though of course there are situations where there are a number of paths to choose from, and other occasions where the ground is too boggy and no path is visible at all. Foggy conditions are another problem, particularly in the Lake District. In these instances a compass is essential to help you find the correct path.

In the Lakes in particular there are a number of high-level alternatives to the main route, and fit trekkers should, if the weather allows, seriously consider taking them. Though harder, the rewards in terms of the views and sense of achievement make it all worthwhile.

HOW LONG DO YOU NEED?

I've heard about an athlete who completed the entire Coast to Coast path in just 37 hours. I've read about a walker who did it in eight days. I know somebody who did it in ten. But excepting these superhuman achievements, for most people, the Coast to Coast trail takes a minimum of fourteen days.

Indeed, even with a fortnight in which to complete the trail, many people still find it fairly tough going, and it doesn't really allow you time to look around places such as Grasmere or Richmond which each deserve a day in themselves. So, if you can afford to build a couple of rest days into your itinerary, you'll be glad you did.

Of course, if you're fit there's no reason why you can't go a little faster if that's what you want to do, though you will end up having a different sort of trek to most of the other people on the route. For where theirs is a fairly relaxing holiday, yours will be more of a sport as you compete against the clock and try to reach the finishing line as quickly as possible. There's nothing wrong with this approach, though you obviously won't see as much as those who take their time. Nevertheless, *chacun à son goût*, as the French probably say. However, what you mustn't do is try to push yourself too fast. That road leads only to exhaustion, injury or, at the absolute least, an unpleasant time.

When deciding how long to allow for their trek, those intending to camp and carry their own luggage shouldn't underestimate just how much a heavy pack can slow you down. On pp30-2 there are some suggested itineraries covering different walking speeds. If you've only got a few days, don't try to walk it all; concentrate, instead, on one area such as the Lakes or North York Moors. You can always come back and attempt the rest of the walk another time.

Practical information for the walker

ACCOMMODATION

The trail guide (Part 4) lists a fairly comprehensive selection of places to stay along the full length of the trail. You have three main options: camping, staying in hostels/bunkhouses, or using B&Bs/hotels. Few people stick to just one of these options the whole way, preferring, for example, to camp most of the time but spend every third night in a hostel, or perhaps take a hostel where possible but splash out on a B&B every once in a while.

The table on pp28-9 provides a quick snapshot of what type of accommodation is available in each of the towns and villages along the way, while the tables on pp30-2 provide some suggested itineraries. The following is a brief introduction to what to expect from each type of accommodation.

Camping

It's possible to camp all along the Coast to Coast path, though few people do so every night. You're almost bound to get at least one night where the rain falls relentlessly, soaking equipment and sapping morale, and it is then that most campers opt to spend the next night drying out in a hostel or B&B somewhere. There are, however, many advantages with camping. It's more economical, for a start, with most campsites charging somewhere between £2 and £5. There's rarely any need to book, except possibly in the very high season, and even then you'd be highly unlucky not to find somewhere. There's also the freedom that carrying your accommodation with you brings, allowing you to stop for the night pretty much where and when you like.

The campsites vary: some are just the back gardens of B&Bs or pubs; others are full-blown caravan sites with a few spaces put aside for tents. Showers are usually available, occasionally for a fee though more often than not for free. Note that few if any youth hostels on the Coast to Coast path now accept campers. Note, too, that some of the bigger towns such as Richmond and Grasmere do not have recognized campsites, with the nearest being around three miles away.

Wild camping (ie camping outside of a regular campsite; see p49) is also possible along the route but please do not make camp in a field without first gaining permission from the landowner. The three best wild campsites are said to be Grisedale Tarn (between Grasmere and Patterdale), Innominate Tarn (by the Hay Stacks on the high route between Ennerdale Bridge and Borrowdale) and Angle Tarn (between Patterdale and Shap).

Remember that camping is not an easy option; the route is wearying enough without carrying your accommodation around with you. Should you decide to camp, therefore, we advise you to consider employing one of the baggage-carrying companies mentioned on pp20-1 (though this does, of course, mean that it will cost more and that you lose a certain amount of freedom, as you'll have to agree at least a day before with the company your destination for the night – and stick to it – so that you and your bag can be reunited every evening.)

Bunkhouses/camping barns

The term 'bunkhouse' or 'camping barn' can mean many different things. In some cases it's nothing more than a drafty old barn in a farmer's field with a couple of wooden benches to sleep on. In at least one exceptional case, however, bunkhouse can also mean a room at the back of a pub that's identical to regular B&B accommodation except that there is a bunk-bed rather than a double bed in the room. Most, however, are nearer in style to the former and sleeping bags are necessary in these places. While not exactly the lap of luxury, a night in a bunkhouse/camping barn is probably the nearest non-campers will get to sleeping outside, while at the same time providing campers with a shelter from the elements should the weather look like taking a turn for the worse. Some of the better bunkhouses/camping barns, especially those maintained by the YHA, provide a shower and simple kitchen with running water and perhaps a kettle, though little in the way of pots, pans, cutlery or crockery.

Hostels

Youth hostels are plentiful along the Coast to Coast path and if you haven't visited one recently – and thus the words 'youth' and 'hostel' still conjure up images of cold, crowded dorms, uncomfortable beds, lousy food and strict staff who take a sadistic pleasure in treating you like schoolchildren – we advise you to take a second look. The YHA (Youth Hostel Association) has in fact got some of the most interesting accommodation on the path, from two pretty country houses at Grasmere to a converted chapel at Kirkby Stephen and a former shepherd's bothy at Black Sail, the most isolated accommodation on the route. Each hostel comes equipped with a whole range of facilities, from drying rooms to washing machines, televisions to pool tables and fully equipped kitchens for guests to use. Many also have a shop selling a selection of groceries, snacks and souvenirs and some are even connected to the internet. All offer breakfast and/or dinner, some offer a packed lunch, and a couple even have a licence to sell alcohol. They are also good places to meet fellow walkers, swap stories and compare blisters.

Weighed against these advantages is the fact that beds are still arranged in dormitories, some of them quite large, thereby increasing your chances of sharing your night with a heavy snorer. The curfew (usually 11pm) is annoying, too. A couple of the hostels also suffer from a shortfall in adequate washing facilities, with only one or two showers to be shared between 15 to 20 people. Nor is it possible to stay in hostels every night, for there are some areas where hostels don't exist and when they do they are occasionally at least a mile or two off the path. If you are travelling in April/May or September, at the beginning or end of the walking season, you may find many shut for two or three days per week, or that they have been taken over by school groups and walkers are shut out.

❏ Should you book your accommodation in advance?

When walking the Coast to Coast path, it's essential that you have your night's accommodation booked by the time you set off in the morning, particularly if you're planning to stay in a hostel, bunkhouse, B&B or guesthouse. Nothing is more deflating than to arrive at your destination at the end of a long day only to find that you've then got to walk on a further five miles or so, or even take a detour off the route, because everywhere in town is booked.

That said, there's a certain amount of hysteria regarding the booking of accommodation, with many websites, B&Bs and other organizations insisting that you have to start booking at least six months in advance if you wish to have any chance of getting accommodation on the route. Whilst it's true that the earlier you book the more chance you'll have of getting precisely the accommodation you require, booking so far in advance does leave you vulnerable to changing circumstances: booking a full six months before setting foot on the trail is all very well if everything goes to plan, but if you break your leg just before you're due to set off or, God forbid, there's another outbreak of foot and mouth, all you're going to end up with is a lot of lost deposits. By not booking so far in advance, you give yourself the chance to shift your holiday plans to a later date should the unforeseen arise.

In my experience, the situation is not as bad as some suggest, at least not outside the high season (by 'high season' I mean the summer period coinciding with the long school holidays in the UK – from the middle of July to the first week of September). Outside this period, and particularly in April/May or September, as long as you're flexible and willing to take what's offered – with maybe even a night or two in a youth hostel if that's all there is – you should get away with booking just a few nights in advance, or indeed often just the night before. The exceptions to this rule are at the weekends, when everywhere is busy and it's essential you find somewhere as soon as you can, and in places such as Danby Wiske or Blakey Moor where accommodation is very limited.

In summary, therefore, my advice is this. Firstly, it's always worth phoning ahead to book your accommodation. If you are staying in **B&Bs** and walking in high season, this should be done two to three months in advance, particularly if you have a preference for specific B&Bs. If, on the other hand, you're not too bothered which B&B you stay in, are trekking in April/May or September, and don't mind the occasional possibility of having to walk a mile or two off the route to get a room, you can probably get away with booking your accommodation by ringing around a night or two before. If you can book at least a few nights in advance, however, so much the better, and at weekends it's essential you book as soon as you can.

If you're planning on staying in **youth hostels** the same applies though do be careful when travelling out of high season as many hostels close for a couple of days each week and shut altogether from around November to Easter. Once again, it's well worth phoning at least one night before, and well before that if it's a weekend, to make sure the hostel isn't fully booked or shut. **Campers**, whatever time of year, should always be able to find somewhere to pitch their tent, though ringing in advance can't hurt and will at least confirm that the campsite is still open.

(Try to pick up the YHA's annual brochure, or visit their website, to find out the exact opening dates of each of the hostels.) Even in high season most are not staffed during the day and walkers have to wait until 5pm before checking in. Furthermore, it is rumoured that most youth hostels will save your booked bed only until 6pm – though to be fair, I never came across this rule on the route and if it does exist it doesn't seem to be rigidly enforced. And finally, the cost of staying in a hostel, once breakfast has been added on, is in most instances not that much cheaper (around £15-20 for members) than staying in a B&B.

Booking a hostel Despite the name, anybody of any age can join the YHA. This can be done at any hostel, or by contacting the **Youth Hostels Association of England and Wales** (☎ 0870 770 6113, 🖥 www.yha.org.uk). The cost of a year's membership is £15.50. Having secured your membership, youth hostels are easy to book, either online or by ringing each individual hostel separately. The hostels also offer a booking service and will reserve your bed at the next stop on the path for you. The hostels in the Lake District also have their own booking service on ☎ 015394 31117. Since non members have to pay £3 more per night it is worth joining if you expect to stay in a hostel for more than six nights in a year.

Bed and breakfast

Bed and Breakfasts (B&Bs) are a great British institution and many of those along the Coast to Coast are absolutely charming, with buildings often three or four hundred years old. There's nothing mysterious about a B&B; as the name suggests, they provide you with a bed in a private room, and breakfast – a hearty, British-style cooked one (see opposite) unless you specify otherwise beforehand – though they range in style enormously. Most B&Bs have both en suite rooms and rooms with shared facilities, though even with the latter the bathroom is never more than a few feet away. These rooms usually contain either a double bed (known as a double room), or two single beds (known as a twin room). Family rooms are for three or more people. Solo trekkers should take note: single rooms are not so easy to find so you'll often end up occupying a double room, for which you'll have to pay a single supplement (see below).

Some B&Bs provide an evening meal (see below); if not, there's nearly always a pub or restaurant nearby or, if it's far, the owner will usually give you a lift to and from the nearest place with food. Be aware that a lot of B&Bs on the route are non-smoking establishments. Always let the owner know if you have to cancel your booking so they can offer the bed to someone else.

B&B prices B&Bs in this guide start at around £18 per person for the most basic accommodation to over £40 for the most luxurious en suite places in a popular tourist haunt like Grasmere. Most charge around £20-25 per person. A typical single supplement is between £5 and £10. An evening meal (usually around £10-12) is often provided, but you may need to book in advance.

Guesthouses, hotels, pubs and inns

The difference between a B&B and a guesthouse is minimal, though some of the better **guesthouses** are more like hotels, offering evening meals and a lounge for guests. **Pubs and inns** also offer bed and breakfast accommodation, and prices are no more than in a regular B&B. **Hotels** do usually cost more, however, and some might be a little incensed with a bunch of smelly trekkers turning up and treading mud into their carpet. Most on the Coast to Coast walk, however, are used to seeing trekkers and welcome them warmly. Prices in hotels start at around £35 per person.

Others

In addition to the accommodation types listed above there are also **holiday cottages**, stationary **caravans** and even one or two **adventure centres** along the route, though these tend to cater more to people staying for at least a few days rather than just one night.

FOOD AND DRINK

Breakfast

Stay in a B&B and you'll be filled to the gills with a cooked English breakfast. This usually consists of a bowl of cereal followed by a plateful of eggs, bacon, sausages, mushrooms, tomatoes, and possibly baked beans or black pudding, with toast and butter, and all washed down with coffee, tea and/or juice. Enormously satisfying the first time you try it, by the fourth or fifth morning you may start to prefer the lighter continental breakfast. Alternatively, and especially if you are planning an early start, you might like to request a packed lunch instead of this filling breakfast and just have a cup of coffee before you leave.

Only the larger youth hostels offer breakfast; usually it is a good meal but they charge an additional £4-5.

Lunch

Your landlady or youth hostel can usually provide a packed lunch at an additional cost, though of course there's nothing to stop you preparing your own (though do bring a penknife if you plan to do this). There are some fantastic locally made cheeses and pickles that can be picked up along the way, as well as some wonderful bakers still making bread in the traditional way (the bakery at Reeth springs to mind here; see p158). Alternatively, stop in a pub (see Evening meals below).

Remember, too, to plan ahead: certain stretches of the walk are devoid of eating places (the stretch from Patterdale to Shap for example) so read ahead about the next day's walk in Part 4 to make sure you never go hungry.

Cream teas

Never miss a chance to avail yourself of the treats on offer in the tearooms of Cumbria and Yorkshire. Nothing relaxes and revives like a decent pot of tea, and the opportunity to accompany it with a jam and cream scone (a combination known as a cream tea) or a cake or two is one that should not be passed up.

Evening meals

If you don't book a meal at your B&B you may find that in many of the villages, the pub is the only place to eat out. **Pubs** are as much a feature of the walk as moorland and sheep, and in some cases the pub is as much of a tourist attraction as any stone circle or ruined abbey. Most of them have become highly attuned to the desires of walkers and offer lunch and evening meals (with often a few local dishes and usually a couple of vegetarian options), some locally brewed beers, a garden to relax in on hot days and a roaring fire to huddle around on cold ones. The standard of the food varies widely, though is usually served in big portions, which is often just about all walkers care about at the end of a long day.

That other great British culinary institution, the **fish 'n' chip shop**, can also be found along the route. Larger towns also have Chinese and Indian **takeaways**; these are usually the last places to serve food in the evenings, staying open until at least 11pm.

Self-catering

There is a grocery shop of some description in most of the places along the route, though most of these are small (and often combined with the post office) and whether you'll be able to find precisely what you went in for is doubtful. If self-catering, therefore, your menus will depend on what you can find. The path is quite trekker-friendly, however, in that a couple of these small stores such as the one at Rosthwaite sells Camping Gaz (which you can also pick up in the bigger towns such as Grasmere, Kirkby Stephen and Richmond). Part 4 goes into greater detail about what can be found where.

Drinking water

There are plenty of ways of perishing on the Coast to Coast trail but given how frequently it rains and how damp the north of England is, thirst probably won't be one of them. Be careful, though, for on a hot day in some of the remoter parts of the Lake District after a steep climb or two you'll quickly dehydrate, which is at best highly unpleasant and at worst mightily dangerous. Always carry some water with you and aim in hot weather to drink three or four litres per day. Don't be tempted by the water in the multitude of streams that you come across. If the cow or sheep faeces in the water don't make you ill, the chemicals from the pesticides and fertilizers used on the farms almost certainly will. Using iodine or another purifying treatment will help to combat the former though there's little you can do about the latter. It's a lot safer to fill up from taps instead.

MONEY

Banks are few and far between on the Coast to Coast path. There's a NatWest at Shap, a Barclays and an HSBC at Kirkby Stephen, and Richmond has branches of all the major banks, but outside of these places there's nothing. The **post office** thus provides a very useful service. You can get cash (by cheque or debit card) for free at a post office counter if you bank with certain banks including the following: Barclays, Alliance & Leicester, Co-op, Smile, Cahoot or Lloyds TSB. A number of post offices also play host to the village **cashpoint** (usually a Link machine). These machines are useful for people who cannot get cash from the counter but a number of these are privately operated and charge £1.25-1.75 whatever amount is withdrawn. Another way of getting money in your hand is to use the **cashback** system: find a store that will accept a debit card and ask them to advance cash against the card. A number of the local village stores, such as those in Reeth and Robin Hood's Bay, will do this, though you'll usually have to spend a minimum of £5 with them first.

❏ Information for foreign visitors

● **Currency** The British pound (£) comes in notes of £100, £50, £20, £10, £5 and coins of £2 and £1. The pound is divided into 100 pence (usually referred to as 'p', pronounced pee) which comes in silver coins of 50p, 20p 10p and 5p and copper coins of 2p and 1p.

● **Rates of exchange** Up-to-date exchange rates can be found at ▢ www.xe.com/ucc.

● **Business hours** Most **shops** and main **post offices** are open at least from Monday to Friday 9am-5pm and Saturday 9am-12.30pm. Many choose longer hours and some open on Sundays as well. However, some also close early one day a week, often Wednesday or Thursday. **Banks** are usually open 10am-4pm Monday to Friday.

New licensing laws came into effect in November 2005. Since then **pub** opening hours have become more flexible and every landlord has to apply for a licence for the hours he/she wants to open – up to 24 hours a day seven days a week – so each pub may have different opening hours. However, it is likely that most pubs on the Coast to Coast route will continue to open between 11am and 11pm and some may still close in the afternoon.

● **National holidays** Most businesses are shut on 1 January, Good Friday (March/April), Easter Monday (March/April), the first and last Monday in May, the last Monday in August, 25 December and 26 December.

● **School holidays** School holiday periods in England are generally as follows: a one-week break late October, two weeks around Christmas and the New Year, a week mid-February, two weeks around Easter, and from late July to early September.

● **Travel/medical insurance** The European Health Insurance Card (EHIC) entitles EU nationals (on production of the EHIC card) to necessary medical treatment under the UK's National Health Service while on a temporary visit here. However, this is not a substitute for proper medical cover on your travel insurance for unforeseen bills and for getting you home should that be necessary. Also consider cover for loss and theft of personal belongings, especially if you are camping or staying in hostels, as there will be times when you'll have to leave your luggage unattended.

● **Weights and measures** Britain is attempting to move towards the metric system but there is much resistance. Most food is now sold in metric weights (g and kg) but most older people still think in the imperial weights of pounds (lb) and ounces (oz). Milk is sold in pints, as is beer in pubs, yet most other liquid is sold in litres. Road signs and distances are always given in miles rather than kilometres and the population remains split between those who are happy with centigrade, kilograms and metres and those who still use fahrenheit, pounds and feet and inches.

● **British Summer Time (BST)** BST starts the last Sunday in March, ie the clocks go forward one hour, and ends the last Sunday in October ie the clocks go back one hour.

● **Telephone** The international access code for Britain is +44, followed by the area code minus the first 0, and then the number you require. To call a number with the same area code as the phone you are calling from you can omit the code. It is cheaper to phone at weekends and after 6pm and before 8am on weekdays. Mobile phone reception is quite unreliable except when in the vicinity of urban areas. In hilly country head for high ground where a weak signal can often be picked up.

● **Emergency services** For police, ambulance, fire and mountain rescue dial ☎ 999.

With few local stores, pubs or B&Bs accepting credit or debit cards, and few places where you can get money out along the way, it is essential to carry plenty of cash (I usually reckon on £50 per person) with you, though keep it safe and out of sight (preferably in a moneybelt). A chequebook could prove very useful as a back-up, so that you don't have to keep on dipping into your cash reserves. **Travellers' cheques** can be cashed only at banks, foreign exchanges and some of the large hotels.

OTHER SERVICES

Grasmere (the YHA), Patterdale (at the YHA), Kirkby Stephen (at the library) and Richmond (library) all have **public internet access**. In addition, the pubs at Ingleby Cross (Blue Bell Inn) and Danby Wiske (The White Swan) also offer an internet service. Most small villages have a **post office** that doubles as the local store, and nearby you'll usually find a **phone box**.

There are **outdoor equipment shops** and **pharmacies** in the larger towns of Grasmere, Kirkby Stephen and Richmond and **tourist information centres** at Kirkby Stephen, Ullswater (near Patterdale), Reeth and Richmond.

WALKING COMPANIES

It is, of course, possible to turn up with your boots and backpack at St Bees and just start walking without planning much other than your accommodation (about which, see the box on p15). The following companies, however, are in the business of making your holiday as stress-free and enjoyable as possible.

Baggage carriers

There are several baggage-carrying companies serving the Coast to Coast route, from national organizations such as Sherpa to companies that consist of little more than one man and his van. With all these services you can book up to the last moment, usually up to around 9 o'clock the previous evening, though it's cheaper if you book in advance. All stipulate a maximum weight per bag of around 15-20kg. The cost is around £5-6 to take your bag to your next destination. Nearly all these services offer an accommodation-booking service as well.

Two of the better known are Sherpa and Packhorse. **Sherpa Van** (☎ 020 8577 2717; 🖳 www.sherpavan.com) is a nationwide company that serves all the major walking trails in Britain, delivering luggage from one place to another from April to October.

Packhorse (☎ 017683 71777; 🖳 www.cumbria.com/packhorse) based at Kirkby Stephen, are a reliable and thoroughly organized outfit who quite rightly receive regular recommendations from their customers. In addition to transporting your luggage, the company also offers a daily passenger service between St Bees and Robin Hood's Bay, allowing passengers to travel along with the luggage, and hop off wherever they want, from £5.75 a stage (phone Packhorse for approximate times). One bus departs Kirkby Stephen at 8.30am, arriving at St Bees at 10.15am, before travelling via the pick-up points back to Kirkby Stephen. A second bus also leaves Kirkby Stephen at 8.30am, stopping at the drop-off points before reaching Robin Hood's Bay at 3.30pm, then travelling directly back to Kirkby Stephen to arrive at 5.45pm. (In other words, the buses stop at the various drop-off points only when travelling from west to east.) The cost of travelling directly from Kirkby Stephen to St Bees or Robin Hood's Bay to Kirkby Stephen is £21 per person. As if that wasn't enough help they also have a secure parking lot in Kirkby Stephen, where one can leave the car for the duration of the walk (£2.50 per day).

This service has two important consequences for trekkers. Firstly, it means that, should you be attempting the walk from west to east and need to miss out a stage for some reason, you can get the Packhorse bus to pick you up and drive you to the end of the next stage. The second important consequence is that you can use Kirkby Stephen as your base, hitching a lift on the Packhorse van to St Bees and the start of the walk, and another at the end of the walk back from Robin Hood's Bay. Thus you can leave your car in Kirkby Stephen for the duration of the walk (which is better than the alternative of leaving it in St Bees and travelling all the way back from the east coast to pick it up again). Or you can buy a return train ticket from your home to Kirkby Stephen, which is cheaper than having to buy one ticket to St Bees, and another from Robin Hood's Bay.

Other companies offering a similar service include **Coast to Coast Holiday & Baggage Services** (☎ 01642 489173; 🖳 www.coasttocoast-holidays.co.uk) and **Brigantes Walking Holidays** (☎ 01729 830463; 🖳 www.Brigantesenglish walks.com); they can also arrange accommodation.

Self-guided holidays

Self-guided basically means that the company will organize accommodation, baggage transfer, transport to and from the walk and various maps and advice, but leave you on your own to actually walk the path. In addition to these, don't forget the specialist Coast to Coast websites (see box p38) that can also book accommodation and provide details of the walk.

● **Contours Walking Holidays** (☎ 017684 80451, 🖳 www.contours.co.uk; Gramyre, 3 Berrier Rd, Greystoke, Cumbria, CA11 OUB. Offers six different itineraries covering the Coast to Coast, from the strenuous to the simple.

● **Discovery Travel** (☎ 01904 766564, 🖳 www.discoverytravel.co.uk; 12 Towthorpe Rd, Haxby, York, YO32 3ND. Offers the Coast to Coast walk either as one walk or divided into two separate one-week stages. Also, unusually, offer the walk from east to west.

● **Explore Britain** (☎ 01740-650900, 🖳 www.xplorebritain.com; 6 George St, Ferryhill, Co Durham, DL17 0DT).

● **Instep Linear Walking Holidays** (☎ 01903 766475, 🖳 www.instep hols.co.uk; 35 Cokeham Rd, Lancing, West Sussex, BN15 0AE).

● **Packhorse** (scc opposite; Chestnut IIouse, Crosby Garrett, Kirkby Stephen, Cumbria CA17 4PR), offer ten itineraries from £289 (six nights) to £809 (17 nights).

● **Sherpa Expeditions** (☎ 020 8577 2717, 🖳 www.sherpa-walking-holi days.co.uk; 131a Heston Rd, Hounslow, Middlesex, TW5 0RF).

Group/guided walking tours

If you don't trust your map-reading skills or simply prefer the company of other walkers as well as an experienced guide, the following companies will be of interest to you. Packages nearly always include meals, accommodation, transport arrangements, minibus back-up and baggage transfer. Have a good look at each of the companies' websites before booking as each has their own speciality and it's important to choose one that's suitable for you.

● **Contours Walking Holidays** (see p21) Offers the entire Coast to Coast path in two one-week sections, which run consecutively for those who wish to tackle the route in one go.

● **Countrywide** (☎ 01707 386800, 🖳 www.countrywidewalking.com; Box 43, Welwyn Garden City, AL8 6PQ) No specific Coast to Coast itinerary but this walking specialist does offer packages to Grasmere, Richmond, the Yorkshire Dales and the North York Moors.

● **Footpath Holidays** (☎ 01985 840049, 🖳 www.footpath-holidays.com; 16 Norton Bravant, Near Warminster, Wiltshire, BA12 7BB) Runs hotel-based guided walking tours along the Coast to Coast path. They divide the path into three different sections of approximately 70 miles each, enabling you to tackle one section at a time, or string all three sections together for the complete trail.

● **HF Holidays** (☎ 020 8905 9556, 🖳 www.hfholidays.co.uk; Imperial House, Edgware Rd, London, NW9 5AL) Not cheap, but an extremely reliable and frequently recommended company offering the Coast to Coast path in its entirety from east to west, with departures currently six times per year. They also offer an alternative Coast to Coast that avoids many of the ups and downs.

● **Sherpa Expeditions** (see p21) Sherpa offer a few guided tours each year.

TAKING DOGS ALONG THE COAST TO COAST PATH

The Coast to Coast is a dog-friendly path, though it is extremely important that dog owners behave in a responsible way. Dogs should always be kept on leads while on the footpath to avoid disturbing wildlife, livestock and other walkers. Dog excrement should be cleaned up and not left to decorate the boots of others; take a pooper scooper or plastic bag if you are walking with a dog.

It is particularly important to keep your dog on a lead when crossing fields with livestock in them, especially around lambing time (see box p51) which can be as early as February or as late as the end of May. Most farmers would prefer it if you did not bring your dog at all at this time.

In addition, in certain areas on the Coast to Coast trail (particularly between Shap and Kirkby Stephen) there are notices ordering owners to keep their dogs on a lead to protect endangered ground-nesting birds, particularly between March and June; dogs can frighten them off and possibly cause them to desert their nests.

Remember when planning and booking your accommodation that you will need to check if your dog will be welcome. Some inns and hotels charge extra for a dog.

Budgeting

England is not a cheap place to go travelling, and while the north may be one of the cheaper parts of it, the towns and villages on the Coast to Coast route are more than used to seeing tourists and charge accordingly. You may think before you set out that you are going to try to keep your budget to a minimum by camping every night and cooking your own food, but it's a rare trekker who sticks to this rule. Besides, the B&Bs and pubs on the route are amongst the Coast to Coast's major attractions, and it would be a pity not to sample the hospitality in at least some of them.

If the only expenses of this walk were accommodation and food, budgeting for the trip would be a piece of cake. Unfortunately, in addition to these there are all the little **extras** that push up the cost of your trip: for example beer, cream teas, stamps and postcards, internet use, buses here and there, baggage carriers, phone calls, laundry, film, souvenirs, entrance fees. It's surprising how much these add up so allow £50-100 over your basic budget.

CAMPING

You can survive on as little as £10-12 per person if you use the cheapest campsites, don't visit a pub, avoid all the museums and tourist attractions in the towns, cook all your own food from staple ingredients ... and generally have a pretty miserable time of it. Even then, unforeseen expenses will probably nudge your daily budget into double figures. Include the occasional pint, and perhaps a pub meal every now and then, and the figure will be nearer £15 per day.

BUNKHOUSES, CAMPING BARNS AND HOSTELS

The current charge for staying in a **YHA hostel** is £11-14 for members. Whack on another £4 for breakfast, though you can use their self-catering facilities to prepare one yourself. There is also lunch (a small packed lunch costs £3.40 and a standard one £4.30) and an evening meal (£5.50) to consider, which means that, overall, it will cost £20-25 per day, or £30-35 to live in a little more comfort, enjoy the odd beer and go out for the occasional meal.

There are a few bunkhouses and camping barns along the Coast to Coast. They vary in quality and price (from around £5-6 to £10-15).

B&BS, GUESTHOUSES AND HOTELS

B&B prices start at £18 per person per night but can be twice this. Add on the cost of food for lunch and dinner and you should reckon on about £35 minimum per day. Staying in a guesthouse or hotel will probably cost more. Remember that there is often a supplement of £5-10 for single occupancy of a room.

When to go

SEASONS

Britain is a notoriously wet country and the north of England is an infamously damp part of it. Rare indeed are the trekkers who have managed to walk the Coast to Coast path without suffering at least one downpour on the way; three or four per trek are more likely, even in summer. That said, it's equally unlikely that you'll spend a fortnight in the area and not see any sun at all, and even the most cynical of walkers will have to admit that, during the walking season at least, there are more sunny days than showery ones. That **walking season**, by the way, starts at Easter and builds to a crescendo in August, before steadily tailing off in September. By the end of September few indeed are the trekkers on the trail, and in October many places close down for the winter.

Spring

Find a couple of dry weeks in springtime and you're in for a treat. The wild flowers are beginning to come into bloom, lambs are skipping in the meadows, the grass is green and lush and the path is not yet badly eroded. Of course, finding a dry fortnight in spring (around the end of March to mid-June) is not easy but occasionally there's a mini-heatwave during this season. Another advantage with walking at this time is that there will be few trekkers and finding accommodation is relatively easy. Easter is the exception, the first major holiday in the year when people flock to the Lake District and other national parks.

Summer

Summer, on the other hand, can be a bit *too* busy and, in somewhere popular like the Lakes over a weekend in August, little short of insufferable. Still, the chances of a prolonged period of sunshine are of course higher at this time of year than any other, the days are much longer and the heather is in bloom at this time, too, turning the hills a fragrant purple. If you crave the company of other trekkers summer will provide you with the opportunity of meeting hundreds of them, though do remember that you must book your accommodation well in advance. Despite the higher than average chance of sunshine, take clothes for any eventuality – it will still rain at some point.

Autumn

September is a wonderful time to walk, when many of the tourists have returned home and the path is clear. I think that the weather is usually reliably sunny, too, at least at the beginning of September, though I admit I don't have any figures to back this claim. The B&Bs and hostels will still be open, at least until the end of the month. By then the weather will begin to get a little wilder and the nights will start to draw in. The walking season is almost at an end.

Winter

A few people trek the Coast to Coast in winter, putting up with the cold temperatures, damp conditions and short days for the chance to experience the trail without other tourists. Much of the accommodation will be closed too. But whilst it may also be a little more dangerous to walk at this time, particularly if taking one of the high-level routes through the Lakes, if you find yourself walking on one of those clear, crisp, wintry days it will all seem worth it.

RAINFALL

At some point on your walk, it will rain; if it doesn't, it's fair to say that you haven't really lived the full Coast to Coast experience properly.

The question, therefore, is not whether you will be rained on, but how often. But as long as you dress accordingly and take note of the safety advice given on p53, this shouldn't be a problem.

Do, however, think twice about tackling some of the high-level alternatives if the weather is very inclement, and don't do so on your own.

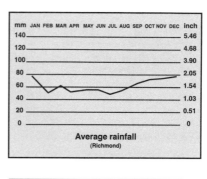

Average rainfall
(Richmond)

DAYLIGHT HOURS

If walking in autumn, winter or early spring, you must take account of how far you can walk in the available light. It won't be possible to cover as many miles as you would in summer. Remember, too, that you will get a further 30-45 minutes of usable light before and after sunrise and sunset depending on the weather. In June, because the path is in the far north of England, those coming from the south may be surprised that there's enough available light for walking until at least 10pm. Conversely, in late spring, late autumn and winter you will be equally amazed how quickly the nights draw in.

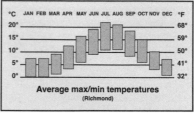

Average max/min temperatures
(Richmond)

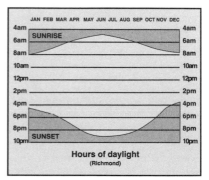

Hours of daylight
(Richmond)

ANNUAL EVENTS

Thanks largely to its popularity with tourists, Grasmere has over the past few years become something of a mecca for those interested in those peculiarly Lakeland sports such as fell running, and Cumberland and Westmoreland wrestling. The annual **Grasmere Lakeland Sports and Show**, the origins of which date back around 300 years, takes place at the end of August. Other sports featured include tug-of-war, hound-trailing and the more recent addition of mountain-biking. If you are in the Lakes at this time, don't miss the opportunity of witnessing this unique event.

As you'd probably expect, Grasmere also hosts an annual **Art and Book Festival** at one of Wordsworth's old houses, Dove Cottage. The festival usually takes place in January.

The villages of Swaledale, which include Keld, Muker, Thwaite, Gunnerside and Reeth, hold an annual music festival. The **Swaledale Festival** usually takes place at the end of May to early June. The festival has an annual theme (eg stringed instruments), and in addition to the music there are all kinds

---

❏ HIGHLIGHTS

The best day and weekend walks on the Coast to Coast

The following suggested trails are for those who cannot, for whatever reason, complete the entire path in one go. They are, in my opinion, the best parts of the Coast to Coast path, and are all described in more detail in Part 4. However, because the Coast to Coast path is so varied and encompasses so many different landscapes and experiences, it is fair to say that none of them will, by themselves, fully capture the glory of the path. Nevertheless, they are all, in their own way, delightful. They are written in the order in which they appear on the trail. Please see the guide section and pp40-5 for details of public transport to and from the start and finish of each walk.

Day walks

● **Ennerdale Bridge to Borrowdale** 14.5 miles/23km (pp82-93) The first truly gorgeous stretch of the Coast to Coast, combining the glories of Ennerdale Water with the tribulations of Loft Beck. Lengthy, slightly precarious if the weather closes in, and arduous too, particularly if taking the High Stile alternative, this is nevertheless a worthy, brutal introduction to the delights and rigours of Coast to Coast walking.

● **Borrowdale to Grasmere** 9.5 miles/15km (pp94-105) A walk of contrasts, this trail takes you from quiet, relatively 'untouristy' Rosthwaite to 'Wordsworth-ville', the ever-popular Grasmere. Not an easy walk, it can be a spectacular one if the day is clear and the high-level alternative is taken, with views to fells near and far.

● **Grasmere to Patterdale** 10 miles/16km (pp105-14) Just a simple up-and-down, though the 'down' can be complicated by detours up St Sunday or Helvellyn which provide better views. Simply splendid.

● **Patterdale to Shap** 16 miles/25.5km (pp114-23) One of the longest stages on the Coast to Coast trail. Not a classic, perhaps, though perfectly pleasant, and one of the most varied too as you leave the Lakes for a long trek by Haweswater, followed by a trudge through sheep and cattle fields to Shap Abbey. Complete this without too much trouble and you should have no trouble completing the entire trail.

(continued opposite)

of other activities from art exhibitions and guided walking trails to craft work-shops; information can be found and tickets bought on the dedicated website ▣ www.swaledale-festival.org.uk.

Richmond Live is a pop music festival usually held over one weekend in July or August. For details visit the website ▣ www.richmondlive.org. Robin Hood's Bay hosts a **folk music weekend**, usually on the first weekend of June. For something a bit different, if you happen to be in the village in winter don't miss the **Victorian weekend** at the beginning of December, where the town turns out in 19th-century costume. It's all good fun, with quizzes, recitals, con-certs and demonstrations, and it's all in aid of charity too.

In addition to the events outlined above, all kinds of **agricultural shows** take place annually in towns and villages on the Coast to Coast trail. These shows are an integral and traditional part of life all over rural England and par-ticularly in the Lake District. Too numerous to list here, details of all the shows can be found by looking at the websites of the places concerned, of which you'll find a number on p38.

❏ HIGHLIGHTS

Day walks *(continued from opposite)*

● **Osmotherley/Ingleby Cross to Clay Bank Top/Blakey Ridge** 12-21 miles/19-33.5km (pp189-92) Relive one of the longest and most arduous days on the walk as you tackle the Yorkshire Moors. Lightweights can duck out at Clay Bank Top, hav-ing prearranged accommodation at one of the nearby villages. Tough trekkers can carry on to Blakey Ridge and the splendid Lion Inn.

● **The Esk Valley: Glaisdale to Grosmont** 3.5 miles/5.5km (see pp203-5) Not so much a trek as a pub crawl, this path takes you along the Esk Valley following the course of the river through woodland and along country tracks, with inn-laden vil-lages en route. Grosmont, at the end of the trail, has trains and buses to return you to Scarborough, Whitby, or the beginning of the trail.

● **Grosmont to Robin Hood's Bay** 15.5 miles/25km (pp206-18) Not a classic, with a lot of walking on roads by the standards of the Coast to Coast, but mentioned here because of the unmissable delights of Little Beck Woods, the pleasant sweetness of the villages at the start and finish, the windswept cliff-top tramp at the end, and the fact that you can pretend you've done the entire Coast to Coast path when you arrive in Robin Hood's Bay.

Weekend walks

In addition to the walk described below, a number of the day walks can be combined to make a two-day trek, particularly those in the Lake District.

● **Kirkby Stephen to Reeth** 26 miles/42km (pp138-59) Anybody who manages to scramble over the Pennines and negotiate the boggy ground down to the old mining village of Keld deserves a reward of some sort, and picturesque Swaledale is just that. As an encore, masochists can take the higher, 'official' route over the moors to Reeth. These days, however, most people seem to settle for a gentle stroll down the dale, passing through or near the villages of Muker, Gunnerside and Thwaite on their way to Reeth.

PLANNING YOUR WALK

VILLAGE AND

Place name (Places in brackets are a short walk off the Coast to Coast path)	Distance from previous place approx miles/km	Cash Machine	Post Office	Tourist Information Centre (TIC) Point (TIP)
St Bees		✔	✔	TIP
Sandwith	5/8			
Moor Row	3/5		✔	
Cleator	1/1.5			
Ennerdale Bridge	5/8 (via Dent)			
Seatoller	13/21			TIC§
Borrowdale (Longthwaite, Rosthwaite, Stonethwaite)	1.5/2.5 (to R'thwaite)		✔	
Grasmere	9.5/15 (from R'thwaite)	✔	✔	
Patterdale	10/16 (direct valley route)		✔	TIC at Glenridding
Shap	16/25.5	✔	✔	
(Orton)	8/13		✔	
Kirkby Stephen	20/32 (from Shap)	✔	✔	TIC
Keld	13/21			
(Thwaite)	2/3			
(Muker)	3.5/5.5 (from Keld)		✔	
(Gunnerside)	2.5/4 (from Muker)		✔	
Reeth	4/6.5 (from Gunnerside) 11/17.5 (from Keld on official high path)	✔	✔	TIC
Marrick	3/5			
Richmond	7.5/12	✔	✔	TIC
Colburn	3/5			
Catterick Bridge	2.5/4			
Bolton-on-Swale	2/3.5			
Danby Wiske	6/10			
Oaktree Hill	2/3.5			
Ingleby Cross	6.5/10.5		✔	
(Osmotherley)	3/5 (from Ingleby Cross)		✔	
Clay Bank Top (Urra and Great Broughton)	12/19 (from Ingleby Cross)			
Blakey Ridge	9/14.5			
Glaisdale	10/16		✔	
Egton Bridge	2/3			
Grosmont	1.5/2.5		✔	TIP
Littlebeck	3.5/5.5			
Hawsker	7.5/12			
Robin Hood's Bay	4.5/7.5		✔	

TOTAL DISTANCE 191.5 miles/307km

DISTANCE Distances are between places directly on the Coast to Coast path

TOWN FACILITIES

Eating Place ✓=one; 𝒲=a few; 𝒲𝒲=4 +	Food Store	Campsite	Hostels YHA/ H (IndHostel)/ B (Barn or Bunkhouse)	B&B-style accommodation ✓=one; 𝒲=a few; 𝒲𝒲=4+	Place name (Places in brackets are a short walk off the Coast to Coast path)
𝒲𝒲	✓	✓		𝒲𝒲	**St Bees**
		✓	B		**Sandwith**
✓	✓			𝒲	**Moor Row**
	✓			✓	**Cleator**
𝒲		✓	B/ YHA (5miles/8km)	𝒲𝒲	**Ennerdale Bridge**
✓		✓	YHA (1mile/1.5km)	𝒲	**Seatoller**
𝒲	✓	✓	B/YHA	𝒲𝒲	**Borrowdale**
			(Longthwaite, Rosthwaite, Stonethwaite)		
𝒲𝒲	✓		YHA/H	𝒲𝒲	**Grasmere**
𝒲		✓	YHA	𝒲𝒲	**Patterdale**
𝒲𝒲	✓	✓	B	𝒲𝒲	**Shap**
𝒲	✓	✓		𝒲	**(Orton)**
𝒲𝒲	✓	✓	YHA	𝒲	**Kirkby Stephen**
	✓(campsite)	✓	YHA	𝒲	**Keld**
✓				𝒲	**(Thwaite)**
✓				𝒲	**(Muker)**
𝒲					**(Gunnerside)**
𝒲𝒲	✓	✓	YHA (1¼miles/2km)	𝒲𝒲	**Reeth**
	✓			✓	**Marrick**
𝒲𝒲	✓(2miles/3km)		B (2miles/3km)	𝒲𝒲	**Richmond**
✓		✓		✓	**Colburn**
	✓	✓		✓	**Catterick Bridge**
		✓			**Bolton-on-Swale**
✓		✓		𝒲	**Danby Wiske**
		✓	B	✓	**Oaktree Hill**
✓	✓		H	𝒲	**Ingleby Cross**
𝒲𝒲	✓		YHA	𝒲	**(Osmotherley)**
✓				𝒲	**Clay Bank Top** (Urra and Great Broughton)
✓		✓		𝒲	**Blakey Ridge**
✓	✓			𝒲	**Glaisdale**
𝒲				𝒲	**Egton Bridge**
✓	✓	✓		𝒲	**Grosmont**
		✓		✓	**Littlebeck**
✓				𝒲	**Hawsker**
𝒲𝒲	✓	✓	YHA (1mile/1.5km)	𝒲𝒲	**Robin Hood's Bay**

§ = closed at the time of writing but may re-open soon

PLANNING YOUR WALK

Itineraries

Most people tackle the Coast to Coast from west to east, mainly because this will allow them to walk 'with the weather at their back' (because most of the time the winds blow off the Atlantic from the west, so by walking from west to east you will have the wind blowing with you rather than against you). It is usual for people to attempt it in one go, though a number of companies (see p20-2) offer the chance of tackling it in two stages, dividing the walk at Kirkby Stephen or Keld.

Part 4 of this book has been written from west to east (though there is of course nothing to stop you from tackling it in the opposite direction, and there are advantages in doing so – see opposite). To help you plan your walk look at the **planning map** (see opposite inside back cover) and the **table of village/town facilities** (on pp28-9), which gives a run-down on the essential information you will need regarding accommodation possibilities and services. You could follow one of the suggested itineraries (see below, and pp31-2) which

STAYING IN B&Bs

Night	Relaxed pace Place	Approx Distance miles/km	Medium pace Place	Approx Distance miles/km	Fast pace Place	Approx Distance miles/km
0	St Bees		St Bees		St Bees	
1	Cleator	9/14.5	Ennerdale Br	14/22.5	Ennerdale Br	14/22.5
2	Ennerdale Br	5/8	Borrowdale§	14.5/23	Borrowdale§	14.5/23
3	Borrowdale§	14.5/23	Grasmere	9.5/15	Patterdale	19.5/31
4	Grasmere	9.5/15	Patterdale	10/16	Shap	16/25.5
5	Patterdale	10/16	Shap	16/25.5	K. Stephen	20/32
6	Shap	16/25.5	K. Stephen	20/32	Reeth	24/38.5
7	Orton	8/13	Keld	13/21	Richmond	10.5/17
8	K. Stephen	13/21	Reeth	11/17.5	Ingleby Cross	23/37
9	Keld	13/21	Richmond	10.5/17	Blakey Ridge	21/33.5
10	Reeth	11/17.5	Danby Wiske	14/22.5	Grosmont	13.5/21.5
11	Richmond	10.5/17	Osmotherley	12/19	R. Hood's Bay	15.5/25
12	Danby Wiske	14/22.5	Clay Bank Top§	11/17.5		
13	Ingleby Cross	9/14.5	Grosmont	22.5/36		
14	Clay Bank Top§	12/19	R. Hood's Bay	15.5/25		
15	Blakey Ridge	9/14.5				
16	Glaisdale	10/16				
17	Littlebeck	7/11				
18	R. Hood's Bay	12/19				

§ **Borrowdale** includes Longthwaite, Rosthwaite & Stonethwaite

Clay Bank Top includes Urra & Great Broughton

are based on preferred type of accommodation and walking speeds. There is also a list of recommended linear day and weekend walks on pp26-7 which cover the best of the Coast to Coast path, all of which are well served by public transport. The public transport map is on p45.

Once you have an idea of your approach turn to Part 4 for detailed information on accommodation, places to eat and other services in each village and town on the route. Also in Part 4 you will find summaries of the route to accompany the detailed trail maps.

WHICH DIRECTION?

There are a number of advantages in tackling the path in a west to east direction, not least the fact that the prevailing winds will, more often than not, be behind you. If you are walking alone but wouldn't mind some company now and again you'll find that most of the other Coast to Coast walkers are heading in your direction too. However, there is also something to be said for leaving the Lake District – many people's favourite part of the British Isles, let alone the favourite part of the path – until the end of the walk.

CAMPING					
Relaxed pace		**Medium pace**		**Fast pace**	
Place	**Approx Distance**	**Place**	**Approx Distance**	**Place**	**Approx Distance**
Night	miles/km		miles/km		miles/km
0 St Bees		St Bees		St Bees	
1 Egremont	11/17.5	Ennerdale Br	14/22.5	Ennerdale Br	14/22.5
2 Ennerdale Br	7/11	Borrowdale§	14.5/23	Borrowdale§	14.5/23
3 Seatoller	13/21	Grasmere*	9.5/15	Patterdale	19/30.5
4 Grasmere*	11/17.5	Patterdale	10/16	Shap	16/25.5
5 Patterdale	10/16	Shap	16/25.5	K. Stephen	20/32
6 Shap	16/25.5	Kirkby Stephen	20/32	Reeth	24/38.5
7 Orton	8/13	Keld	13/21	Applegarth	8/13
8 Kirkby Stephen	13/21	Reeth	11/17.5	Danby Wiske	17/27
9 Keld	13/21	Applegarth	8/13	Osmotherley	12/19
10 Reeth	11/17.5	Danby Wiske	16.5/26.5	Blakey Ridge	20/32
11 Applegarth	8/13	Osmotherley	12/19	Grosmont	13.5/21.5
12 Danby Wiske	16.5/26.5	Blakey Ridge	20/32	R Hood's Bay	15.5/25
13 Osmotherley	12/19	Grosmont	13.5/21.5		
14 Clay Bank Top§	11/17.5	R. Hood's Bay	15.5/25		
15 Blakey Ridge	9/14.5				
16 Grosmont	13.5/21.5				
17 Littlebeck	3.5/5.5				
18 R. Hood's Bay	12/19				

* No campsite but alternative accommodation is available
§ **Borrowdale** includes Longthwaite, Rosthwaite & Stonethwaite
Clay Bank Top includes Urra & Great Broughton

PLANNING YOUR WALK

PLANNING YOUR WALK

STAYING IN CAMPING BARNS/BUNKHOUSES/HOSTELS

Night	Relaxed pace Place	Approx Distance miles/km	Medium pace Place	Approx Distance miles/km	Fast pace Place	Approx Distance miles/km
0	St Bees		St Bees		St Bees	
1	Sandwith	3/5	Sandwith	3/5	Sandwith	3/5
2	Ennerdale Br	12/19	Ennerdale YHA	15.5/25	Ennerdale YHA	15.5/25
3	Black Sail	8.5/13.5	Borrowdale§	10.5/17	Borrowdale§	10.5/17
4	Borrowdale§	5.5/9	Grasmere	10/16	Patterdale	20/32
5	Grasmere	10/16	Patterdale	10/16	Shap	16/25.5
6	Patterdale	10/16	Shap	16/25.5	K. Stephen	20/32
7	Shap	16/25.5	K. Stephen	20/32	Reeth [Grinton]	25.5/41
8	Orton*	8/13	Keld	13/21	Applegarth	9.5/15
9	K. Stephen	13/21	Reeth [Grinton]	12.5/20	Osmotherley	28.5/46
10	Keld	13/21	Applegarth	9.5/15	Blakey Ridge*	20/32
11	Reeth [Grinton]	12.5/20	Danby Wiske*	16.5/26.5	Grosmont*	13.5/21.5
12	Applegarth	9.5/15	Osmotherley	12/19	R. Hood's Bay	15.5/25
13	Danby Wiske*	16.5/26.5	Clay Bank Top§*	11/17.5		
14	Osmotherley	12/19	Glaisdale*	19/30.5		
15	Clay Bank Top§*	11/17.5	R. Hood's Bay	19/30.5		
16	Blakey Ridge*	9/14.5				
17	Glaisdale*	10/16				
18	Littlebeck*	7/11				
19	R. Hood's Bay	12/19				

*No camping barns, bunkhouses or hostels but
alternative accommodation is available
§ **Borrowdale** includes Longthwaite, Rosthwaite & Stonethwaite
Clay Bank Top includes Urra & Great Broughton

SUGGESTED ITINERARIES

The itineraries in the boxes on pp30-1 and above are based on different accommodation types – camping, camping barns/bunkhouses/hostels, and B&Bs – with each one divided into three alternatives depending on your walking speed. They are only suggestions so feel free to adapt them. **Don't forget** to add your travelling time before and after the walk.

SIDE TRIPS

The Coast to Coast path is long enough and few walkers upon it will be tempted by side trips that involve yet more walking. Yet the path cuts through possibly the richest trekking territory in England, and there are plenty of opportunities for short (or long) diversions off the trail should you wish. Such side trips are beyond the scope of this book but a quick glance at an Ordnance Survey map will give you some idea of the alternative trails and side trips available.

Wainwright's series of guides to Lakeland fells describes other walks around the Lake District in further detail. Certainly an ascent of some of the hills in the area gives an entirely different perspective of the Lakeland landscape. Old favourites include Great Gable, Striding Edge on Helvellyn, High Street and England's highest mountain Scafell Pike (978m).

What to take

Deciding how much to take can be difficult. Experienced walkers know that you should take only the bare essentials but at the same time you must ensure you have all the equipment necessary to make the trip safe and comfortable.

KEEP IT LIGHT

Experienced backpackers know that there is some sort of complicated formula governing the success of a trek, in which the enjoyment of the walk is inversely proportional to the amount carried. Carrying a heavy rucksack slows you down, tires you out and gives you aches and pains in parts of the body that you never knew existed. It is imperative, therefore, that you take time packing and that you are ruthless when you do: if it's not essential, don't take it.

HOW TO CARRY IT

If you are using one of the baggage-carrier services, you must contact them beforehand to find out what their regulations are regarding the weight and size of the luggage you wish them to carry. Even if you are using one of these services, you will still need to carry a small **daypack** with you filled with those items that you will need during the day: water bottle/pouch, this book, sunscreen, sun hat, wet-weather gear, some food, camera, money and so on.

If you have decided to forego the services of the baggage carriers, you will have to consider your **rucksack** even more carefully. Ultimately its size will depend on where you are planning to stay and how you are planning to eat. If you are camping and cooking for yourself you will probably need a 65- to 75-litre rucksack, which should be large enough to carry a small tent, sleeping bag, cooking equipment, crockery, cutlery and food. Those not carrying their home with them should find a 40- to 60-litre rucksack sufficient.

When choosing a rucksack, make sure it has a stiffened back and can be adjusted to fit your own back comfortably. Don't just try the rucksack out in the shop: take it home, fill it with things and then try it out around the house and out for a short walk. Only then will you be certain that the rucksack is properly adjusted; make sure the hip belt and chest strap (if there is one) are fastened tightly as this helps distribute the weight with most of it being carried on the hips. Put a small daypack inside the rucksack, as this will be useful to carry things in when leaving the main pack at the hostel or B&B. Finally, it's also a good idea to keep everything wrapped in plastic bags inside the rucksack, and I usually place all these bags inside a bin-bag which then goes inside the rucksack. That way, even if it does pour with rain, everything should remain dry.

FOOTWEAR

Boots
Only a decent pair of strong, durable trekking boots are good enough to survive the rigours of the Coast to Coast path. Don't be tempted by a spell of hot weather into bringing something flimsier: the bogs and marshes on the trail never dry out and there are few things less agreeable in life than walking along a trail with saturated socks and boots. Make sure, too, that your boots provide good ankle support for the ground is rough and stony and twisted ankles are commonplace. Make sure your boots are waterproof as well: these days most people opt for a synthetic waterproof lining (Gore-Tex or similar), though a good quality leather boot with dubbin should prove just as reliable in keeping your feet dry.

In addition, many people bring an extra pair of shoes or trainers to wear off the trail. This is not essential but if you are using one of the luggage-carrying services and you've got some room in your luggage why not?

Socks
If you haven't got a pair of the modern hi-tech walking socks the old system of wearing a thin liner sock under a thicker wool sock is just as good. Bring a few pairs of each.

CLOTHES

In a country notorious for its unpredictable climate, it is imperative that you pack enough clothes to cover every extreme of weather, from burning hot to bloomin' freezing. Modern hi-tech outdoor clothes come with a range of fancy names and brands, but they all still follow the basic two- or three-layer principle, with an inner base layer to transport sweat away from your skin, a mid-layer for warmth and an outer layer to protect you from the wind and rain.

A thin lightweight **thermal top** of a synthetic material is ideal as the base layer as it draws moisture (ie sweat) away from your body. Cool in hot weather and warm when worn under other clothes in the cold, pack at least one thermal top. Over the top in cold weather a mid-weight **polyester fleece** should suffice. Fleeces are light, more water-resistant than the alternatives (such as a woolly jumper), remain warm even when wet, and pack down small in rucksacks; thus they are ideal trekking gear.

Over the top of all this a **waterproof jacket** is essential. 'Breathable' jackets cost a small fortune (though prices are falling all the time) but prevent the build-up of condensation.

Leg wear
Many walkers find trekking trousers an unnecessary investment. Any light, quick-drying trouser should suffice. Jeans are heavy and dry slowly and are thus

not recommended. A pair of waterproof trousers *is* more than useful, however, while on really hot sunny days you'll be glad you brought your shorts. Thermal **longjohns** take up little room in the rucksack and could be vital if the weather starts to get really cold.

Gaiters are not necessary but, again, those who bring them are always glad they did, for they provide extra protection when walking through boggy ground and when the vegetation around the trail is dripping wet after bad weather.

Underwear
Three or four changes of underwear is fine. Any more is excessive, any less unhygienic. Because backpacks can cause bra straps to dig painfully into the skin, women may find a **sports bra** more comfortable.

Other clothes
Don't leave home without a **sun hat** and **gloves** – you'd be surprised how cold it can get up on the fells even in summer.

TOILETRIES

Once again, take the minimum. **Soap**, **towel**, a **toothbrush** and **toothpaste** are pretty much essential (although those staying in B&Bs will find that most provide soap and towels anyway). Some **toilet paper** could also prove vital on the trail, particularly if using public toilets (which occasionally run out).

A **plastic trowel** is also useful for digging holes when defecating outdoors (see pp48-9). Other items: **razor**; **deodorant**; **tampons/sanitary towels** and a high-factor **sun-screen** should cover just about everything.

FIRST-AID KIT

A small first-aid kit could prove useful for those emergencies that occur along the trail. Suggestions for what should be in this kit include **aspirin** or **parac-etamol**; **plasters** for minor cuts; **moleskin**, **Second Skin** or some other treatment for blisters; a **bandage** for holding dressings, splints, or limbs in place and for supporting a sprained ankle; **elastic knee support** for a weak knee; a small selection of different-sized **sterile dressings** for wounds; **porous adhesive tape**; **antiseptic wipes**; **antiseptic cream**; **safety pins**; **tweezers**; and **scissors**.

GENERAL ITEMS

Essential items are a **map**, **torch**, **water bottle/pouch**, **spare batteries**, **penknife**, **watch**, **whistle** (see p52 for details of the international distress signal), some **emergency food** and a **watch** (preferably with an alarm to help you make an early start each day). Those with weak knees may need a **walking pole** or **sticks**. If you know how to use it properly a **compass** is extremely handy and in the Lakes it becomes essential. Some people find a **mobile phone** invaluable too, though note that in the Lakes reception is usually available only on the fells.

Useful items include a **book** for evenings or train/bus journeys, some **plastic bags** to put rubbish in, a pair of **sunglasses**, **binoculars** and a **camera**.

CAMPING GEAR

Both campers and those intending to stay in the various bunkhouses en route will find a sleeping bag essential. A two- to three-season bag should suffice for summer. In addition, campers will need a decent bivvy bag or tent, a sleeping mat, fuel and stove, and cutlery/pans, a cup and a scrubber for washing up.

MONEY

Cash machines (ATMs) are infrequent along the Coast to Coast path, particularly in the first half through the Lakes, though their numbers are growing as post offices and shops along the trail install them. Banks are even rarer, with only Kirkby Stephen, Shap and Richmond boasting any. Not everybody accepts **debit** or **credit cards** as payment either – though most B&Bs and restaurants now do. As a result, you should always carry a fair amount of cash with you, just to be on the safe side. A **cheque book** from a British bank is useful in those places where credit cards are not accepted. See also p18 and pp28-9.

Crime on the trail is thankfully rare but it's always a good idea to carry your money safely in a **moneybelt**.

MAPS

The hand-drawn maps in this book cover the trail at a scale of 1:20,000 and this large scale, combined with the notes and tips written on the maps, should be enough to stop you losing your way. Nevertheless, it's always a good idea to have a contour map of the region through which you are walking, which could prove invaluable should you need to abandon the path and find the quickest route down because of, for example, bad weather. They also help you to identify local features and landmarks and devise possible side trips.

Unfortunately, the two Outdoor Leisure strip maps produced by the Ordnance Survey (☎ 08456 050505, 🖳 www.ordnancesurvey.co.uk) that covered the entire trail at a scale of 1:27,777 are out of print (although it may be possible to get second-hand copies; look for sheets OL33 covering the trail from St Bees to Keld and OL34 covering it from Keld to Robin Hood's Bay). In their place the Ordnance Survey now have a series of maps at a scale of 1:25,000 but in order to cover the whole trail you will need eight maps. The trouble here, of course, is one of weight and expense. The details are: Explorer series 303 (for St Bees); Outdoor Leisure (OL) 4 for the western Lake District; OL 5 for the eastern Lake District; OL 19 for the upper Eden Valley (Kirkby Stephen); OL 30 for Swaledale; Explorer series 304 for Richmond and the Vale of Mowbray; OL 26 for the western North York Moors; and OL 27 for the eastern half to Robin Hood's Bay.

While it may be extravagant to buy all of these maps, members of the **Ramblers' Association** (see box p38) can borrow up to 10 maps for a period of six weeks at 30p per map from their library.

The alternative is to go for the strip maps produced by both Harvey Maps and Footprint, both of which cover the trail over two maps at a scale of

1:40,000. The problem here is that they only cover a narrow strip either side of the trail and consequently give little opportunity for exploring further afield.

RECOMMENDED READING

Most of the following books can be found in the tourist information centres; the centre at Richmond has a particularly good supply of books about the path and the places en route. As well as stocking many of the titles listed below, the tourist offices also have a number of books about the towns and villages en route, usually printed by small, local publishers.

General guidebooks

We have to mention here Wainwright's original *A Coast to Coast Walk (Wainwright Pictorial Guides)*, a veritable work of art and now, after some doubt, reprinted by local publisher, Frances Lincoln. For those who have been bitten by the trekking bug there are plenty of other titles in the Wainwright oeuvre, including a number on the Lakeland fells and a *Pennine Way Companion*. As an alternative, *Wainwright's Coast to Coast Walk* (Mermaid Books) has the additional selling point of photos by Derry Brabbs. One for the coffee table is *Coast-to-Coasting* by John Gillham and Ronald Turnbull (a runner who completed the Coast to Coast in just four days!). Although not exclusively about Wainwright's trail – indeed, there are eight walks in this guide – the beauty of the photographs is reason enough to buy this tome. Sticking with the Wainwright theme, for some late-night reading why not take Wainwright to bed with you? Hunter Davies's *Wainwright: The Biography* (Orion Press) is a wonderfully absorbing account of this most complex of men.

For general guidebooks, both Rough Guides and Lonely Planet publish guides to England; though neither, it must be said, covers the Coast to Coast trail in adequate detail. Better is Lonely Planet's *Walking in Britain* by David Else.

Other guidebooks

Other guides to the trail include Cicerone's *The Coast to Coast Trail: A Long-Distance Walking Guide* by Terry Marsh and *Coast to Coast Walk (Walking Country Series)* by Paul Hannon (Hillside Publications). There are also a couple of accommodation guides, including Doreen Whitehead's long-running publication *Coast to Coast Bed & Breakfast Accommodation Guide*.

If you are a seasoned long-distance walker, or even new to the game and like what you see, check out the other titles in the Trailblazer series; see p223-4.

Flora and fauna field guides

Collins *Bird Guide* with its beautiful illustrations of British and European birds continues to be the favourite field guide of both ornithologists and laymen alike. For only £3.99 Andrew Branson's *Wild Flowers of Britain and Europe* (Bounty Books) is the best-value pocket-sized guide available to the flora you'll encounter on the Coast to Coast path.

PLANNING YOUR WALK

❏ SOURCES OF FURTHER INFORMATION

Online trail information

🖥 www.coast2coast.co.uk Vying with the website immediately below for the title of best online guide, this one run by Sherpavan, is crammed full of useful information and should be a compulsory stop for any net-head looking to do the trail. They also have an online shop for books and maps and an accommodation-/luggage-transfer booking service (see p20). Perhaps best of all, however, they have a bulletin board where trekkers can share their experiences and those who have yet to try the trail can post any questions they might have.

🖥 www.coasttocoastguides.co.uk Richmond-based organization and another excellent website with books and maps for sale and a thorough accommodation guide.

Tourist information organizations

● **Tourist Information Centres (TICs)** TICs are based in towns throughout Britain and provide all manner of locally specific information and an accommodation-booking service. There are four centres relevant to the Coast to Coast path: **Ullswater** (near Patterdale, p114), **Kirkby Stephen** (p136), **Reeth** (p158) and **Richmond** (p167). In addition there are a number of unofficial information centres, such as the post office in Patterdale.

● **Yorkshire Tourist Board** (☎ 01904 621756; 🖥 www.ytb.org.uk) The tourist board oversees all the local tourist information centres in the county. It's a good place to find general information about the county and information on outdoor activities and local events. They can also help with arranging holidays and accommodation.

● **Cumbria Tourist Board** (☎ 015394 44444; 🖥 www.cumbria-the-lake-district.co.uk) Performing much the same role as the Yorkshire board above but, of course, for the county encompassing the Lake District.

Organizations for walkers

● **The Backpackers' Club** (🖥 www.backpackersclub.co.uk; 24 Chequers Place, Cholsey, Wallingford, Oxfordshire, OX10 9PF) A club aimed at people who are involved or interested in lightweight camping through walking, cycling, skiing, canoeing, etc.

The club produce a quarterly magazine, provide members with a comprehensive advisory and information service on all aspects of backpacking, organize weekend trips and also publish a farm pitch directory. Membership is £12 per year.

● **The Long Distance Walkers' Association** (🖥 www.ldwa.org.uk) An association for people with the common interest of long-distance walking. Membership includes a journal three times per year giving details of challenge events and local group walks as well as articles on the subject.

Information on over 500 long-distance paths is presented in the LDWA's *Long Distance Walkers' Handbook*. Membership is currently £10 per year.

● **The Ramblers' Association** (☎ 020 7339 8500, 🖥 www.ramblers.org.uk; 2nd Floor, Camelford House, 87-90 Albert Embankment, London SE1 7TW). Looks after the interests of walkers throughout Britain. They publish a large amount of useful information including their *Yearbook* (£5.99 to non-members), a full directory of services for walkers.

Getting to and from the Coast to Coast path

Both St Bees and Robin Hood's Bay are quite difficult to reach. For this reason, many people are now opting to use Kirkby Stephen as their base. Not only is this town well connected by public transport (it lies on the Carlisle to Leeds line) but it is also the home of several baggage-carrying companies, some of whom offer taxi services to the start at St Bees and other destinations on the

❏ **GETTING TO BRITAIN**

Air Manchester is the nearest major international airport to St Bees but for most foreign visitors one of the London airports is likely to be their entry point to the country. Nevertheless, if you've no business in London do check out flights to Manchester, which enjoys good connections with most of continental Europe as well as North America. From Manchester airport to St Bees it's about 2½ hours by car. Leeds Bradford (convenient for Kirkby Stephen) and Teeside (7 miles/11km outside Darlington and useful for Richmond; also the nearest airport to Robin Hood's Bay), are also worth investigating but are served mainly by domestic flights.

A number of **budget airlines** (namely 🖳 www.easyjet.com, 🖳 bmibaby.com and 🖳 www.ryanair.com) fly from many of Europe's major cities to Manchester and the London terminals of Stansted and Luton, with a few now flying to Gatwick and Heathrow too. From London it is around four hours to Carlisle by train, from where you can catch a second train back down the coast to St Bees; see p40.

From Europe by train Eurostar (🖳 www.eurostar.com) operates the high-speed passenger service via the Channel Tunnel between Paris and London (2½-3 hours) and Brussels and London (2-2½ hours). The Eurostar terminal in London is currently at Waterloo station but is scheduled to move to St Pancras station in mid-2007.

Both Waterloo and St Pancras have connections to the London Underground and to all other main railway stations in London; Euston is the station for trains to Carlisle (for St Bees), while Kings Cross serves departures to Whitby.

From Europe by bus Eurolines (🖳 www.eurolines.com) have a huge network of long-distance bus services connecting over 500 cities in 25 European countries to London. Check carefully, however: often, once such expenses as food for the journey are taken into consideration, it often does not work out that much cheaper than taking a flight, particularly when compared to the prices of some of the budget airlines.

From Europe by car Eurotunnel (🖳 www.eurotunnel.com) operates the shuttle train service for vehicles via the Channel Tunnel between Calais and Folkestone taking one hour between the motorway in France and the motorway in Britain.

P&O Ferries (🖳 www.poferries.com) and Hoverspeed (🖳 www.hoverspeed .com) run frequent ferries between Calais and Dover. The journey takes about 75 minutes. There are countless other ferries plying routes between all the major North Sea and Channel ports of mainland Europe and the ports on Britain's eastern and southern coasts.

Coast to Coast path, and will also bring customers back to Kirkby Stephen at the end of their walk. See pp20-1 for details of a few of these companies.

If you want to make your own way to St Bees, it's best to catch a train from Carlisle or a bus/walk from Whitehaven. For Robin Hood's Bay, the Whitby to Scarborough bus calls in at the top of the town half a dozen times a day, with both of these towns well connected by rail.

NATIONAL TRANSPORT

All train **timetable and fare information** can be found at National Rail Enquiries (☎ 08457 484950, 24hrs), or on the web at ⌨ www.nationalrail.co .uk. Alternatively you can look on the websites of the train companies concerned (⌨ www.virgin.com/trains, ⌨ www.gner.co.uk and ⌨ www.northern rail.org). Timetables and tickets are also available on ⌨ www.thetrainline.com and ⌨ www.qjump.co.uk.

The principal coach (long-distance bus) operator in Britain is **National Express** (☎ 08705 808080, open 8am-10pm daily; ⌨ www.nationalexpress .com), though **Megabus** (☎ 0900 160 0900, ⌨ www.megabus.com) has two services a day between London and Glasgow via Manchester (£26 return).

Coach travel is generally cheaper (though with the excellent Virgin Value train fares that is not always true) but longer than travel by train.

Getting to St Bees
● **Train** At the time of writing there were 11 services a day **from London** to Carlisle, each taking between 3½ and 4½ hours. It is possible to catch the 10.15am from London Euston to arrive at Carlisle at 1.39pm, thus giving you 40 minutes to make your way to the platform for the 14.20 St Bees departure. Virgin also has services from the south coast, the south-west and Scotland to Carlisle.

Between Carlisle (see box below) and St Bees, there are 5-8 trains a day, Mon-Sat. (The service to Whitehaven, four miles up the road from St Bees, is more frequent with 15-16/day Monday to Saturday and 3/day on Sunday.)

Note: St Bees is a request stop – you must inform the conductor of your desire to alight there. Otherwise the train won't stop and you could end up

---

❑ **Carlisle**
Carlisle has a Link **cashpoint** inside the station lobby (to the left as you enter from platform 4) as well as toilets and a buffet (café) on the platform. A **train information office** (Mon-Sat 8am-7.30pm, Sun 11am-7.30pm) sits just inside the station's main entrance.

If you get stuck overnight there's a couple of **hotels** including one right by the entrance, and if you've time to kill the imposing **citadel**, rearing up to your left as you leave the station, is worth at least a quick peek. Erected in 1810, the walls were designed by Thomas Telford to replace the original fortifications built on the order of Henry VIII in 1542. A stroll to the **castle** (daily 9.30am-6pm), cathedral and **Tullie House Museum and Art Gallery** (Mon-Sat 11am-5pm, Sun noon-5pm), all on Castle St in the centre of town, should be in order for those with more time to spare.

❑ **Whitehaven**
If you arrive early and want to look around first, a couple of sights worth mentioning are the **Georgian harbour** and the adjoining **Beacon**, housing Whitehaven's **museum** (Tue-Sun 10am-5.30pm; entry £4.40); and the **Rum Story** (daily 10am-5pm), in Jefferson's, the oldest wine merchants in Britain, which is also at the harbour.

spending your first night sampling the delights of Barrow-in-Furness or Sellafield.

I have been told that, should the train from London to Carlisle be delayed, causing you to miss your connection to St Bees, you can inform the railway staff at Carlisle and they'll put you on the next train to Whitehaven (see box above), from where a taxi will take you free-of-charge to St Bees. Whether they're still operating this service by the time you read this is uncertain, but it's certainly worth enquiring.

Coming **from Manchester Piccadilly** there are nine trains a day Monday to Saturday to Barrow-in-Furness; the Sunday service is less regular and may require a change of train. From Barrow in Furness to St Bees there are 6-8/day Monday to Saturday (no Sunday service).

● **Coach/bus** The nearest National Express coach service runs to Whitehaven from London, four miles north of St Bees. Alternatively, National Express has services to Carlisle from several towns and cities in Britain. From Carlisle Stagecoach operates two services (No 300/1 daily and No 600 Mon-Sat) to Whitehaven. From Whitehaven trekkers have the options of walking or taking a taxi, bus (see box p43) or train (see above) to St Bees.

● **Car** You can of course drive to St Bees and leave your car (for a fee) at a B&B there. The nearest motorway is the M6 to Carlisle which joins the M1 just outside Coventry. From the south, leave the M1 at junction 36 (the Southern Lakes turn-off), then take the A590 till it meets the A5092; this then meets the A595 (to Whitehaven) and turn off just before Egremont.

Getting to Robin Hood's Bay
● **Train** Robin Hood's Bay is, if anything, even harder to get to than St Bees. The nearest rail station is at Whitby: trekkers coming up from London to Robin Hood's Bay need to change twice, at Darlington and Middlesbrough, in order to reach Whitby, from where they can catch a bus to the Bay (20 minutes). The train journey takes about five hours. A better way, perhaps, involving only one change of train, is to catch one of the fourteen services operated by GNER from London to Scarborough (changing at York) and then take a bus from there to the Bay. The bus journey is longer (approximately 40 minutes) but the train journey is only around three hours including changes.

● **Coach/bus** National Express operates one direct service a day to Whitby (leaving London Victoria at 1pm, arriving at Whitby at 8.40pm) and two which involve a change at Leeds (depart London Victoria at 9.30am and 11.30am arriving at Whitby at 5.39pm and 7.34pm respectively). The last bus (93) for the 20-minute journey from Whitby to Robin Hood's Bay leaves at 10.05pm.

● **Car** It's not entirely straightforward to get to Robin Hood's Bay by car either, though compared to public transport it is at least the simplest. From London it's probably best to head up to Doncaster on the M1/A1(M), then the M18/A19 to York. From there you can head north-east to Scarborough on the A64, then the A171 heading towards Whitby, turning off on the B1447 for Robin Hood's Bay.

Coming from the west, from Manchester take the M62 north-east to Leeds, then the A64 all the way to Scarborough, from where you pick up the A171 as outlined above.

Getting to Kirkby Stephen

● **Train** Kirkby Stephen lies on the Carlisle to Settle line. Coming from London, (Kings Cross) take a train to Leeds (just over two hours, operated by GNER), which also lies on the Carlisle to Settle line, and catch a train to Kirkby Stephen from there (Mon-Sat 6-7/day, Sun 3/day). The journey takes just under two hours.

● **Car** The A685 runs through the town, though there are plans for a bypass to be constructed in the near future. The trans-Pennine A66 (which shadows the Coast to Coast path to the north) crosses the A685 just four miles north of the town. The nearest motorway, the M6, is 22 miles west of the A66 interchange.

LOCAL TRANSPORT

Public transport is limited along the Coast to Coast path. While most places do have some sort of bus service, these services are irregular and often just three or four times per day. Usually the choice of destination is limited too, with often the nearest big town being the only choice.

Old roadsign with distances in miles and furlongs. In case you've forgotten, eight furlongs equals one mile.

If you have difficulty getting through to the transport companies in the box on pp43-4, you can contact **traveline** (☎ 0870 608 2608, 7am-9pm; 🖳 www.traveline.org.uk) which has public transport information for the whole of the UK.

For information about Cumbria contact Stagecoach North West or Cumbria County Council (see box opposite) and ask for a copy of Stagecoach's publication, *The Lakesrider*, which gives details of buses, trains and ferries in the county and is published twice a year.

Brief details of local transport services for each town and village are given in the route guide.

◻ PUBLIC TRANSPORT SERVICES

Notes
- Services on Bank Holiday Mondays are usually the same as Sunday services
- Services generally operate at the same frequency in both directions
- Frequencies given are between 9am and 6pm
- In most areas in addition to the standard single (one-way) and return tickets there are a variety of special tickets and passes so check before travelling to see if any are relevant to your plans
- In rural areas where there are no fixed bus stops it is usually possible to 'hail and ride' a passing bus though it is important to stand where visibility is good and also somewhere where it would be safe for the driver to stop.

Services

Northern Rail Ltd (🖳 www.northernrail.org, ☎ 08457 484950)
- See p40 for details of the services from Carlisle to Barrow-in-Furness/Lancaster via Whitehaven and St Bees
- Leeds to Carlisle via Kirkby Stephen, Mon-Sat 5-6/day (1/day continues to Glasgow Central), Sun 3/day
- Middlesbrough to Whitby via Glaisdale, Egton and Grosmont, Mon-Sat 4-5/day, Sun 4/day June to September

North York Moors Railway (enquiries ☎ 01751-472508, talking timetable ☎ 01751 -473535, 🖳 www.northyorkshiremoorsrailway.com or 🖳 www.nymr.demon.co.uk)
Grosmont to Pickering and vice versa, daily Mar-Oct plus in holiday periods such as Christmas/New Year and February half-term, weekends only at other times; 4-8/day depending on the time of year

Stagecoach North West (🖳 www.stagecoachbus.com)/**Cumbria County Council** (☎ 01228 606705, 🖳 www.cumbria.gov.uk/roads-transport)

20	Whitehaven to St Bees via Sandwith, Mon-Sat 5-6/day, no Sunday service
6	Whitehaven to Muncaster via Moor Row & Egremont, Mon-Sat 3-4/day
X6	Whitehaven to Millom via Egremont and Muncaster, Sun 4/day
22	Whitehaven to Egremont via Cleator Moor and Cleator, Mon-Sat hourly, no Sunday service
830	St Bees to Egremont via Cleator, Mon-Sat 3-4/day
219	Cockermouth to Cleator Moor via Ennerdale Bridge, Mon-Sat 3-4/day
300/301	Whitehaven to Carlisle, Mon-Sat hourly, Sun 1/every two hours
77/77A	Keswick to Keswick (Honiston Rambler) a circular route via Buttermere, Honister YHA and Seatoller, Mar-Oct 4/day in each direction
79	Keswick to Seatoller (Borrowdale Rambler) via Rosthwaite, Mar-Oct Mon-Sat 1-2/hr, Sun hourly; Oct-Mar Mon-Sat hourly
555	Keswick to Lancaster via Grasmere, Ambleside, Windermere and Kendal, Mon-Sat hourly, Sun hourly (Easter to Oct only)
	Keswick to Carlisle connecting service, Mon-Sat 3/day, Sun 2/day
599	Grasmere to Bowness/Kendal (Open-top Lakeland Experience) via Ambleside and Windermere, Mar-Aug daily 3/hr; Aug-Oct daily 2/hr
517	Bowness to Glenridding (Kirkstone Rambler) via Patterdale Hotel, Mar-Jul and Aug-Oct Sat, Sun and Public Holidays 3/day; Jul-Aug daily 3/day
208	Patterdale Hotel to Keswick (Ullswater Connexion), May-July and Aug-Oct Sat, Sun and Public Holidays only 5/day; July-Aug daily 5/day

(continued overleaf)

PLANNING YOUR WALK

❏ Public transport services

Stagecoach North West *(continued from p43)*

106   Penrith to Kendal via Shap & Orton (various operators), Mon-Sat 3-6/day
108   Penrith to Patterdale Hotel, Mon-Sat 4-5/day, Mar-Oct only Sun 4/day
111   Penrith to Burnbanks Village (Haweswater Rambler), Tue and Sat 5/day
      (connects with trains from Leeds or Carlisle 2/day); Sun July-Aug 3/day
563   Penrith (bus and rail stations) to Kirkby Stephen, Mon-Sat 5-6/day
564   Kirkby Stephen to Kendal, Mon-Sat 4/day

Arriva North East (☎ **0870 102 1088**, 🖳 **www.arrivabus.co.uk/northeast**)

29   Richmond to Darlington, Mon-Sat 3-4/day
30   Keld to Richmond via Thwaite, Muker (Farmer's Arms), Gunnerside Bridge
      and Reeth, Mon-Thu 2/day, Fri 1/day, Sat 3/day; plus Gunnerside Bridge to
      Richmond Mon-Fri 3/day and Reeth to Richmond Mon-Fri 2/day
30A   Reeth to Richmond, Sat 2/day
830   Hawes Dales Countryside Museum via Thwaite, Muker, Gunnerside Bridge,
      Reeth, Grinton, Richmond, Scotch Corner and Darlington, May-Oct;
      Sunday 1/day plus Hawes to Richmond 1/day and Reeth to Richmond 2/day
34   Richmond to Darlington via Colburn Lanes and Catterick Village, Mon-Sat
      10/day, Sun 4/day, Bank Holidays hourly 8.54am-2.54pm + two services
X59   Askrigg to Darlington via Richmond, Mon-Fri 1/day
47   Richmond to Brompton-on-Swale, Mon-Sat 3-4/day
X26   Catterick Village to Darlington via Colburn and Richmond, 1/hr daily
27   Catterick Garrison to Darlington via Richmond, Sun hourly
X27   Catterick Garrison to Darlington via Richmond, Mon-Sat hourly
28   Catterick Garrison to Darlington via Richmond, Mon-Sat hourly
54   Richmond to Marne Barracks via Colburn, Mon-Fri 7-8/day
X54   Richmond to Darlington via Catterick Garrison and Colburn, Sat 1/hr daily
93   Scarborough to Middlesbrough via Robin Hood's Bay, Hawsker Village and
      Whitby, Mon-Sat 6/day, Sun 1-2/day; Scarborough to Whitby daily 1-2/hr

Moorsbus Network (☎ **01845 597000**, 🖳 **www.moors.uk.net/moorsbus**)

M2   Helmsley to Stokesley via Gt Broughton and Clay Bank, 3/day (2/day
      connect with the M9) Mon-Sat, Sun Mar-Oct only, daily July-Aug plus Fri,
      Sat and Tue early June-Sep
M9   Osmotherley (The Cross) to Stokesley via Lord Stones Café, 2/day and via
      Clay Bank 1/day Sun Mar-Oct plus daily July-Aug

Abbotts of Leeming (☎ **01677 422858**)

80   Stokesley to Northallerton via Osmotherley, Mon-Sat 5/day plus 1/day
      Northallerton to Osmotherley
89   Stokesley to Northallerton via Gt Broughton and Osmotherley, Mon-Sat
      4-5/day, Sun Mar-Oct 4/day

M&D Minicoaches (☎ **01947-895418**)

99   Whitby to Lealholm via Grosmont, Egton, and Glaisdale, Mon-Sat 3-5/day.
      This is a hail and ride service.

Postbus (☎ **08457-740740**, 🖳 **www.royalmail.com/postbus**)

261   Penrith bus station to Patterdale Hotel via Penrith rail station and
      Glenridding, Mon-Fri 1/day, leaves Penrith Bus Station at 17.45 and
      Patterdale Hotel for the return journey at 18.25; nine seats available.

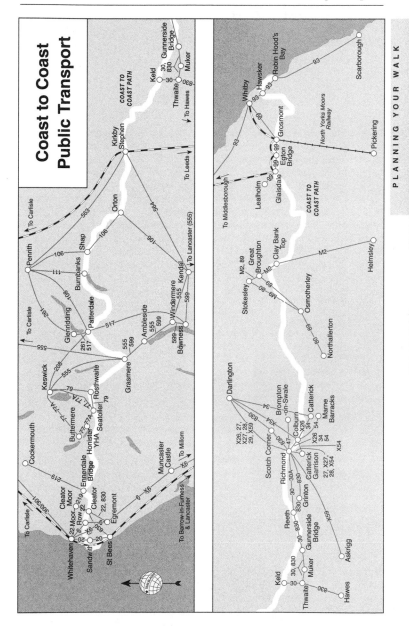

Coast to Coast Public Transport

Minimum impact

In this chaotic world in which people live their lives at an increasingly frenetic pace, many of us living in overcrowded cities and working in jobs that offer little free-time, the great outdoors is becoming an essential means of escape. Walking in the countryside is a wonderful means of relaxation and gives people the time to think and rediscover themselves.

Of course, as the popularity of the countryside increases so do the problems that this pressure brings. It is important for visitors to remember that the countryside is the home and workplace of many others. Walkers in particular should be aware of their responsibilities. Indeed a walker who respects and understands the countryside will get far more enjoyment from their trip.

By following a few simple guidelines while walking the Coast to Coast path you can have a positive impact, not just on your own well-being but also on local communities and the environment, thereby becoming part of the solution.

Support local businesses

ECONOMIC IMPACT

Rural businesses and communities in Britain have been hit hard in recent years by a seemingly endless series of crises. Most people are aware of the country code; not dropping litter and closing the gate behind you are still as pertinent as ever, but in light of the economic pressures that local countryside businesses are under there is something else you can do: buy local.

Buy local

Look and ask for local produce to buy and eat. Not only does this cut down on the amount of pollution and congestion that the transportation of food creates, so-called 'food miles', but also ensures that you are supporting local farmers and producers – the very people who have moulded the countryside you have come to see and who are in the best position to protect it. If you can find local food which is also organic so much the better.

Support local businesses

If you spend £1 in a local business 80p of that pound stays within the local economy where it can be spent again and again to do the most good for that community and landscape. If, on the other hand, you spend your money in a branch

---

❑ **Nourishing facts to ponder while walking**
● A supermarket provides one job for every £250,000 spent, compared with a village shop which provides one job for every £50,000 spent.
● Britain imports 125,000 tonnes of lamb and exports 102,000 tonnes annually.
● A small portion of chicken breast can cost £3 in a supermarket; farmers get little more than £1 for an entire chicken.
● The UK imports 126 million litres of liquid milk and exports 270 million litres of liquid milk in the same year.
● 40-80% of the antibiotics used in farming are thought to be unnecessary. Overuse has already made some drugs ineffective.
● Every kilogram of pesticide used on the land costs the water companies £7.57 to remove from our groundwater supplies.
● The total cost of car use for an out-of-town supermarket – including air pollution, CO_2 emissions, congestion, noise and accidents – is estimated to be £50,000 per week higher than for an equivalent market in the town centre.

---

of a national or multinational chain store, restaurant or hotel the situation is reversed; only 20% (mainly the staff wages) stays within the local economy and the other 80% is effectively lost to that community as it's siphoned off to pay for goods, transport and profit. The more money which circulates locally and is spent on local labour and materials, the more power the community has to effect the change it wants to see; a world of difference from the corporatization of the countryside which we are currently witnessing.

Encourage local cultural traditions and skills
No part of the countryside looks the same. Buildings, food, skills, and language evolve out of the landscape and are moulded over hundreds of years to suit the locality. Discovering these cultural differences is part of the pleasure of walking in new places. Visitors' enthusiasm for local traditions and skills brings awareness and pride, nurturing a sense of place; an increasingly important role in a world where economic globalization continues to undermine the very things that provide security and a feeling of belonging.

ENVIRONMENTAL IMPACT

A walking holiday in itself is an environmentally friendly approach to tourism. The following are some ideas on how you can go a few steps further in helping to minimize your impact on the environment while walking the Coast to Coast path.

Use public transport whenever possible
Public transport along the Coast to Coast trail is not bad (though it can be a little infrequent at times), with just about everywhere served by at least one bus or train a day. Public transport is always preferable to using private cars as it benefits everyone: visitors, locals and the environment.

Never leave litter
'Pack it in, pack it out'. Leaving litter shows a total disrespect for the natural world and others coming after you. As well as being unsightly litter kills

MINIMUM IMPACT & OUTDOOR SAFETY

wildlife, pollutes the environment and can be dangerous to farm animals. **Please** carry a plastic bag so you can dispose of your rubbish in a bin in the next village. It would be very helpful if you could pick up litter left by other people too.
● **Is it OK if it's biodegradable?** Not really. Apple cores, banana skins, orange peel and the like are unsightly, encourage flies, ants and wasps and ruin a picnic spot for others. Using the excuse that they are natural and biodegradable just doesn't cut any ice. When was the last time you saw a banana tree in the north of England?
● **The lasting impact of litter** A piece of orange peel left on the ground takes six months to decompose; silver foil 18 months; a plastic bag 10 years; clothes 15 years; and an aluminium can 85 years.

Erosion
● **Stay on the main trail** The effect of your footsteps may seem minuscule but when they are multiplied by several thousand walkers each year they become rather more significant. Avoid taking shortcuts, widening the trail or taking more than one path; your boots will be followed by many others. This is particularly true on the Coast to Coast path which has become a victim of its own success, with a number of sections of the trail now badly eroded. Indeed, over the Pennines the authorities have now established three trails, with each to be used for four months a year, thereby limiting the amount of erosion on any one trail.
● **Consider walking out of season** Maximum disturbance by walkers coincides with the time of year when nature wants to do most of its growth and repair. In high-use areas, like that along much of the Coast to Coast path, the trail is often prevented from recovering.

Walking at less busy times eases this pressure while also generating year-round income for the local economy. Not only that, but it may make the walk a more relaxing experience with fewer people on the path and less competition for accommodation.

Respect all wildlife
Care for all wildlife you come across along the path; it has as much right to be there as you. Tempting as it may be to pick wild flowers leave them so the next people who pass can enjoy them too. Don't break branches off or damage trees in any way.

If you come across wildlife keep your distance and don't watch for too long. Your presence can cause considerable stress, particularly if the adults are with young, or in winter when the weather is harsh and food is scarce.

Young animals are rarely abandoned. If you come across young birds keep away so that their mother can return.

The code of the outdoor loo
'Going' in the outdoors is a lost art worth reclaiming, for your sake and everyone else's. As more and more people discover the joys of the outdoors this is

(**Opposite**): On the trail between Helvellyn (see p109) and Patterdale in the Lake District. (Photo © Henry Stedman).

becoming an important issue. In some parts of the world where visitor pressure is higher than in Britain, walkers and climbers are required to pack out their excrement. This could soon be necessary here. Human excrement is not only offensive to our senses but, more importantly, can infect water sources.

● **Where to go** Wherever possible **use a toilet**. Public toilets are marked on the trail maps in this guide and you will also find facilities in pubs, cafés and campsites along the Coast to Coast path. If you do have to go outdoors choose a site at least **30 metres away from running water**.

Use a stick or trowel to **dig a small hole** about 15cm (6") deep to bury your excrement in. It decomposes quicker when in contact with the top layer of soil or leaf mould. Then stir loose soil into your deposit as this speeds up decomposition. Do not squash it under rocks as this slows down the composting process. If you have to use rocks to cover it make sure they are not in contact with your faeces.

● **Toilet paper and sanitary towels** Toilet paper takes a long time to decompose whether buried or not. It is easily dug up by animals and may then blow into water sources or onto the path.

The best method for dealing with it is to **pack it out**. Put the used paper inside a paper bag which you then place inside a plastic bag (or two). Then simply empty the contents of the paper bag at the next toilet you come across and throw the bag away. You should also pack out **tampons** and **sanitary towels** in a similar way; they take years to decompose and will be dug up and scattered about by animals.

Wild camping

Unfortunately wild camping is not encouraged within the national parks which make up the majority of the walk. In any case there are few places where it is a viable option.

This is a shame since wild camping is an altogether more fulfilling experience than camping on a designated site. Living in the outdoors without any facilities provides a valuable lesson in simple, sustainable living where the results of all your actions, from going to the loo to washing your plates, can be seen.

If you do insist on wild camping always ask the landowner for permission. Follow these suggestions for minimizing your impact and encourage others to do likewise.

● **Be discreet** Camp alone or in small groups, spend only one night in each place and pitch your tent late and move off early.

● **Never light a fire** Accidental fire is a great fear for farmers and foresters. Never make a camp fire and take matches and cigarette butts out with you to dispose of safely. Aside from that, the deep burn caused by camp fires, no matter how small, damages the turf which can take years to recover. Cook on a camp stove instead.

MINIMUM IMPACT & OUTDOOR SAFETY

(**Opposite**) **Top:** Bivvying at Applegarth (see p162), Yorkshire Dales National Park. **Bottom:** Taking a break at The Lion Inn, Blakey Ridge. Pubs are as much a feature of the Coast to Coast path as are moorland and sheep. (Photos © Jim Manthorpe).

● **Don't use soap or detergent**   There is no need to use soap; even biodegradable soaps and detergents pollute streams. You won't be away from a shower for more than a day or so. Wash up without detergent; use a plastic or metal scourer, or failing that, a handful of fine pebbles or some bracken or grass.

● **Leave no trace**   Learn the skill of moving on without leaving any sign of having been there: no moved boulders, ripped up vegetation or dug drainage ditches. Make a final check of your campsite before departing; pick up any litter that you or anyone else has left, so leaving the place in a better state than you found it.

ACCESS

Britain is a crowded island with few places where you can wander as you please. Most of the land is a patchwork of fields and agricultural land and the land through which the Coast to Coast path marches is no different. However, there are countless public rights of way, in addition to the Coast to Coast path, that criss-cross the land.

This is fine, but what happens if you feel a little more adventurous and want to explore the moorland, woodland and hills that can also be found near the walk.

Right to roam

The Countryside & Rights of Way Act 2000 (CRoW), or 'Right to Roam' as dubbed by walkers, came into effect in full on 31 October 2005 after a long campaign to allow greater public access to areas of countryside in England and Wales deemed to be uncultivated open country; this essentially means moorland, heathland, downland and upland areas. Some land is covered by restrictions (ie high-impact activities such as driving a vehicle, cycling, horse-riding are not permitted) and some land is excluded (such as gardens, parks and cultivated land). Full details are given on www.countrysideaccess.gov.uk.

With more freedom in the countryside comes a need for more responsibility from the walker. Remember that wild open country is still the workplace of farmers and home to all sorts of wildlife. Have respect for both and avoid disturbing domestic and wild animals.

The Countryside Code

The countryside is a fragile place which every visitor should respect. The Countryside Code seems like common sense but sadly some people still appear to have no understanding of how to treat the countryside they walk in. Everyone visiting the countryside has a responsibility to minimize the impact of their visit so that other people can enjoy the same peaceful landscapes; it doesn't take much effort.

The Countryside Code has now been revised, in part because of the changes brought about by the CRoW Act (see

> ❏ **The Countryside Code**
> ● Be safe – plan ahead and follow any signs
> ● Leave gates and property as you find them
> ● Protect plants and animals, and take your litter home
> ● Keep dogs under close control
> ● Consider other people

above) and was relaunched in July 2004. Below is an expanded version of the new Countryside Code, launched under the logo 'Respect, Protect and Enjoy':

● **Be safe** The Coast to Coast path is pretty much hazard free but you're responsible for your own safety so follow the simple guidelines outlined on pp52-4.

● **Leave all gates as you found them** Normally a farmer leaves gates closed to keep livestock in but may sometimes leave them open to allow livestock access to food or water. Leave them as you find them and if there is a sign, follow the instructions.

● **Leave livestock, crops and machinery alone** Help farmers by not interfering with their means of livelihood.

● **Take your litter home** 'Pack it in, pack it out'. Litter is not only ugly but can be harmful to wildlife. Small mammals often become trapped in discarded cans and bottles. Many walkers think that orange peel and banana skins do not count as litter. Even biodegradable foodstuffs attract common scavenging species such as crows and gulls to the detriment of less dominant species. See pp47-8.

● **Keep your dog under control** Across farmland dogs should be kept on a lead. During lambing time they should not be taken with you at all (see box opposite and p22).

● **Enjoy the countryside and respect its life and work** Access to the countryside depends on being sensitive to the needs and wishes of those who live and work there. Being courteous and friendly to those you meet will ensure a healthy future for all based on partnership and co-operation.

> ❏ **Lambing**
> Lambing takes place from mid-March to mid-May when dogs should not be taken along the path. Even a dog secured on a lead can disturb a pregnant ewe.
>
> If you see a lamb or ewe that appears to be in distress contact the nearest farmer.

● **Keep to paths across farmland** Stick to the official path across arable or pasture land. Minimize erosion by not cutting corners or widening the path.

● **Use gates and stiles to cross fences, hedges and walls** The Coast to Coast path is well supplied with stiles where it crosses field boundaries. On some of the side trips you may find the paths less accommodating. If you have to climb over a gate because you can't open it always do so at the hinged end.

● **Guard against all risk of fire** See p49.

● **Help keep all water clean** Leaving litter and going to the toilet near a water source can pollute people's water supplies. See pp47-9 for more advice.

● **Take special care on country roads** Drivers often go dangerously fast on narrow winding lanes. To be safe, walk facing the oncoming traffic and carry a torch or wear highly visible clothing when it's getting dark.

● **Protect wildlife, plants and trees** Care for and respect all wildlife you come across along the Coast to Coast path. Don't pick plants, break trees or scare wild animals. If you come across young birds that appear to have been abandoned leave them alone.

● **Make no unnecessary noise** Enjoy the peace and solitude of the outdoors by staying in small groups and acting unobtrusively.

MINIMUM IMPACT & OUTDOOR SAFETY

Outdoor safety

AVOIDANCE OF HAZARDS

With good planning and preparation most hazards can be avoided. This information is just as important for those out on a day walk as for those walking the entire Coast to Coast path. Always make sure you have suitable **clothes** to keep you warm and dry, whatever the conditions (see pp34-5) and a spare change of inner clothes. Carrying plenty of food and water is vital too.

A compass, whistle, torch, map and first-aid kit should be carried; this is discussed further on p35. The **emergency signal** is six blasts on the whistle or six flashes with a torch.

Safety on the Coast to Coast path

Sadly every year people are injured or killed walking the Coast to Coast path. The most dangerous section is in the Lake District, where the altitudes and the unpredictable weather combine to lead walkers to their doom. Mountain rescue teams are locally based and are staffed by volunteers who are ready 24 hours a day 365 days of the year.

In an emergency phone ☎ 999 as normal, and the police will activate the service. These rescue teams rely on donations (the Patterdale's running costs are estimated to be £30,000 per annum), and are called out on average about 60 times a year. There is another rescue team based at Kirkby Stephen.

All rescue teams should be treated as very much the last resort, however, and it's vital you take every precaution to ensure your own safety:

● Avoid walking on your own if possible, particularly on the Lakeland fells.
● Make sure that somebody knows your plans for every day that you are on the trail. This could be a friend or relative whom you have promised to call every night, or the owner of the B&B you plan to stay in at the end of each day's walk. That way, if you fail to turn up or call that evening, they can raise the alarm.
● If the weather closes in suddenly and fog or mist descends while you are on the trail, particularly on the moors or fells, and you become uncertain of the correct trail, do not be tempted to continue. Just wait where you are and you'll find that mist often clears, at least for long enough to allow you to get your bearings. If you are still uncertain, and the weather does not look like improving, return the way you came to the nearest point of civilization, and try again another time when conditions have improved.
● Always fill your water bottle/pouch at every opportunity and have some high-energy snacks.
● Always carry a torch, compass, map, first-aid kit, whistle and wet-weather gear with you.

● Wear strong sturdy boots with good ankle support and a good grip, not trainers.
● Be extra vigilant if walking with children.

Dealing with an accident

● Use basic first aid to treat the injury to the best of your ability.
● Work out exactly where you are. If possible leave someone with the casualty while others go to get help. If there are only two people, you have a dilemma. If you decide to get help leave all spare clothing and food with the casualty.
● In an emergency dial ☎ 999.

WEATHER FORECASTS

The Coast to Coast suffers from enormously unpredictable weather, so it's vital that you always try to find out what the weather is going to be like before you set off for the day.

Many hostels and tourist information centres will have pinned up somewhere a summary of the weather forecast. Alternatively you can call the premium-rate weather line (see below). Pay close attention to it and alter your plans for the day accordingly. That said, even if the forecast is for a fine sunny day, always assume the worst and pack some wet-weather gear.

Telephone forecasts

These are frequently updated and generally reliable. Calls are charged at the expensive premium rate: **Weather Call** ☎ 09068 500419 (Cumbria), ☎ 09068 500417 (Yorkshire).

Online forecasts

For detailed weather outlooks, including local five-day forecasts, log on to 🖳 www.bbc.co.uk/weather or 🖳 www.metoffice.gov.uk.

BLISTERS

It is important to break in new boots before embarking on a long trek. Make sure the boots are comfortable and try to avoid getting them wet on the inside. Air your feet at lunchtime, keep them clean and change your socks regularly. If you feel any hot spots stop immediately and apply a few strips of zinc oxide tape and leave it on until it is pain free or the tape starts to come off.

If you have left it too late and a blister has developed you should surround it with 'moleskin' or any other blister kit to protect it from abrasion. Popping it can lead to infection. If the skin is broken keep the area clean with antiseptic and cover with a non-adhesive dressing material held in place with tape.

HYPOTHERMIA

Also known as exposure, hypothermia occurs when the body can't generate enough heat to maintain its normal temperature, usually as a result of being wet, cold, unprotected from the wind, tired and hungry. It is usually more of a problem in upland areas such as in the Lakes and on the moors.

MINIMUM IMPACT & OUTDOOR SAFETY

Hypothermia is easily avoided by wearing suitable clothing, carrying and eating enough food and drink, being aware of the weather conditions and checking the morale of your companions.

Early signs to watch for are feeling cold and tired with involuntary shivering. Find some shelter as soon as possible and warm the victim up with a hot drink and some chocolate or other high-energy food. If possible give them another warm layer of clothing and allow them to rest until feeling better. If allowed to worsen, strange behaviour, slurring of speech and poor co-ordination will become apparent and the victim can quickly progress into unconsciousness, followed by coma and death. Quickly get the victim out of wind and rain, improvising a shelter if necessary. Rapid restoration of bodily warmth is essential and best achieved by bare-skin contact: someone should get into the same sleeping bag as the patient, both having stripped to the bare essentials, placing any spare clothing under or over them to build up heat. Send urgently for help.

HEAT EXHAUSTION AND HEATSTROKE

Not an ailment that you would normally associate with the north of England, heatstroke is a serious problem nonetheless. Symptoms of **heat exhaustion** include thirst, fatigue, giddiness, a rapid pulse, raised body temperature, low urine output and, if not treated, delirium and finally a coma. The best cure is to drink plenty of water.

Heatstroke is another matter altogether, and even more serious. A high body temperature and an absence of sweating are early indications, followed by symptoms similar to hypothermia (see above) such as a lack of co-ordination, convulsions and coma. Death will follow if treatment is not given instantly. Sponge the victim down, wrap them in wet towels, fan them, and get help immediately.

SUNBURN

It can happen, even in northern England and even on overcast days. The only surefire way to avoid it is to stay wrapped up, but that's not really an option. What you must do, therefore, is to smother yourself in sunscreen (with a minimum factor of 15) and apply it regularly throughout the day. Don't forget your lips, nose, the back of your neck and even under the chin to protect you against rays reflected up off the ground.

PART 3: ENVIRONMENT AND NATURE

Conserving the Coast to Coast path

Britain is an overcrowded island, and England is the most densely populated part of it. As such, the English countryside has suffered a great deal of pressure from both over-population and the activities of an ever more industrialized world. Thankfully, there is some enlightened legislation to protect the surviving pockets of forest and heathland.

Outside of these fragments, it is interesting to note just how much man has altered the land that he lives on. Whilst the aesthetic costs of such intrusions are open to debate, what is certain is the loss of biodiversity that has resulted. The last wild boar was shot near the Coast to Coast trail a few centuries ago (see box p135); add to that the extinction of bear and wolf, as well as, far more recently, a number of other species lost or severely depleted over the decades and you get an idea of just how much of an influence man has over the land, and how that influence is all too often used negatively.

There is good news, however. In these enlightened times when environmental issues are quite rightly given more precedence, many endangered species, such as the otter, have increased in number thanks to the active work of voluntary conservation bodies. There are other reasons to be optimistic. The environment is no longer the least important issue in party politics and this reflects the opinions of everyday people who are concerned about issues such as conservation on both a global and local scale.

GOVERNMENT AGENCIES AND SCHEMES

Since 1 April 2005, the **Countryside Agency**, **English Nature** and the environment section of the **Rural Development Service** (RDS) have operated as a 'confederation of partners' with regard to responsibility for the protection and conservation of rural, urban and coastal areas in England. (Prior to this the Countryside Agency and English Nature were independent agencies, and the RDS was a core part of the Department for the Environment, Food and Rural Affairs.)

Subject to the Natural Environment and Rural Communities Bill being passed by Parliament (although there is now a chance that this may be delayed) these three organizations will be united formally on 1 October 2006 with the creation of a new agency, **Natural England**. A new **Commission for Rural Communities** will also be established; its role will be to act as an independent adviser and watchdog for rural people, particularly communities suffering economic disadvantage.

Natural England

Natural England will be a single body responsible for identifying, establishing and funding: National Parks, Areas of Outstanding Natural Beauty (both previously managed by the Countryside Agency), National Nature Reserves, Sites of Special Scientific Interest, and Special Areas of Conservation (all previously managed by English Nature).

The highest level of landscape protection is the designation of land as a **national park** which recognizes the national importance of an area in terms of landscape, biodiversity and as a recreational resource. At the time of writing there were nine national parks in England. Three of these are bisected by the Coast to Coast path (Lake District, Yorkshire Dales and North York Moors national parks). This designation does not signify national ownership and these are not uninhabited wildernesses, making conservation a knife-edged balance between protecting the environment and the rights and livelihoods of those living in the parks.

The second level of protection is **Area of Outstanding Natural Beauty** (AONB), of which there are 37 in England covering some 15% of the country. The only AONB passed on the Coast to Coast trail covers the North Pennines including Nine Standards Rigg. Their primary objective is conservation of the natural beauty of a landscape. As there is no statutory administrative framework

---

❏ Statutory bodies

● **Department for Environment, Food and Rural Affairs** (☎ 020-7238 6951, 🖳 www .defra.gov.uk; Nobel House, 17 Smith Sq, London SW1P 3JR) Government ministry responsible for sustainable development in the countryside.

● **Natural England** (At the time of writing contact details for Natural England were not known; however, it is likely that the offices of the Countryside Agency and English Nature will be able to advise). **Countryside Agency** (☎ 01242 533222; 🖳 www.countryside.gov.uk; John Dower House, Crescent Place, Cheltenham GL50 3RA) Statutory body charged with improving the quality of the countryside for everyone. Designates National Parks and AONBs; manages England's National Trails and provides most of the funding and resources for path maintenance. **English Nature** (☎ 01733 455000; 🖳 www.english-nature.org.uk; Northminster House, Peterborough PE1 1UA) Government agency championing the conservation of wildlife, geology and wild places in England.

● **English Heritage** (☎ 0870 333 1181, 🖳 www.english-heritage.org.uk) Organization whose central aim is to make sure that the historic environment of England is properly maintained. It is officially known as the Historic Buildings and Monuments Commission for England. Mount Grace Priory (see box p186) is managed by English Heritage.

● **Lake District National Park Authority** (☎ 01539 724555; 🖳 www.lake-district.gov.uk) The government authority charged with managing the Lake District.

● **Yorkshire Dales National Park Authority** (🖳 www.yorkshiredales.org.uk)

● **North York Moors National Park Authority** (☎ 01439 770657; 🖳 www. moors.uk.net).

None of the three park authorities listed above has much in the way of specific Coast to Coast trail information on their websites, though they might be worth contacting to find out the latest developments to the path.

THE ENVIRONMENT & NATURE

for their management, this is the responsibility of the local authority within whose boundaries they fall.

Other levels of protection are National Nature Reserves and Sites of Special Scientific Interest. **National Nature Reserves** (NNR), of which there are 215 (including Smardale in Cumbria), are places where the priority is protection of the wildlife habitats and geological formations. They are either owned or managed by English Nature/Natural England or by approved organizations such as wildlife trusts. **Local nature reserves** (LNR) are managed locally; there are two in Cumbria and 15 in North Yorkshire.

Sites of Special Scientific Interest (SSSI) range in size from little pockets protecting wild flower meadows, important nesting sites or special geological features, to vast swathes of upland, moorland and wetland. SSSIs, of which there are over 4000 in England, are a particularly important designation as they have some legal standing. They are managed in partnership with the owners and occupiers of the land who must give written notice before initiating any operations likely to damage the site and who cannot proceed without consent from English Nature/Natural England. Many SSSIs are also either a NNR or a LNR.

Special Areas of Conservation (SAC) is an international designation which came into being as a result of the 1992 Earth Summit in Rio de Janeiro, Brazil. This European-wide network of sites is designed to promote the conservation of habitats, wild animals and plants, both on land and at sea. At the time of writing 236 land sites in England had been designated as SACs. Every land SAC is also an SSSI.

Environmental Stewardship Scheme

In March 2005 the Environmental Stewardship Scheme (ESSs) replaced the Environmentally Sensitive Area (ESA) scheme and the Countryside Stewardship Scheme (CSS); these covered areas that fell outside the SSSI remit, or any of the other designations, but which were deemed to be 'important' nonetheless.

The crucial difference with both ESSs (and ESAs) is that they are voluntary and provide a way through which farmers are enticed to adopt low-impact agricultural practices by being offered financial incentives. With the ESA, farmers entered into a ten-year management agreement with the **Department for Environment, Food and Rural Affairs** (DEFRA) but for ESSs the agreement is five years. In both cases the stricter the management controls the higher the payments. This, in its own small way, is a step closer to seeing all land as worthy of protection so that it can be left in a decent state for future generations.

CAMPAIGNING AND CONSERVATION ORGANIZATIONS

These voluntary organizations started the conservation movement in the mid-19th century and are still at the forefront of developments. Independent of government but reliant on public support, they can concentrate their resources either on acquiring land which can then be managed purely for conservation purposes, or on influencing political decision-makers by lobbying and campaigning.

THE ENVIRONMENT & NATURE

❑ **Campaigning and conservation organizations**
● The umbrella organization for the 47 wildlife trusts in the UK is **The Wildlife Trusts** (☎ 0870 036 7711, 🖳 www.wildlifetrusts.org), The Kiln, Waterside, Mather Rd, Newark, Nottinghamshire, NG24 1WT; Two relevant to the Coast to Coast path are **Cumbria Wildlife Trust** (☎ 01539 816300, 🖳 www.wildlifetrust.org.uk/cumbria) and **Yorkshire Wildlife Trust** (🖳 www.york shire-wildlife-trust.org.uk).
● **Royal Society for the Protection of Birds** (RSPB; ☎ 01767 680551, 🖳 www .rspb.org.uk; The Lodge, Sandy, Beds SG19 2DL) The largest voluntary conservation body in Europe focusing on providing a healthy environment for birds and wildlife and with over 150 reserves in the UK including one at Haweswater (see pp117-18).
● **National Trust** (☎ 0870 458 4000, 🖳 www.nationaltrust.org.uk; PO Box 39, Warrington WA5 7WD) A charity with 3.4 million members which aims to protect, through ownership, threatened coastline, countryside, historic houses, castles and gardens, and archaeological remains for everybody to enjoy. Seatoller (see p90) is a National Trust village.
● **British Trust for Conservation Volunteers** (BTCV; ☎ 01302 572244, 🖳 www .btcv.org; 163 Balby Rd, Doncaster DN4 0RH) Encourages people to value their environment and take practical action to improve it.
● **Campaign to Protect Rural England** (CPRE; ☎ 020 7981 2800, 🖳 www .cpre.org.uk; 128 Southwark St, London SE1 0SW) A charity whose members care about the countryside and campaign for it to be protected and enhanced.
● **Friends of the Earth** (☎ 020 7490 1555, 🖳 www.foe.co.uk; 26-8 Underwood St, London N1 7JQ) International organization campaigning for a better environment for all.
● **Greenpeace** (☎ 020 7865 8100, 🖳 www.greenpeace.org.uk; Greenpeace House, Canonbury Villas, London N1 2PN) International organization promoting peaceful activism in defence of the environment worldwide.
● **The Land is Ours** (TLIO; ☎ 07961 460171, 🖳 www.tlio.org.uk; 16B Cherwell St, Oxford, OX4 1BG) A campaign, not an organization, which aims to highlight the exclusion of ordinary people from the land.
● **Woodland Trust** (☎ 01476 581135, 🖳 www.woodland-trust.org.uk; Autumn Park, Dysart Rd, Grantham, Lincolnshire NG31 6LL) The trust aims to conserve, restore and re-establish native woodlands throughout the UK.
● **World Wide Fund for Nature** (WWF; ☎ 01483 426444, 🖳 www.wwf.org.uk; Panda House, Weyside Park, Godalming, Surrey GU7 1XR) One of the world's largest conservation organizations, protecting endangered species and threatened habitats.

Managers and owners of land include well-known bodies such as the **Royal Society for the Protection of Birds** (RSPB), with over 150 nature reserves and more than a million members, and the **Campaign to Protect Rural England** (CPRE) which exists to promote the beauty and diversity of rural England by encouraging the sustainable use of land and other natural resources in town and country.

Pressure groups such as **Friends of the Earth**, **Greenpeace** and the **World Wide Fund for Nature** (WWF) also play a vital role in environmental protection by raising public awareness with government agencies when policy needs to be formulated. A huge increase in public interest and support since the 1980s indicates that people are more conscious of environmental issues and believe that it cannot be left to our political representatives to take care of them for us without our voice. See also box opposite.

We are becoming the most powerful lobbying group of all; an informed electorate.

BEYOND CONSERVATION

Pressures on the countryside grow year on year. Western society, whether directly or indirectly, makes constant demands for more oil, more roads, more houses, more cars. At the same time awareness of environmental issues increases and the knowledge that our unsustainable approach to life cannot continue. Some governments appear more willing to adopt sustainable ideals, others less so.

Yet even the most environmentally positive of governments are some way off perfect. It's all very positive to classify parts of the countryside as national parks and Areas of Outstanding Natural Beauty but it will be of little use if we continue to pollute the wider environment; the seas and skies. For a brighter future we need to adopt that sustainable approach to life. It would not be difficult and the rewards would be great.

The individual can play his or her part. Walkers in particular appreciate the value of wild areas and should take this attitude back home with them. This is not just about recycling the odd green bottle or two and walking to the corner shop rather than driving, but about lobbying for more environmentally sensitive policies in local and national government.

The first step to a sustainable way of living is in appreciating and respecting this beautiful, complex world we live in and realizing that every one of us plays an important role within the great web. The natural world is not a separate entity. We are all part of it and should strive to safeguard it rather than work against it. So many of us live in a world that does seem far removed from the real world, cocooned in centrally heated houses and upholstered cars. Rediscovering our place within the natural world is both uplifting on a personal level and important regarding our outlook and approach to life.

❏ **Sustainability websites**

For lovers of the natural world who have ever asked 'but what can I do?', the following websites are a good place to start:

● **The Ecologist Magazine** (🖳 www.theecologist.org) Britain's longest-running environmental magazine.

● **International Society for Ecology and Culture** (🖳 www.isec.org.uk) Promoting locally based alternatives to the global consumer culture to protect biological and cultural diversity.

● **Permaculture Magazine** (🖳 www.permaculture.co.uk) Explains the principles and practice of sustainable living.

● **Resurgence Magazine** (🖳 www.resurgence.gn.apc.org) 'The flagship of the green movement'.

Flora and fauna

The beauty of walking from one side of England to another is that on the way you pass through just about every kind of habitat this country has to offer. From woodland and grassland to heathland, beach and bog, the variety of habitats is surpassed only by the number of species of flower, tree and animal that each supports.

The following is not in any way a comprehensive guide – if it were, you would not have room for anything else in your rucksack – but merely a brief guide to the more commonly seen flora and fauna of the trail, together with some of the rarer and more spectacular species.

MAMMALS

The Coast to Coast path is alive with all manner of native species, and the wide variety of habitats encountered on the way means that the wildlife is varied too. Unfortunately, most of these creatures are shy and many are nocturnal, and walkers can consider themselves extremely lucky if during their trek they see more than three or four species.

One creature that you will see everywhere along the walk, from the cliffs at St Bees to the fields outside Robin Hood's Bay, is the **rabbit** (*Oryctolagus cuniculus*). Timid by nature, most of the time you'll have to make do with nothing more than a brief and distant glimpse of their white tails as they stampede for the nearest warren at the first sound of your footfall. Because they are so numerous, however, the laws of probability dictate that you will at some stage get close enough to observe them without being spotted; trying to take a decent photo of one of them, however, is a different matter.

If you're lucky you may also come across **hares**, often mistaken for rabbits but much larger, more elongated and with longer back legs and ears.

Rabbits used to form one of the main elements in the diet of the **fox** (*Vulpes vulpes*), one of the more adaptable of Britain's native species. Famous as the scourge of chicken coops, their reputation as indiscriminate killers is actually unjustified: though they will if left undisturbed kill all the chickens in a coop in what appears to be a mindless and frenzied attack, the fox will actually eat all their victims, carrying off and storing the carcasses in underground burrows for them and their families to eat at a later date. These days, however, you are far more likely to see a fox in towns, where they survive mostly on the scraps and leftovers of the human population, rather than in the country. While generally considered nocturnal, it's not unusual to encounter a fox during the day too, often lounging in the sun near their den.

One creature that is strictly nocturnal, however, is the **bat**, of which there are 14 species in Britain, all protected by law. Your best chance of spotting one is just after dusk while there's still enough light in the sky to make out their flitting forms as they fly along hedgerows, over rivers and streams and around street lamps in their quest for moths and insects. The most common species in Britain is the pipistrelle (*Pipistrellus pipistrellus*).

The Lakes offer one of the few chances in England to see the rare **red squirrel** (*Sciurus vulgaris*). While elsewhere in the country these small, tufty-eared natives have been usurped by their larger cousins from North America, the **grey squirrel** (*Sciurus carolinensis*), in the Lakes the red squirrel maintains a precarious foothold. In Patterdale a count of the local red squirrel population is organized annually; contact the YHA there for details. A number also hang around Gillerthwaite YHA in Ennerdale.

Patterdale also offers walkers on the Coast to Coast their best chance of seeing the **badger** (*Meles meles*). Relatively common throughout the British Isles, these nocturnal mammals with their distinctive black-and-white-striped muzzle are sociable animals that live in large underground burrows called setts, appearing after sunset to root for worms and slugs. One creature which you almost certainly won't encounter, though they are said to exist in the Lakes, is the **pine marten** (*martes martes*). Extremely rare in England since being virtually wiped out during the 19th century for their pelts and their reputation as vermin, there are said to be a few in the valley of Ennerdale.

In addition to the above, keep a look out for other fairly common but little seen species such as the carnivorous **stoat** (*Mustela erminea*), its smaller cousin the **weasel** (*Mustela nivalis*), the **hedgehog** (*Erinaceus europaeus*) – these days, alas, most commonly seen as roadkill – and a number of species of **voles**, **mice** and **shrews**.

One of Britain's rarest creatures, the **otter** (*Lutra lutra*), is enjoying something of a renaissance thanks to concerted conservation efforts. Though more common in the south-west, otters are still present in the north of England. At home both in salt and freshwater, they are a good indicator of a healthy unpolluted environment. Don't come to the north expecting otter sightings every day. If you see one at all you should consider yourself *extremely* fortunate, for they remain rare and very elusive. There are said to be some in Swaledale.

A surprisingly large number of trekkers encounter deer on their walk. Mostly this will be the **roe deer** (*Capreolus capreolus*), a small native species that likes to inhabit woodland, though can also be seen grazing in fields. As with most creatures, your best chance of seeing one is very early in the morning, with sightings particularly common in Ennerdale, the upper end of Swaledale and the Vale of Mowbray. Britain's largest native land mammal, the **red deer** (*Cervus elaphus*), is rarely seen on the walk though it does exist in small pockets around the Lakes.

REPTILES

The **adder** is the only common snake in the north of England, and the only poisonous one of the three species in Britain. They pose very little risk to walkers – indeed, you should consider yourself extremely fortunate to see one, providing you're a safe distance away. They only bite when provoked, preferring to hide instead. The venom is designed to kill small mammals such as mice, voles and shrews, so deaths in humans are very rare, but a bite can be extremely unpleasant and occasionally dangerous to children or the elderly. You are most likely to encounter them in spring when they come out of hibernation and during the summer when pregnant females warm themselves in the sun. They are easily identified by the striking zigzag pattern on their back. Should you be lucky enough to encounter one, enjoy it but leave it undisturbed.

BIRDS

The Coast to Coast is without doubt an ornithologist's dream. The seaside cliffs, woods, moorland and hedgerows encountered on the path provide homes for a wealth of different species including the golden eagle, Britain's rarest and most majestic bird, and a flock of feral parrots.

GUILLEMOT
L: 450MM/18"

The red sandstone cliffs above St Bees (see p74) have been owned by the RSPB since 1973 and dotted along the trail are viewpoints where you can gaze down at the nesting seabirds. This is in fact the only colony of cliff-nesting seabirds in north-west England to which birds return year after year to lay their eggs and hatch chicks. The most common of the seabirds is the **guillemot** (*Uria aalge*), with an estimated minimum of 5000 crowding onto the cliff's open ledges, including the rare **black guillemot** (*Cepphus grylle*); indeed, the cliffs are believed to be the only place where this rare sub-species nests in England. **Razorbills** (*Alca torda*), a close relative of the guillemot, are also present, as are **puffins** (*Fratercula arctica*), though their numbers seldom rise above two dozen or so. **Kittiwakes** (*Rissa tridactyla*), **fulmars** (*Fulmarus glacialis*) and **gulls** (family *Larus*) are also present, while a little further inland **ravens** (*Corvus corax*) and **peregrine falcons** (*Falco peregrinus*) nest.

Away from the coast, the rarest species in England is the **golden eagle** (*Aquila chrysaetos*), a pair of which had set up an eyrie near the Coast to Coast trail, on the way down to Haweswater Reservoir from Kidsty Pike (see p115). Enthusiastic twitchers could be seen peering up the valley most hours of the day, and there was also a 24hr guard keeping watch to protect it from the predations of the egg collectors. This was the only pair of breeding golden eagles

BLACK GUILLEMOT
L: 350MM/13.5"

GOLDEN EAGLE
L: 910MM/36"

in England. Sadly, at the time of writing the female eagle had not been seen for some time with speculation that she had died. If this is the case we can only hope that an eagle from Scotland comes in to replace her. The first wild **ospreys** (*Pandion haliaetus*) to breed in England for centuries are also present in the Lakes, though not near the trail.

Other birds of prey include **kestrel** (*Falco tinnunculus*), **buzzard** (*Buteo buteo*), **barn owl** (*Tyto alba*) and **short-eared owl** (*Asio flammeus*).

One of the most common birds seen on the path, particularly in the latter half of the walk, is the **pheasant** (*Phasianus colchicus*). Ubiquitous on the moors, the male is distinctive thanks to its beautiful long, barred tail feathers, brown body and glossy green-black head with red head-sides, while the female is a dull brown. Another way to distinguish them is by the distinctive strangulated hacking sound they make together with the loud flapping of wings as they fly off.

Another reasonably common sight on the moors of Yorkshire is the **lapwing** (*Vanellus vanellus*), also known as the peewit. Black and white with iridescent green upperparts and approximately the size of a pigeon or tern, the lapwing's most distinctive characteristic is the male's tumbling, diving swooping flight pattern when disturbed, believed to be either a display to attract a female or an attempt to distract predators from its nest, which is built on the ground.

Less common but still seen by most walkers is the **curlew** (*Numenius arquata*), another bird that, like the lapwing, is associated with coastal and open fields, moors and bogs. With feathers uniformly streaked grey and brown, the easiest way to identify this bird is by its thin elongated, downward curling beak. Both the lapwing and the curlew are actually wading birds that nest on the moors in the spring, but which winter by the coast. Other birds that make their nest on open moorland and in fields include the **redshank** (*Tringa totanus*), **golden plover** (*Pluvialis apricaria*), **snipe** (*Gallinago gallinago*), **dunlin** (*Calidris alpina*) and **ring ouzel** (*Turdus torquatus*).

Somewhat ironically, these birds have benefited from the careful management of the moors which is mainly done to protect the populations of game birds such as **black grouse** (*Tetrao tetrix*).

In the deciduous woodland areas on the trail, look out for **treecreepers** (*Certhia familiaris*), **tits** (family *Paridae*, including

LAPWING/PEEWIT
L: 320MM/12.5"

CURLEW
L: 600MM/24"

THE ENVIRONMENT & NATURE

blue, coal and great), **nuthatches** (*Sitta europaea*), **pied flycatchers** (*Ficedula hypoleuca*) and **redstarts** (*Phoenicurus phoenicurus*), while in the conifers watch out for **crossbills** (*Loxia curvirostra*) and **siskins** (*Carduelis spinus*).

Finally, for something completely different, if you have time do take a trip down to the River Eden below Kirkby Stephen where walkers swear they have seen a flock of **parrots** that escaped from captivity and appear to be thriving.

FLOWERS

Spring, is the time to come and see the spectacular displays of colour on the Coast to Coast path. Alternatively, arrive in August and you'll see the heathers carpeting the moors in a blaze of purple flowers.

BLACK GROUSE
L: 580MM/23"

The coastal meadows

The coastline is a harsh environment subjected to strong, salt-laced winds. One plant that does survive in such conditions, and which will probably be the first you'll encounter on the path, is **gorse** (*Ulex europeous*) with its sharp-thorned bright yellow, heavily perfumed flowers. Accompanying it are such cliff-top specialists as the pink-flowering **thrift** (*Armeria maritima*) and white **sea campion** (*Silene maritima*) and **fennel** (*Foeniculum vulgare*), a member of the carrot family which grows to over a metre high.

Woodland and hedgerows

From March to May **bluebells** (*Hyacinthoides non-scripta*) proliferate in the woods along the Coast to Coast, providing a wonderful spectacle. Little Beck (see p208) and Clain (see p190) woods are particularly notable for these displays. The white **wood anemone** (*Anemone nemorosa*) and the yellow **primrose** (*Primula vulgaris*) also flower early in spring. **Red campion** (*Silene dioica*), which flowers from late April, can be found in hedgebanks along with **rosebay willowherb** (*Epilobium augustifolium*) which also has the name fireweed due to its habit of colonizing burnt areas.

In scrubland and on woodland edges you'll find **bramble** (*Rubus fruticosus*), a common vigorous shrub, responsible for many a ripped jacket thanks to its sharp thorns and prickles. **Blackberry** fruits ripen from late summer into autumn. Fairly common in scrubland and on woodland edges is the **dog rose** (*Rosa canina*) which has a large pink flower, the fruits of which are used to make rose-hip syrup.

Other flowering plants common in wooded areas and in hedgerows include the tall **foxglove** (*Digitalis purpurea*) with its trumpet-like flowers, **forget-me-not** (*Myosotis arvensis*) with tiny, delicate blue flowers and **cow parsley** (*Anthriscus sylvestris*), a tall member of the carrot family with a large globe of white flowers which often covers roadside verges and hedgebanks.

Spear Thistle
Cirsium vulgare

Common Knapweed
Centaurea nigra

Sea Campion
Silene maritima

Bell Heather
Erica cinerea

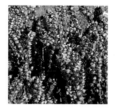

Heather (Ling)
Calluna vulgaris

Violet
Viola riviniana

Devil's-bit Scabious
Succisa pratensis

Harebell
Campanula rotundifolia

Bluebell
Endymion non-scriptus

Marsh Marigold (Kingcup)
Caltha palustris

Meadow Buttercup
Ranunculis acris

Cowslip
Primula veris

Tormentil
Potentilla erecta

Birdsfoot-trefoil
Lotus corniculatus

Ox-eye Daisy
Leucanthemum vulgare

Common Ragwort
Senecio jacobaea

Primrose
Primula vulgaris

Dandelion
Taraxacum officinale

Gorse
Ulex europaeus

Rowan tree
Sorbus aucuparia

Rosebay Willowherb
Epilobium angustifolium

Lousewort
Pedicularis sylvatica

Herb-Robert
Geranium robertianum

Scarlet Pimpernel
Anagallis arvensis

Hemp-nettle
Galeopsis speciosa

Ransoms (Wild Garlic)
Allium ursinum

Yarrow
Achillea millefolium

Foxglove
Digitalis purpurea

Meadow Cranesbill
Geranium pratense

Water Avens
Geum rivale

Common Vetch
Vicia sativa

Heartsease (Wild Pansy)
Viola tricolor

Germander Speedwell
Veronica chamaedrys

Early Purple Orchid
Orchis mascula

Thrift (Sea Pink)
Armeria maritima

Red Campion
Silene dioica

Heathland and scrubland

There are three species of heather. The most dominant one is **ling** (*Calluna vulgaris*), with tiny flowers on delicate upright stems. The other two species are **bell heather** (*Erica cinera*), with deep purple bell-shaped flowers, and **cross-leaved heath** (*Erica tetralix*) with similarly shaped flowers of a lighter pink, almost white colour. Cross-leaved heath prefers wet and boggy ground. As a result, it usually grows away from bell heather which prefers well-drained soils.

Heather is an incredibly versatile plant which is put to many uses. It provides fodder for livestock, fuel for fires, an orange dye and material for bedding, thatching, basketwork and brooms. It is still sometimes used in place of hops to flavour beer, and the flower heads can be brewed to make good tea. It is also incredibly hardy and thrives on the denuded hills, preventing other species from flourishing. Indeed, recently highland cattle have been brought to certain areas of the moors to graze on the heather, allowing other species a chance to grow.

Not a flower but worthy of mention is the less attractive species, **bracken** (*Pteridium aquilinum*), a vigorous non-native fern that has invaded many heathland areas to the detriment of native species.

Grassland

There is much overlap between the hedge/woodland-edge habitat and that of pastures and meadows. You will come across **common birdsfoot-trefoil** (*Lotus corniculatus*), **Germander speedwell** (*Veronica chamaedrys*), **tufted** and **bush vetch** (*Vicia cracca* and *V. sepium*) and **meadow vetchling** (*Lathyrus pratensis*) in both.

Often the only species you will see in heavily grazed pastures are the most resilient. Of the thistles, the three most common species are **creeping thistle**, **spear thistle** and **marsh thistle** (*Cirsium arvense, C.vulgare* and *C. palustre*). Among them you may find **common ragwort** (*Senecio jacobaea*), **yarrow** (*Achillea millefolium*), **sheep's** and **common sorrel** (*Rumex acetosella* and *R. acetosa*), and **white** and **red clover** (*Trifolium repens* and *T. pratense*).

Other widespread grassland species include **harebell** (*Campanula rotundifolia*), delicate yellow **tormentil** (*Potentilla erecta*) which will often spread up onto the lower slopes of mountains along with **devil's-bit scabious** (*Succisa pratensis*). Also keep an eye out for orchids such as the **fragrant orchid** (*Gymnaadenia conopsea*) and **early purple orchid** (*Orchis mascula*).

TREES

It seems incredible that, before man and his axe got to work, most of the bleak, empty moors and windswept Lakeland fells were actually covered by trees. These days, the biggest and most ubiquitous areas of tree cover are the ghastly pine plantations of Ennerdale and other places in the Lakes. But the overgrazing of land by sheep and, to a lesser extent, deer, which eat the young shoots of trees, has ensured that the ancient forests have never returned. Yet there are still small patches of indigenous woodland on the Coast to Coast path. Perhaps the most interesting are the Atlantic Oakwoods at Borrowdale, including Johnny's Wood (see p88) on the way to Longthwaite. The woods are owned and cared for by the National Trust and are actually correctly known as temperate rainforest, the moist Atlantic cli-

OAK LEAVES SHOWING GALLS

HAZEL (WITH FLOWERS)

ASH (WITH SEEDS)

mate creating a landscape of boulders covered by liverworts and ferns, under **oaks** (*Quercus petraea*) dripping in moss and lichen. There are other areas of woodland in the Lakes, including Easedale Woods on the way into Grasmere and Glenamara Park, just before Patterdale, which has some truly spectacular mature trees. One interesting thing about oak trees is that they support more kinds of insects than any other tree in Britain and some of these insects affect the oak in interesting ways. The eggs of the gall-fly, for example, cause growths on the leaves, known, appropriately enough, as galls. Each of these contains a single insect. Other kinds of gall-flies lay eggs in stalks or flowers, leading to flower galls – growths the size of currants.

Oak woodland is a diverse habitat and not exclusively made up of oak. Other trees that flourish in oak woodland include **downy birch** (*Betula pubescens*), its relative the **silver birch** (*Betula pendula*), **holly** (*Ilex aquifolium*), and **hazel** (*Corylus avellana*) which has traditionally been used for coppicing (where small trees are grown for periodic cutting). Further east there are some examples of limestone woodland. **Ash** (*Fraxinus excelsior*) and oak dominate, along with **wych elm** (*Ulmus glabra*), **sycamore** (*Acer*) and **yew** (*Taxus*).

The **hawthorn** (*Crataegus monogyna*) also grows on the path, usually in isolated pockets on pasture. These species are known as pioneer species and play a vital role in the ecosystem by improving the soil. It is these pioneers, particularly the **rowan** (*Sorbus aucuparia*) and hawthorn, that you will see growing all alone on inaccessible crags and ravines. Without interference from man, these pioneers would eventually be succeeded by longer-living species such as the oak. In wet, marshy areas and along rivers and streams you are more likely to find **alder** (*Alnus glutinosa*).

ALDER (WITH FLOWERS)

THE ENVIRONMENT & NATURE

Using the guide

The trail guide has been described from west to east and divided into 13 stages. Though each of these roughly corresponds to a day's walk, do not assume that this is the only way to structure the trek. There are so many places to stay en route that – except for a couple of stretches where there is no accommodation – you can pretty much divide up the walk whichever way you want. This is even more true if you have your own camping gear, in which case you can pitch your tent virtually anywhere, as long, of course, as you first have permission from the landowner.

On pp30-2 are tables to help you plan an itinerary. To provide further help, practical information is presented on the trail maps, including walking times, places to stay, camp and eat, as well as shops for supplies. Further service details are given in the text under the entry for each settlement.

TRAIL MAPS

Scale and walking times

The trail maps are to a scale of 1:20,000 (1cm = 200m; $3^1/_8$ inches = one mile). Walking times are given along the side of each map; the arrow shows the direction to which the time refers. Black triangles indicate the points between which the times have been taken. These times are merely a tool to help you plan and are not there to judge your walking ability. Hopefully, after a couple of days you'll know how fast you walk compared to the time bars and can plan your days more accurately as a result. **See note on walking times in the box on p71**.

Up or down?

The trail is shown as a dashed line. An arrow across the trail indicates the slope; two arrows show that it is steep. Note that the arrow points towards the higher part of the trail. If, for example, you are walking from A (at 80m) to B (at 200m) and the trail between the two is short and steep, it would be shown thus: A- - - - >>- - - -B. Reversed arrow heads indicate downward gradient.

Accommodation

Accommodation marked on the map is either on or within easy reach of the trail. Many B&B proprietors whose accommodation is a mile or two off the trail will offer to collect walkers from the nearest point on the trail and deliver them back again next morning. This is particularly true of the B&Bs at Great Broughton and Urra, where walkers are collected at Clay Bank Top (see p192). Details of each place are given in the accompanying text. The number of rooms of each type is given at the beginning of each entry, ie S=Single, T=Twin room, D=Double room, F=Family room (sleeps at least three people). The rates are also given; these are *per person* per night prices. As an example: £20/15 sgl/dbl means the rate is £20 for a single room, £15 per person in a double. Unless otherwise specified, the rates are for the summer high season.

Other features

Features are marked on the map when they are pertinent to navigation. In order to avoid cluttering the maps and make them unusable, not all features have been marked each time they occur.

The route guide

ST BEES

Nestling at the mouth of Pow Beck ('beck' is a local term meaning stream), St Bees is the perfect starting point for a long-distance walk: attractive, friendly and compact, with enough facilities to set you up for the trail yet nothing so captivating that you'll want to delay the start of your walk. The village is definitely agricultural in character: many of the buildings along the main street were originally farm buildings dating back to the 17th century and there's even an ancient **pinfold** on Outrigg. This construction – a simple, circular, stone-walled enclosure – was used to house stray sheep and cattle that had been recovered from the surrounding hills. The livestock would remain in the

pinfold until the farmer could afford to pay a fine to retrieve them.

The town's main sight is its red sandstone **Priory church**, once part of a thriving 12th-century Benedictine priory dedicated to the saints Bega and Mary. Original Norman features include the impressively elaborate Great West Door and, standing opposite, the curious carved Dragon Stone, a door lintel from the 12th century.

The church is believed to stand on a site that had been holy to Christians for centuries prior to the monastery's foundation and has seen over eight hundred years of unbroken worship since then. Not even the dissolution of the monasteries ordered

---

❏ **Who was St Bees?**

St Bees is actually a corruption of St Bega, an Irish princess who fled her native country sometime between the 6th and 9th centuries to avoid an arranged marriage with a Norwegian prince. Landing on England's north-west coast, so the story goes, St Bega lived as a hermit and became renowned for the good deeds she carried out for the locals. And that's about it really, or at least it would be, if it wasn't for the legends that have grown up over the centuries. In the most famous of these, St Bega approaches the local landlord, Lord Egremont, for some land for a convent she wished to found. Egremont, clearly not the most generous of men, promised St Bega all the land covered by snow the next day; which, seeing as the next day happened to be midsummer's day, was not as generous an offer as it first appeared. Miraculously, however, snow did fall that day and St Bega was able to build her convent, around which the village was built. There's a statue of St Bega just to the west of the railway station on Station Rd.

by Henry VIII in 1538, which led to the closure of this and every other priory you'll come across on the Coast to Coast path, could stop the site from being used by the villagers as their main centre of worship, even though Henry's commissioners had removed the lead from the roof, and the whole building, for much of the 16th century, was left open to the elements. Restoration began in the early 17th century, with a major overhaul of the building taking place in the 19th. Thankfully, however, the architects kept intact much of the church's sturdy Norman character and that is the church's most impressive feature today.

As with quite a few of the larger churches on the route, there's a table just inside the door with various pamphlets on the history of both the church and the village, each costing only about 20p. Don't miss the glass case in the southern aisle displaying a shroud and a lock of woman's hair unearthed in the recent excavation of a 14th-century grave; and the graveyard to the north of the church, where you'll find the shaft of a stone cross from the 10th century (in other words, older than every other part of the church), with its Celtic decorations still visible. Incidentally, the **grammar school** across the road from the church is one of the most venerable in Cumbria, having been founded on his deathbed in 1583 by a local man, Edmund Grindal, who had risen to become Archbishop of Canterbury during the reign of Elizabeth I. His birthplace, on the junction of Finkle St and Cross St, is the oldest surviving house in St Bees.

Services

There's a small **general store** (Mon-Fri 8.30am-7.30pm, Sat 9am-5pm) on Main St. If that's closed, try the **post office** (Mon, Tue, Thu & Fri 6am-5.30pm, Wed 6am-

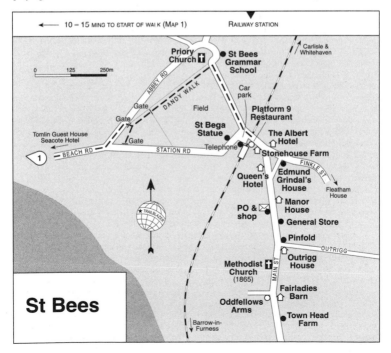

St Bees

← 10 – 15 MINS TO START OF WALK (MAP 1)   RAILWAY STATION

Carlisle & Whitehaven

Priory Church
● **St Bees Grammar School**

0   125   250m

ABBEY RD
DANDY WALK

Gate   Field

Car park

Platform 9 Restaurant

Gate

St Bega Statue

Tomlin Guest House
Seacote Hotel

Gate   STATION RD   Telephone

The Albert Hotel
Stonehouse Farm

1   = BEACH RD =

FINKLE ST

Queen's Hotel

Edmund Grindal's House

Fleatham House

★ TRAILBLAZER

Manor House

PO & shop

General Store

● **Pinfold**

OUTRIGG

Outrigg House

Methodist Church (1865)

MAIN ST

Fairladies Barn

Oddfellows Arms

Town Head Farm

Barrow-in-Furness

7.30pm, Sat 7.30am-7.15pm, Sun 7.15am-12.30pm) just down the road; it stocks similar goods, as well as a few Coast to Coast maps, T-shirts and souvenirs. It is also the home of the local Link **cash machine**, currently the only one you'll see from here to Grasmere. There is also a **tourist information point** by the train station but it has limited information.

One thing the town lacks is a trekking or camping shop, so make sure you have everything you need until at least Seatoller (the first place with any sort of trekking outlet) or, preferably, Grasmere, where there are several trekking/camping shops.

Where to stay

Just 30 metres from the station, *Stonehouse Farm* (☎ 01946 822224; 🖳 www.stonehousefarm.net, 133 Main St; main farmhouse 1S/3D/2F; converted dairy 1F; cottage 1D/1T) is a long-established and reliable B&B. One of only two working farms within St Bees (the other is **Town Head** at the top of the hill beyond Fairladies), Stonehouse has en suite rooms with TV in its main, Georgian, farmhouse, while the dairy next door has been converted into a spacious family suite. On the other side of the farmhouse is an even older cottage (dating back to 1660) where the character of the building with its impressive exposed beams more than compensates for the lack of en suite bathrooms. **Camping** (£3) is also available in the back garden, allowing you to fall asleep to the hooting of the barn owl that's taken up residence in the farm's derelict barn. Finally, long-term parking (£1 per day) is also available. Rates are £26/22.50 sgl/dbl; children are charged according to age, ie a three-year-old pays £3, a 15-year-old £15.

Albert Hotel (1 Finkle St; ☎ 01946 822345, 🖳 www.alberthotelcumbria.co.uk, 7S/3D/3T/2F) is a convenient place to stay right opposite the station. It is clean and comfortable with B&B from £25 per person.

Queen's Hotel (☎ 01946 822287; 4S/8D/3T), on Main St, is probably the main social centre in town, largely thanks to the food served in the bar. A 17th-century freehouse, Queen's has 15 rooms upstairs.

Typically decorated for this part of the world with comfort more important than considerations of fashion, all rooms come with TV and tea-/coffee-making facilities, and all are en suite. Rates are £38/25 sgl/dbl.

Manor House Hotel (Main St; ☎ 01946 822425; 🖳 manorhousehotel@aol.com; 1S/2D/5T) is perhaps the most impressive-looking hotel in St Bees, though I found it was let down by a surly attitude from one of the staff. Nevertheless, it would be churlish to complain about a place where they actively seek walkers' custom, including offering discounts to Coast-to-Coasters. Rates are from £25/35 sgl/dbl per person.

Up at the top of the road, the *Fairladies Barn Guest House* (Main St; ☎ 01946 822718; 🖳 www.fairladiesbarn.co.uk; 5D/4T/1F) is a delight; a large, restored, 17th-century sandstone barn with charming rooms, each en suite with TV, and each different. As such, it's worth looking at a few before deciding which room you wish to stay in. Or you could simply go for the most popular room, the unusually shaped studio flat under the roof at the end of the barn. Single occupancy is possible in all the rooms. Rates are £27.50-22/22.50-20 sgl/dbl depending on the length of stay. If this is full try back down the road at *Outrigg House* (Main St; ☎ 01946 822348, 1S/1T/1D) where you are guaranteed a friendly welcome. Rates are £18 per person.

Away from the main road, *Fleatham House* (High House Rd; ☎ 01946 822341; 🖳 www.fleathamhouse.com; 3S/2D/1T, all en suite) is where Tony Blair, UK Prime Minister, is said to have stayed in an attempt to show solidarity with the north-west's tourist industry following the 2001 foot and mouth crisis. Predictably grand, it lies at the end of a steep driveway at the top of the village and charges an equally steep £55/40 sgl/dbl (midweek rates), or £65 for single occupancy of a double room.

Tomlin Guest House (Map 1, p72; 1 Tomlin House, Beach Rd; ☎ 01946 822284; 🖳 id.whitehead@which.net; 3D/1T) is the closest B&B to the sea, a friendly little place just opposite the large Seacote Hotel. The only disadvantage is that it's a little way from any restaurants that are open in the evening (the Seacote excluded). Nevertheless, it's a cheerful, welcoming little place with a lock-up garage for rent while you walk. Rates sgl/dbl £22.50/18.

Finally, *Seacote Hotel* (Map 1 p72; Beach Rd; ☎ 01946 822300; 🖳 www.seacote.com 83 rooms all en suite) is the rather imposing building by the beach car park. Rooms here are £22.50 per person (£40 for a single) and there are **camping** pitches for £6 in their caravan park (☎ 01946 822777).

Where to eat

The *Queen's Hotel* is definitely the most popular place in town and it's not hard to see why: huge platefuls of warming food (served Mon-Sat 12 noon-2pm, closed Tue lunchtime), 6-9.30pm; Sun 12 noon-2pm, 7-9pm) including pasta bake for £6.25 and meatballs for £6.95, a convivial atmosphere free of gaming machines and jukeboxes, and separate smoking and non-smoking dining-rooms. The bar is known for its real ales and malt whiskies: give the Jennings Bitter a try. The *Oddfellows Arms* at the top

of the hill is similar but cheaper, the atmosphere is more subdued, and the standard of food lower.

Elsewhere, the *Platform 9 Restaurant* (☎ 01946 822600, Tue-Fri & Sun 6-9pm; Sat 6-10pm) is, unsurprisingly, located at the station. The high prices will probably put off most walkers who want to save their extravagant slap-up meal for the end of the trek. If you do decide to indulge early the pork or lamb will set you back £14.95.

Finally, for cream teas and sea views, call in at *Hartley's Tea Rooms* (Map 1 p72). They also sell maps and guides.

Transport (see also pp43-5)

For **trains** to St Bees, see p40. From St Bees there are 5-8 trains/day running north to Carlisle from 7.10am (no service on Sunday), with the last at 6.19pm. Towards Barrow-in-Furness there are 8-9/day, from 6.42am, with the last at 6.42pm.

Bus No 20 runs to and from Whitehaven (5-6/day Mon-Sat; no Sunday/Bank Holiday services).

STAGE 1: ST BEES TO ENNERDALE BRIDGE   MAPS 1-7

There is a lot of variety to this **14-mile (22.5km, $6^{1}/_{4}$hr)** stage, beginning with a cliff-top walk along the Irish Sea and ending with a high-level view across to the Lake District fells. Some who are lacking fitness may find this first day a bit of a struggle, particularly the final haul over Dent and into Ennerdale Bridge. If you think this may be you, and you have the time, consider stopping in Cleator or, a mile or so off the path, Egremont for the first night, before possibly continuing on the second day to the youth hostel at High Gillerthwaite, the eccentric Black Sail, or the youth hostel at Honister Hause.

The Coast to Coast path officially begins from the sea wall in St Bees which protects the village from the Irish Sea. The best way to the shore from 'downtown' St Bees is along **Dandy Walk** (see map p69), so called because the 'dandy' students from the grammar school would walk along this path in their caps and gowns. *(continued on p74)*

❑ **Important note – walking times**
Unless otherwise specified, **all times in this book refer only to the time spent walking.** You will need to add 20-30% to allow for rests, photography, checking the map, drinking water etc. When planning the day's hike count on 5-7 hours' actual walking.

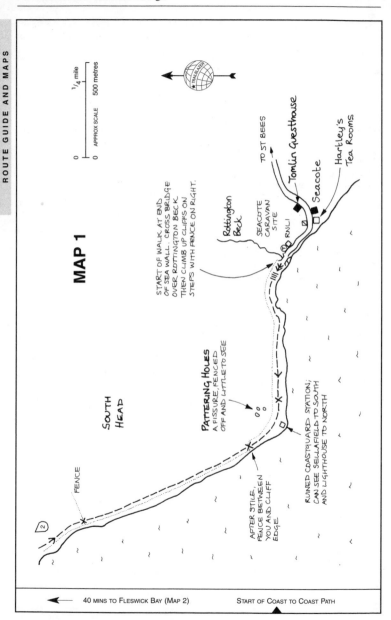

MAP 1

START OF WALK. AT END OF SEA WALL. CROSS BRIDGE OVER ROTTINGTON BECK THEN CLIMB UP CLIFFS ON STEPS WITH FENCE ON RIGHT.

TO ST BEES

Tomlin Guesthouse

Seacote

Hartley's Tea Rooms

Rottington Beck

SEACOTE CARAVAN SITE

RNLI

SOUTH HEAD

PATTERING HOLES
A FISSURE, FENCED OFF AND LITTLE TO SEE

FENCE

2

AFTER STILE, FENCE BETWEEN YOU AND CLIFF EDGE

RUINED COASTGUARD STATION; CAN SEE SELLAFIELD TO SOUTH AND LIGHTHOUSE TO NORTH

0   APPROX SCALE   500 metres
0   1/4 mile

40 MINS TO FLESWICK BAY (MAP 2)

START OF COAST TO COAST PATH

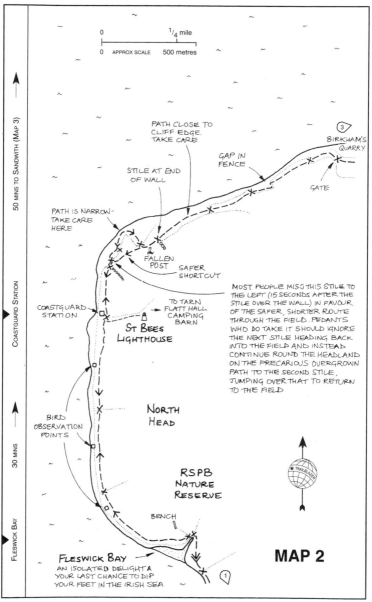

0   ¼ mile

0   APPROX SCALE   500 metres

50 MINS TO SANDWITH (MAP 3)

PATH CLOSE TO
CLIFF EDGE.
TAKE CARE

③ BIRKHAM'S
QUARRY

GAP IN
FENCE

STILE AT END
OF WALL

GATE

PATH IS NARROW-
TAKE CARE
HERE

FALLEN
POST

SAFER
SHORTCUT

MOST PEOPLE MISS THIS STILE TO
THE LEFT (15 SECONDS AFTER THE
STILE OVER THE WALL) IN FAVOUR
OF THE SAFER, SHORTER ROUTE
THROUGH THE FIELD. PEDANTS
WHO DO TAKE IT SHOULD IGNORE
THE NEXT STILE HEADING BACK
INTO THE FIELD AND INSTEAD
CONTINUE ROUND THE HEADLAND
ON THE PRECARIOUS OVERGROWN
PATH TO THE SECOND STILE,
JUMPING OVER THAT TO RETURN
TO THE FIELD

COASTGUARD STATION

COASTGUARD
STATION

TO TARN
FLATT HALL
CAMPING
BARN

St Bees
Lighthouse

NORTH
HEAD

BIRD
OBSERVATION
POINTS

30 MINS

RSPB
NATURE
RESERVE

TRAILBLAZER

FLESWICK BAY

BENCH

FLESWICK BAY
AN ISOLATED DELIGHT &
YOUR LAST CHANCE TO DIP
YOUR FEET IN THE IRISH SEA

MAP 2

①

(continued from p71) Follow Beach Rd to the coast and wet your boots in the Irish sea. Having done so, turn north-west, leaving the sea wall of St Bees to climb up the cliff-top path, steep at first. You are now on the Coast to Coast path, with a fence on one side and a 300-foot (90m) drop on the other.

The cliffs themselves are made of red sandstone, used in the construction of many of the buildings around here. There are some features along the way to help you judge your progress, the first being the **Pattering Holes**, fissures of uncertain origin in the ground beyond the fence by the ruined coastguard's hut.

Progressing further north the small **Fleswick Bay** is reached, a secluded pebble beach surrounded by red sandstone cliffs with some interestingly weathered boulders lying on the shore. It is also your last chance on the trail to dip your feet in the Irish Sea.

This bay marks the dividing line between the constituent parts of St Bees Head: South Head, which you have been walking on up to now, and **North Head** (Map 2), which you now climb up to from the bay. Two features distinguish this latter part of St Bees Head: the three **RSPB observation points**, to the left of the path, which allow you to safely peer over the cliffs and observe the seabirds nesting there (including puffins, terns and England's only colony of black guillemots); and **St Bees Lighthouse**, a little way inland from the path but clearly visible since South Head.

Tarn Flatt Hall (book via the Lakeland Barns Booking Office in Keswick, ☎ 01768 772645), a **camping barn**, is best reached by turning off the path here towards the lighthouse and continuing east for 400m. It sleeps around eight and costs just £6 per person. The barn comes with an electric light, cooking slab and an open fire, with wood available from the farm. **Camping** is also on offer for £4.

After the lighthouse, the path continues up to the tip of North Head before heading east along the coast, eventually turning inland at Birkham's Quarry. Fifteen minutes later, you arrive at Sandwith.

SANDWITH   MAP 3

Sandwith (pronounced *Sanith*) is the first settlement of note that you come to on the trail, almost five miles/8km along the path from St Bees (though, dishearteningly, only two miles/3km as the crow flies!).

There's little here, to be honest, and unless the pub (the Dog and Partridge) is open, little to warrant much of a stay, particularly as you'll probably be wanting to crack on to the Lakes.

The nearest **accommodation** is *Tarn Flatt Hall* (see above).

Transport-wise, **bus** No 20 passes through 5-6/day, Mon-Sat, on its route between St Bees and Whitehaven.

Taking the road alongside the Dog and Partridge, with the chemical works an eyesore to your left, the path crosses the Byerstead Road and, just over half a mile (0.8km) later, the B5345 linking Whitehaven to St Bees.

From the railway tunnel (Map 3) at the foot of the hill the trail crosses fields and a small stream (Scalegill Beck; Map 4), before passing through the nearby tunnel underneath a disused railway. If you were to continue on this road and

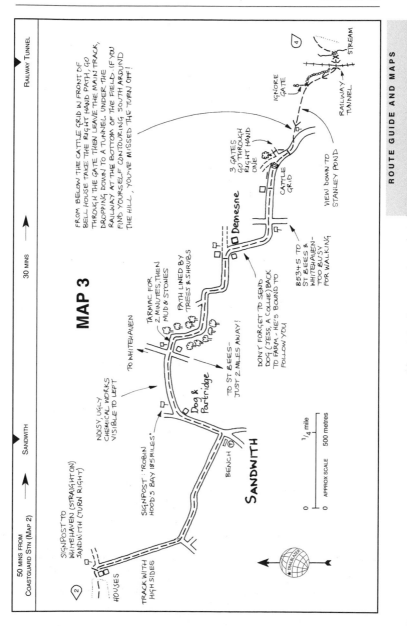

50 MINS FROM
COASTGUARD STN (MAP 2) ▶ SANDWITH ▶ 30 MINS ▶ RAILWAY TUNNEL

② SIGNPOST TO
WHITEHAVEN (STRAIGHT ON)
SANDWITH (TURN RIGHT)

HOUSES

TRACK WITH
HIGH SIDES

MAP 3

NOISY, UGLY
CHEMICAL WORKS
VISIBLE TO LEFT

TO WHITEHAVEN

SIGNPOST :: "ROBIN
HOOD'S BAY 185 MILES"

Dog & Partridge

BENCH

SANDWITH

TO ST BEES -
JUST 2 MILES AWAY!

DON'T FORGET TO SEND
DOG (JESS, A COLLIE) BACK
TO FARM - HE'S BOUND TO
FOLLOW YOU

TARMAC FOR
2 MINUTES, THEN
MUD & STONES

PATH LINED BY
TREES & SHRUBS

Demesne

B5345 TO
ST BEES &
WHITEHAVEN -
TOO BUSY
FOR WALKING

CATTLE
GRID

3 GATES
GO THROUGH
RIGHT HAND
ONE

VIEW DOWN TO
STANLEY POND

FROM BELOW THE CATTLE GRID IN FRONT OF
BELL HOUSE TAKE THE RIGHT HAND PATH, GO
THROUGH THE GATE THEN LEAVE THE MAIN TRACK,
DROPPING DOWN TO A TUNNEL UNDER THE
RAILWAY AT THE BOTTOM OF THE FIELD. (IF YOU
FIND YOURSELF CONTOURING SOUTH AROUND
THE HILL, YOU'VE MISSED THE TURN OFF!

IGNORE
GATE

RAILWAY
TUNNEL

STREAM

④

0 ¼ mile
0 500 metres
APPROX SCALE

then look behind you, you would see, for the final time, St Bees, nestling in the valley of Pow Beck. We, however, advise you to take a right up the steps immediately after the tunnel and join the disused railway as it snakes its way to Moor Row. It's longer but quieter and a whole deal more seductive.

Moor Row has little to delay you save, perhaps, for the **post office and store** (Mon-Fri 6.30am-12.30pm, 1.30-6pm, Sat 8.30am-3.30pm, Sun 8.30am-12.30pm) which sells snacks, chocolate etc. Those who have had enough walking already have the choice of two B&Bs: *Alva House* (☎ 01946 814537, 🖳 www.alva-house.com, 1S/2D/1T/1F) is just before the village by the route of the dismantled railway while *Jasmine House* (☎ 01946 815795, 🖳 www.jasminehousebandb.com; 1S/2D/2F) is at the other end of the village. Rates at both are from £23 per person with the latter also home to a small **teashop**; a packed lunch costs from £3.50 and an evening meal from £3.50 to £10.

The No 6 **bus** passes through 3-4 times a day, Mon-Sat, between Whitehaven and Muncaster Castle. Taking the road south out of Moor Row (signposted to Egremont), leave it via a kissing gate leading into a field. A whole series of kissing gates follows as you cross the dismantled railway once more on your way down into Cleator, arriving by St Leonard's Church.

CLEATOR   MAP 4

Remnants of some 12th-century masonry in Cleator's church give some indication of just how old this village is, though you'll struggle in vain to find much else of antiquity in the plain, identical terraced houses that make up much of the rest of the place. These houses were built for the miners who worked in the nearby iron-ore pits. As the industry collapsed in the latter half of the 20th century, so the town suffered, and continues to do so today. It's a sad but familiar story repeated time and again throughout west Cumbria.

But don't let the village's troubles put you off Cleator. True, the village is not one of the prettiest en route and it's true, too, that for many years the facilities for walkers were minimal. But the village does provide an antidote to the somewhat twee nature of many Lake District hamlets further east and with a great B&B, the walker-friendly **Farren's Family Store** (Mon-Fri 6am-6.45pm; Sat 6.15am-1.30pm, 4.30-6.30pm; Sun 8.30am-2pm) and a **pub** (The Three Tuns) with a colourful landlord, there's enough in Cleator to warrant an overnight stay, should you already be feeling the effects of this first day.

By the way, Cleator is not the same place as Cleator Moor, a bigger town one

mile to the north. As an alternative to Cleator, **Egremont** is only 1½ miles/2.5km away, with more B&Bs such as *Bookwell Garth Guest House* (☎ 01946 820271; 5S/6T/1F), at 16 Bookwell; rates start from £21 (there are no en suite rooms).

Bus No 22 calls in at Cleator on its way (almost hourly Mon-Sat) between Whitehaven and Egremont.

Where to stay

Those on expenses might want to consider the Grade 1 listed *Ennerdale Country House Hotel* (☎ 01946 813907; 🖳 www.feathers.uk.com/ennerdale; 3S/24D or T/3F, all en suite), set in ten acres of landscaped gardens at the top end of town, where each of the rooms comes with an entertainment system with satellite TV, Sony Playstation, videos and a CD player. It all sounds lovely – though it's hardly a typical Coast to Coast place, and at about £99 per person, it ain't cheap! One that is more in keeping with the walk is the extremely pleasant and good value *Chapel Nook* (☎ 01946 810366 or 07801 862234; 🖳 keithrhodes@supanet.com; 2D, one en suite) on Kiln Brow. Rates start at £19.50.

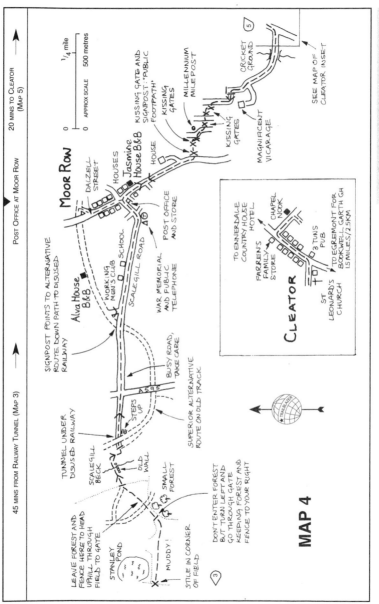

45 MINS FROM RAILWAY TUNNEL (MAP 3)

POST OFFICE AT MOOR ROW

20 MINS TO CLEATOR (MAP 5)

1/4 mile

0

0   APPROX SCALE   500 metres

MAP 4

LEAVE FOREST AND FENCE HERE TO HEAD UPHILL THROUGH FIELD TO GATE

STANLEY POND

MUDDY!

STILE IN CORNER OF FIELD

③

DON'T ENTER FOREST BUT TURN LEFT AND GO THROUGH GATE KEEPING FOREST AND FENCE TO YOUR RIGHT

SMALL FOREST

OLD WALL

SCALEGILL BECK

TUNNEL UNDER DISUSED RAILWAY

STEPS UP

SIGNPOST POINTS TO ALTERNATIVE ROUTE DOWN PATH TO DISUSED RAILWAY

Alva House B&B

WORKING MEN'S CLUB

SCHOOL

SCALEGILL ROAD

POST OFFICE AND STORE

WAR MEMORIAL AND PUBLIC TELEPHONE

A595

BUSY ROAD, TAKE CARE

SUPERIOR ALTERNATIVE ROUTE ON OLD TRACK

Moor Row

DALZELL STREET

HOUSES

Jasmine House B&B

HOUSE

HOUSES

KISSING GATES AND SIGNPOST "PUBLIC FOOTPATH"

KISSING GATES

MILLENNIUM MILEPOST

KISSING GATES

MAGNIFICENT VICARAGE

CRICKET GROUND

⑤

SEE MAP OF CLEATOR INSET

Cleator

TO ENNERDALE COUNTRY HOUSE HOTEL

FARREN'S FAMILY STORE

CHAPEL NOOK

3 TUNS PUB

ST LEONARD'S CHURCH

TO EGREMONT FOR BOOKWELL GARTH GH 1.5 MILES/2.5KM

TRAILBLAZER

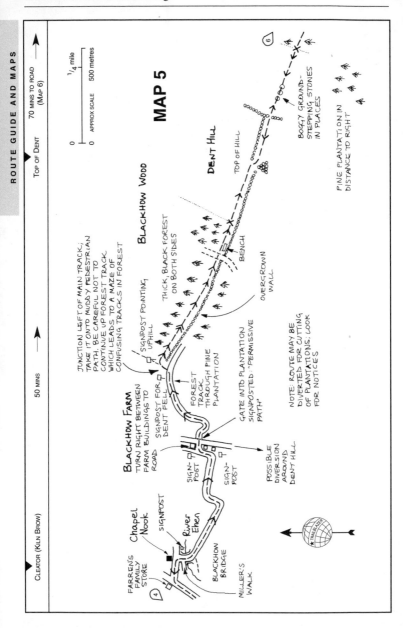

MAP 5

CLEATOR (KILN BROW)

50 MINS

TOP OF DENT

70 MINS TO ROAD (MAP 6)

0 ¼ mile
0 500 metres
APPROX SCALE

JUNCTION LEFT OF MAIN TRACK; TAKE IT ONTO MUDDY PEDESTRIAN PATH. BE CAREFUL NOT TO CONTINUE UP FOREST TRACK WHICH LEADS TO A MAZE OF CONFUSING TRACKS IN FOREST

SIGNPOST POINTING UPHILL

THICK, BLACK FOREST ON BOTH SIDES

BLACKHOW WOOD

DENT HILL

TOP OF HILL

BENCH

OVERGROWN WALL

BOGGY GROUND- STEPPING STONES IN PLACES

PINE PLANTATION IN DISTANCE TO RIGHT

BLACKHOW FARM turn right between farm buildings to FARM ROAD

SIGNPOST FOR DENT FELL

FOREST TRACK THROUGH PINE PLANTATION

GATE INTO PLANTATION SIGNPOSTED: "PERMISSIVE PATH"

NOTE: ROUTE MAY BE DIVERTED FOR CUTTING OF PLANTATIONS: LOOK FOR NOTICES

SIGN-POST

SIGN-POST

POSSIBLE DIVERSION AROUND DENT HILL

Chapel Nook

SIGNPOST

River Ehen

BLACKHOW BRIDGE

MILLER'S WALK

FARREN'S FAMILY STORE

TRAIL BLAZER

❑ Tree-felling on Dent Hill

In the summer of 2003 felling began on the slopes of Dent, a process that had only just come to an end at the time of writing. During the felling the authorities were insisting that walkers take the low road route around Dent starting at Black How Farm.

The original route as indicated on Maps 5 and 6 is now passable again. However, after passing over the top of the hill look out for the signpost by the complicated track junction at the top of the forest. The signpost urges you to turn right which is presumably a measure to guide walkers away from the tree-felling area. Ignore this sign and take a left onto the downhill track as indicated on the maps in this book.

Farren's Family Store in Cleator will probably be able to advise on any further felling/detours. Look too for notices pinned to gates and stiles on Dent.

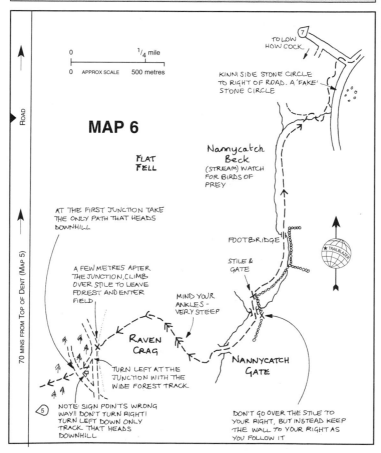

MAP 6

TO LOW
HOW COCK

KINNISIDE STONE CIRCLE
TO RIGHT OF ROAD. A 'FAKE'
STONE CIRCLE

0   ¼ mile

0   APPROX SCALE   500 metres

ROAD

FLAT
FELL

Nannycatch
Beck
(STREAM) WATCH
FOR BIRDS OF
PREY

70 MINS FROM TOP OF DENT (MAP 5)

AT THE FIRST JUNCTION TAKE
THE ONLY PATH THAT HEADS
DOWNHILL

FOOTBRIDGE

A FEW METRES AFTER
THE JUNCTION, CLIMB
OVER STILE TO LEAVE
FOREST AND ENTER
FIELD

STILE &
GATE

★ TRAILBLAZER

MIND YOUR
ANKLES –
VERY STEEP

RAVEN
CRAG

TURN LEFT AT THE
JUNCTION WITH THE
WIDE FOREST TRACK

NANNYCATCH
GATE

NOTE: SIGN POINTS WRONG
WAY!! DON'T TURN RIGHT!
TURN LEFT DOWN ONLY
TRACK THAT HEADS
DOWNHILL

DON'T GO OVER THE STILE TO
YOUR RIGHT, BUT INSTEAD KEEP
THE WALL TO YOUR RIGHT AS
YOU FOLLOW IT

From Cleator it is possible to take the road route around Dent to Ennerdale Bridge though unless the weather is positively treacherous, or you've had enough climbing for the day, take the high route. It would be a shame to miss the view from the summit of Dent Hill (Map 5) and the tranquillity of Nannycatch Beck that lies hidden away at its foot. Long and, this far into the stage, fairly arduous, the climb up Dent takes about 50 minutes from Cleator. At the top there are views to the Lakeland fells ahead and the sea behind, with the gigantic plant of Sellafield to the south-west, the largish town of Egremont before it and, on a good day, the silhouette of the Isle of Man. Many people get lost on their way to Nannycatch Beck. Pay close attention to Map 6 on p79. From Nannycatch, head due north along the beck before veering to the right, still following the course of the water, to the road leading into Ennerdale Bridge. Look for the 'false' **stone circle of Kinniside** on the moor across the road. False, not because it isn't made of stone (it is), nor because it isn't a circle (it is that, too) but because it isn't, as it at first appears, a prehistoric circle (of which we'll be seeing a number of examples on the walk) but a 20th-century one built by a local academic. From the circle, the trail hugs the roadside down to Ennerdale Bridge, with paths constructed firstly to the left and then to the right of the road so walkers do not have to share the tarmac with the traffic.

A mile or so before Ennerdale Bridge is the turn-off to *Low Cock How Farm* (Map 6; ☎ 01946 861354; 🖳 www.walk-rest-ride.co.uk; 1S/1D/2T/1F) with B&B from £25. There's a well-equipped **bunkhouse** (with bedding sleeping up to 12 people) from £11 per person or £15 with breakfast, and **camping** from £5.

ENNERDALE BRIDGE   MAP 7

Ennerdale Bridge is a postcard-pretty little place occupying a wonderful location spanning the River Ehen in one of Britain's least developed valleys. Unfortunately the post office and shop closed at the end of 2005 and the village has been let down somewhat by its accommodation, though the recent reopening of the *Fox and Hounds* (☎ 01946 861373, 2D/2T/2F all en suite) has improved the situation. This tastefully restored inn retains many original features such as the exposed beams. B&B is £35 per person or £45 for a single room.

A reliable B&B option is the large *Shepherd's Arms Hotel* (☎ 01946 861249; 🖳 www.shepherdsarmshotel.co.uk; 4T/4D; 6 en suite), more expensive than any other at £45/37.50 sgl/dbl, though at least that

guarantees crisp white sheets and a good night's sleep.

Other B&Bs in Ennerdale Bridge include: the attractive *Bridge End Cottage* (☎ 01946 861806; 2D; £22 per person) which does good breakfasts and is situated, as the address suggests, right by the bridge on the road into town; further up the road, *Cloggers* (☎ 01946 862487; 1S/1D/1T en suite; £22 per person).

Back in the centre of the village is the *Ennerdale Village Camp Site* (High Bridge Farm; ☎ 01946 861 339). Your first impressions are likely to be negative as you walk down the drive between fields strewn with rusting farm machinery. Nevertheless, the site itself, sitting snugly in a bend in the Ehen, is quiet, pleasant, convenient and, if

---

(Opposite) Top left: Sign beside the disused railway line near Moor Row, Cleator. (Photo © Jim Manthorpe). **Top right**: St Bees Church, parts of which date back to Norman times, is well worth a visit. (Photo © Henry Stedman). **Bottom**: St Bees and the beach. The official start of the Coast to Coast path is by the sea wall. (Photo © Jim Manthorpe).

MOOR ROW
CLEATOR MOOR
FRIZINGTON
ARLECDON
ROWRAH
KIRKLAND

COAST TO COAST
PUBLIC FOOTPATH

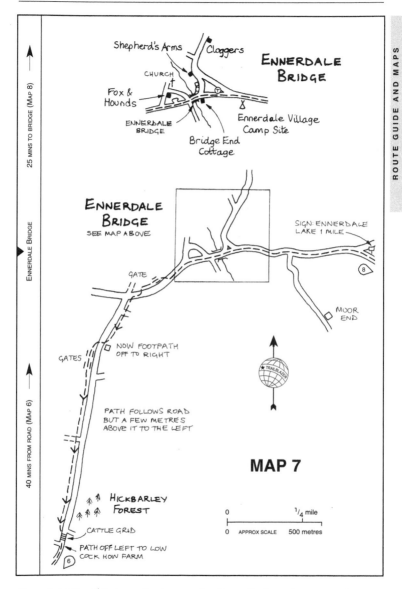

Shepherd's Arms

Cloggers

ENNERDALE
BRIDGE

CHURCH

Fox &
Hounds

ENNERDALE
BRIDGE

Ennerdale Village
Camp Site

Bridge End
Cottage

ENNERDALE
BRIDGE
SEE MAP ABOVE

SIGN: ENNERDALE
LAKE 1 MILE

GATE

8

MOOR
END

NOW FOOTPATH
OFF TO RIGHT

GATES

PATH FOLLOWS ROAD
BUT A FEW METRES
ABOVE IT TO THE LEFT

TRAILBLAZER

MAP 7

HICKBARLEY
FOREST

0   ¼ mile

0   APPROX SCALE   500 metres

CATTLE GRID

PATH OFF LEFT TO LOW
COCK HOW FARM

6

25 MINS TO BRIDGE (MAP 8)

ENNERDALE BRIDGE

40 MINS FROM ROAD (MAP 6)

ROUTE GUIDE AND MAPS

(Opposite): It's a little boggy in places on the ridge-walk alternative route to Grasmere (see p100) but the walking is easy and the views exceptional. (Photo © Henry Stedman).

the sun's out, campers can rightly feel they've bagged a great place, and all for just £4 per person. Be warned, though, that the washing and toilet facilities are minimal.

Food-wise, there is the *Shepherd's Arms*, with good homemade food using local produce and a decent vegetarian selection, and the *Fox and Hounds* (Mon-Fri 12 noon-2pm, 6-9pm; Sat & Sun 12 noon-9pm) with friendly staff and a good

selection of local ales. Most dishes, including the very tasty chicken in a white wine and mushroom sauce, are around £7.25. **Packed lunches** are available from both the Fox and Hounds (£4.50) and Shepherd's Arms Hotel (£5.40).

For **transport**, bus No 219 calls in 3-4 times a day, Mon to Sat, on its way between Cockermouth and Cleator Moor.

STAGE 2: ENNERDALE BRIDGE TO BORROWDALE   MAPS 7-14

As with any day, the enjoyment level of this **$14^{1}/_{2}$-mile (23.5km, $6^{3}/_{4}$hr, low route)** stage depends to a large degree on the weather. Indeed, perhaps more so here than elsewhere: without the sun you cannot fully appreciate the stunted, dappled, mossy forest growing along the southern edge of Ennerdale Water. Without clear conditions you won't have the opportunity to take in the extensive views down to Lake Buttermere from the top of Loft Beck. And if the weather looks like closing in, you'd be foolhardy to attempt the fell-top alternative via Red Pike, as detailed on p90. It's a fairly long walk today, though hostellers are particularly well served on this stage with four hostels spaced out along the route.

The stage's first half involves a stroll along the southern side of **Ennerdale Water**, the path hugging the lakeshore round Robin Hood's Chair – an appropriate name given your final destination, although, as with Robin Hood's Bay, it probably has no real association with the legendary hero – to the very eastern extremity of the lake. It's a lovely walk and flat for the most part, at the end of which you turn north around some sheep enclosures and across the river to join a rather shadeless forest track passing through acre after acre of dull pine plantations. If you're not stopping at Ennerdale Youth Hostel nor wish to take the Red Pike Alternative route, we strongly recommend the path along the southern banks of the River Liza, as shown on Maps 9-11. It's not the official route, but it is a more interesting, wilder one. To join it, keep to the southern side of the Liza and join the bridleway, leaving it just before the gate across the bridleway. From here you join the riverside path, which you follow all the way up to Black Sail.

On the dull, official path on the other side of the river, *Ennerdale Youth Hostel* at **High Gillerthwaite** (Map 10; ☎ 0870 770 5820; 🖳 ennerdale@yha. org.uk; 24 beds; £12) lies between river and road. *High Gillerthwaite Camping Barn* (bookings ☎ 01946 758198; 14 beds) is further up the track. Beds here are only £6; there is a cooking area though no cooking facilities. The hostel is closed during the day so don't rely on filling your water bottle here. Just beyond the camping barn is the start of the alternative trail up to Red Pike, High Stile and Hay Stacks (see p90 and Maps 10a, p91, and 10b, p92).

Continuing on the lower trail, just over 90 minutes after joining the forest track, you emerge above the trees at the head of Ennerdale and *Black Sail Youth Hostel* (Map 11; ☎ 07711 108450; 16 beds, £11). The remotest and smallest of the youth hostels on our route, this former shepherd's bothy is now (cont'd on p87)

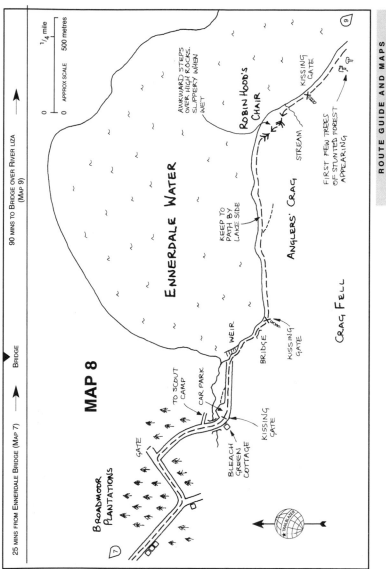

MAP 8

25 MINS FROM ENNERDALE BRIDGE (MAP 7) → BRIDGE → 90 MINS TO BRIDGE OVER RIVER LIZA (MAP 9)

APPROX SCALE
0 — ¼ mile
0 — 500 metres

BROADMOOR PLANTATIONS

GATE

BLEACH GREEN COTTAGE

KISSING GATE

TO SCOUT CAMP

CAR PARK

WEIR

ENNERDALE WATER

BRIDGE

KISSING GATE

CRAG FELL

ANGLERS' CRAG

KEEP TO PATH BY LAKE SIDE

STREAM

FIRST FEW TREES OF STUNTED FOREST APPEARING

ROBIN HOOD'S CHAIR

AWKWARD STEPS OVER HIGH ROCKS, SLIPPERY WHEN WET

KISSING GATE

TIMBLEBECK

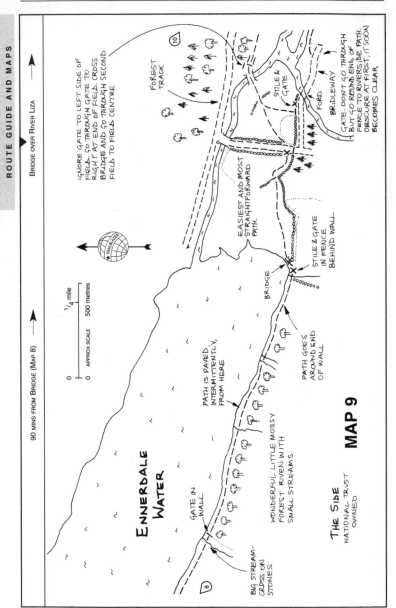

90 MINS FROM BRIDGE (MAP 8)

BRIDGE OVER RIVER LIZA

ENNERDALE WATER

IGNORE GATE TO LEFT SIDE OF FIELD. GO THROUGH GATE TO RIGHT AT END OF FIELD. CROSS BRIDGE AND GO THROUGH SECOND FIELD TO FIELD CENTRE

FOREST TRACK

STILE & GATE

FORD

BRIDLEWAY

GATE. DON'T GO THROUGH BUT GO ROUND END OF FENCE TO RIVER. PATH OBSCURE AT FIRST, IT SOON BECOMES CLEAR

EASIEST AND MOST STRAIGHTFORWARD PATH.

STILE & GATE IN FENCE BEHIND WALL

BRIDGE

PATH IS PAVED INTERMITTENTLY FROM HERE

PATH GOES AROUND END OF WALL

WONDERFUL LITTLE MOSSY FOREST RIVER WITH SMALL STREAMS

THE SIDE
NATIONAL TRUST OWNED

MAP 9

GATE IN WALL

B4G STREAM CROSS ON STONES

0 — ¼ mile
0 — 500 metres
APPROX SCALE

TRAILBLAZER

25 MINS FROM BRIDGE OVER
RIVER LIZA (MAP 9)

TURN-OFF TO RED PIKE

70 MINS TO YH (MAP 11) VIA TWO LOW ROUTES

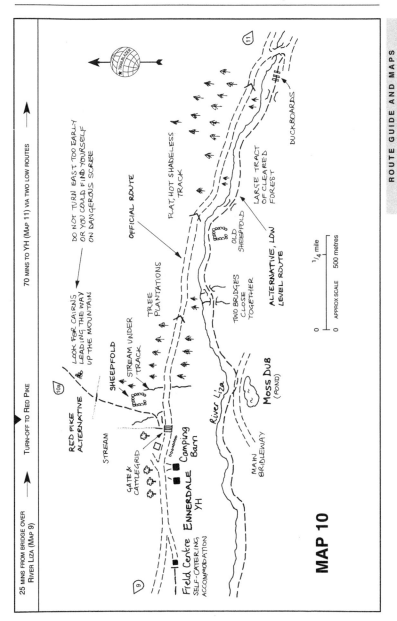

DO NOT TURN EAST TOO EARLY
OR YOU COULD FIND YOURSELF
ON DANGEROUS SCREE

LOOK FOR CAIRNS
LEADING THE WAY
UP THE MOUNTAIN

OFFICIAL ROUTE

FLAT, HOT SHADELESS TRACK

LARGE TRACT
OF CLEARED
FOREST

DUCKBOARDS

RED PIKE
ALTERNATIVE

SHEEPFOLD

STREAM UNDER
TRACK

TREE
PLANTATIONS

OLD
SHEEPFOLD

ALTERNATIVE, LOW
LEVEL ROUTE

TWO BRIDGES
CLOSE
TOGETHER

STREAM

GATE &
CATTLEGRID

Camping
Barn

Ennerdale
YH

River Liza

Moss Dub
(POND)

MAIN
BRIDLEWAY

Field Centre
SELF-CATERING,
ACCOMMODATION

MAP 10

0   APPROX SCALE   500 metres

0   ¼ mile

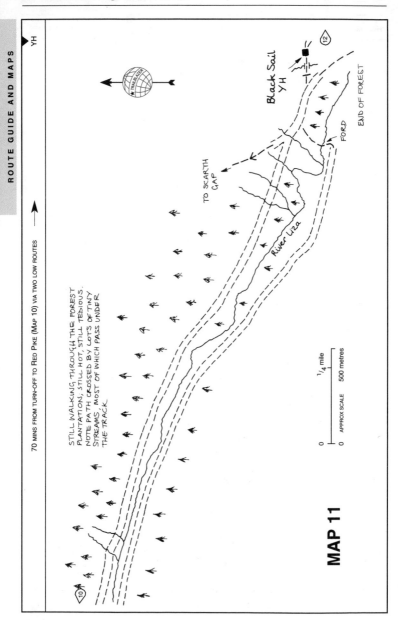

70 MINS FROM TURN-OFF TO RED PIKE (MAP 10) VIA TWO LOW ROUTES →

STILL WALKING THROUGH THE FOREST PLANTATIONS, STILL HOT, STILL TEDIOUS. NOTE PATH CROSSED BY LOTS OF TINY STREAMS, MOST OF WHICH PASS UNDER THE TRACK.

TO SCARTH GAP

River Liza

Black Sail YH

FORD

END OF FOREST

0   ¼ mile
APPROX SCALE
0   500 metres

MAP 11

ROUTE GUIDE AND MAPS

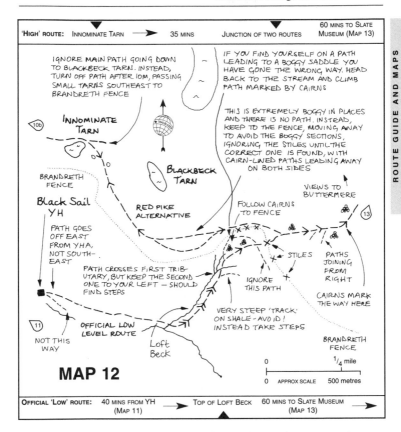

'HIGH' ROUTE: INNOMINATE TARN → 35 MINS JUNCTION OF TWO ROUTES 60 MINS TO SLATE MUSEUM (MAP 13)

IGNORE MAIN PATH GOING DOWN TO BLACKBECK TARN. INSTEAD, TURN OFF PATH AFTER 10M, PASSING SMALL TARNS SOUTHEAST TO BRANDRETH FENCE

IF YOU FIND YOURSELF ON A PATH LEADING TO A BOGGY SADDLE YOU HAVE GONE THE WRONG WAY. HEAD BACK TO THE STREAM AND CLIMB PATH MARKED BY CAIRNS

INNOMINATE TARN

THIS IS EXTREMELY BOGGY IN PLACES AND THERE IS NO PATH. INSTEAD, KEEP TO THE FENCE, MOVING AWAY TO AVOID THE BOGGY SECTIONS, IGNORING THE STILES UNTIL THE CORRECT ONE IS FOUND, WITH CAIRN-LINED PATHS LEADING AWAY ON BOTH SIDES

BLACKBECK TARN

BRANDRETH FENCE

VIEWS TO BUTTERMERE

Black Sail YH

RED PIKE ALTERNATIVE

FOLLOW CAIRNS TO FENCE

PATH GOES OFF EAST FROM YHA, NOT SOUTH-EAST

STILES

PATHS JOINING FROM RIGHT

PATH CROSSES FIRST TRIB-UTARY, BUT KEEP THE SECOND ONE TO YOUR LEFT – SHOULD FIND STEPS

IGNORE THIS PATH

CAIRNS MARK THE WAY HERE

VERY STEEP 'TRACK' ON SHALE-AVOID! INSTEAD TAKE STEPS

NOT THIS WAY

OFFICIAL LOW LEVEL ROUTE

Loft Beck

BRANDRETH FENCE

MAP 12

0   1/4 mile
0   APPROX SCALE   500 metres

OFFICIAL 'LOW' ROUTE: 40 MINS FROM YH (MAP 11) → TOP OF LOFT BECK 60 MINS TO SLATE MUSEUM (MAP 13) →

(cont'd from p82) also the hostel with the biggest reputation, thanks to the manager (the only permanent staff member here). One look at the extensive wine list – far more than one would expect in any youth hostel, let alone one in such an isolated spot as this – provides the first indication that this isn't your typical hostel. The hostel is often left open during the day, providing very welcome shelter when it's raining, with tea (50p) and cake (£1) on sale in the kitchen. Note, however, that Sherpa and a number of other baggage carriers do not deliver to Black Sail.

From the hostel things get a little tricky, with a sharp climb up **Loft Beck** followed by a long descent to Honister Hause (Maps 12-13). In fine weather this section is reasonably straightforward, if a little sweaty. Unfortunately, fine weather can never be guaranteed around these parts, particularly in the afternoon when most people attempt the climb. The ascent up Loft Beck is hard but it's at the top, when you're trying to locate the correct path down to Honister Hause, that real problems can occur: follow Map 12 carefully to negotiate this section.

From **Brandreth Fence**, a fairly clear path contouring the western face of Brandreth and Grey Knotts (Map 13) can be made out, with a number of large cairns along the way to aid navigation in misty conditions. Ahead, the working Hopper Quarry can be seen in the distance on your left. Your path drops gently to Fleetwith and unravels into a number of paths at the **Drum House**. Walking round the Drum House – now little more than a massive pile of stones and slate – you come upon a much more definite path heading off east down the hill. The path's arrow-straight course betrays its previous incarnation as a quarry tramway, now dismantled, and the Drum House's original purpose was to house the cable that operated the tramway that originally ran to the cutting sheds.

At the bottom of the tramway is **Honister Hause**, one of the highest road passes in the Lake District at 332m. The pass plays host to a car park, *Honister YH* (☎ 0870 770 5870; 📧 honister@yha.org.uk; 26 beds; £11) and the **Honister Slate Mine Visitor Centre** (☎ 01768 777230; 🖥 www.honister-slate-mine.co.uk) that serves hot drinks and squash. The No 77 **bus** runs from here to Seatoller (eight minutes) and to Keswick (40 minutes) four times daily, Mar-Oct. The 77A goes via Buttermere to Keswick (60 mins, 4/day, Mar-Oct). From Honister the Coast to Coast path follows the B5289 down little Gatesgarthdale on an old toll road, with both road and path following much the same course. The path loops round to join up with the road again at **Seatoller** (see p90), from where it wends its way through Johnny's Wood into Borrowdale (Map 14).

❑ Honister Slate Mine

The story of mining at Honister begins 400 million years ago when volcanic ash, combined with water and compressed, formed the strong, fine-grained slate that is so popular today. When the glaciers of the last Ice Age retreated across Gatesgarthdale they exposed three parallel veins of this slate in the steep sides of the valley.

The mine (along with the nearby quarry) that tourists are allowed to visit today was reopened in 1997 after an 11-year break in production. When slate was first extracted from Gatesgarthdale, however, is a matter of debate. Certainly by the 1750s slate was being quarried on an industrial scale here, and from 1833, when entrepreneur Sam Wright took over, it was also being mined. As well as the disused tramway that you walk down, there were roads and aerial ropeways to take the slate to the road. The workers who split and finished the slate would live in barracks at Honister during the week; the youth hostel is in fact a converted quarry workers' building.

The slate produced at the Honister mine is green in both senses of the word, being a dull shade of green in colour and, because this is the only slate mine in England (as opposed to an open quarry that scars the land) more environmentally friendly too. The slate from this mine has been used to roof some of Britain's most famous buildings, including both the Ritz Hotel and St James's Palace in London.

The **Visitors' Centre** at Honister is well worth visiting. There are guided tours into the mine daily at 10.30am, 12.30pm and 3.30pm for £8.50 which includes a free cup of tea in the adjacent tearoom. The shop is full of slate souvenirs, from great slabs of the stuff that have been fashioned into coffee tables, to smaller chippings carved into chess pieces, and even smaller flakes that are sold by the bagful. Some of the stuff is lovely – but think twice before purchasing: this walk is hard enough without carrying a full-size slate coffee table on your back for the next fortnight. Thankfully, the website has an online shopping service and they'll deliver the stuff to your home.

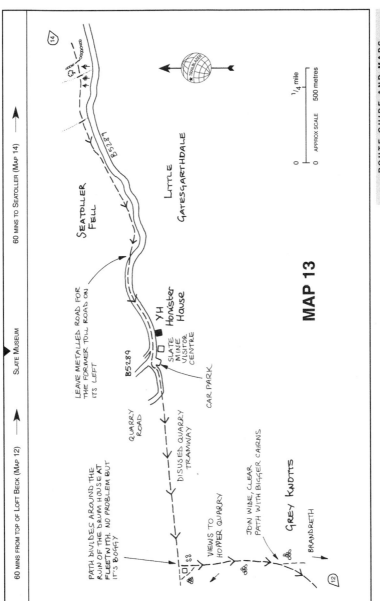

LEAVE METALLED ROAD FOR
THE FORMER TOLL ROAD ON
ITS LEFT

SEATOLLER
FELL

B5289

LITTLE
GATESGARTHDALE

YH Honister
House

SLATE MINE
VISITOR
CENTRE

B5289

CAR PARK

MAP 13

QUARRY
ROAD

DISUSED QUARRY
TRAMWAY

PATH DIVIDES AROUND THE
RUIN OF THE DRUM HOUSE AT
FLEETWITH. NO PROBLEM BUT
IT'S BOGGY

VIEWS TO
HOPPER QUARRY

JOIN WIDE, CLEAR
PATH WITH BIGGER CAIRNS

GREY KNOTTS

BRANDRETH

0   APPROX SCALE   ¹/₄ mile
0   500 metres

ROUTE GUIDE AND MAPS

The Red Pike, High Stile & Hay Stacks route;
Maps 10, 10a, 10b & 12

'*All I ask for, at the end, is a last, long resting place by the side of Innominate Tarn, on Haystacks where the water gently laps the gravelly shore and the heather blooms and Pillar and Gable keep unfailing watch. A quiet place, a lonely place. I shall go to it, for the last time, and be carried: someone who knew me in life will take me there and empty me out of a little box and leave me there alone. And if you, dear reader, should get a bit of grit in your boot as you are crossing Haystacks in the years to come, please treat it with respect. It might be me.*'

Alfred Wainwright *Memoirs of an Ex-Fellwanderer*

In his Coast to Coast guide Wainwright describes this route as suitable only for 'very strong and experienced fellwalkers' in clear weather. While we don't think the group of people who can do this walk is quite as exclusive as Wainwright suggests, we certainly agree that the weather needs to be clear, if only because the views possible at the top – in particular across Buttermere to the north and to Gable and Pillar in the south – demand it. There are no technically difficult parts, though there are some steep ascents and descents which jolt the joints, and route finding on the way up to Red Pike and after Hay Stacks can be tricky. All being well, this alternative route should add about **1½ miles (2.5km, 1¾hr)** to this stage.

This high-level route takes in a number of summits, including Red Pike (755m), High Stile (807m), High Crag (744m) and Hay Stacks (597m), the smallest in height but the most interesting.

There are a couple of places where people go wrong. The first is the climb up to Red Pike, where many branch off eastwards too early: having crossed the stream, continue north-east (following cairns) until you are firmly on the grassy upper reaches of Red Pike (Map 10a). The second problem occurs on Hay Stacks at Innominate Tarn (Map 12), where an obvious path continues east down to Blackbeck Tarn, but the correct route, all but invisible, branches off from this path just 10m from Innominate.

The path soon atrophies to nothing, but not before a fence (Brandreth Fence) has come into view (or at least fenceposts), which you can follow all the way to a union with the regular route up Loft Beck.

If the weather closes in while you are on Hay Stacks you may prefer to continue on the clear trail to Blackbeck, mentioned above, to the working quarry, from where you can follow the works road down to Honister (see p88).

SEATOLLER   MAP 14

The National Trust village of Seatoller has a bar and café, a hiking shop and trekking agency, a car park, and a post-box and a couple of B&Bs; not bad for a hamlet that can't contain, in this author's opinion, more than 20 houses.

The *Yew Tree* is a great place to get out of the rain (and at 3500mm per year, the rainfall in Seatoller is considerably greater than that of Keswick just 8 miles/13km further down the valley, which gets less than 1500mm annually). It consists of a **bar**,

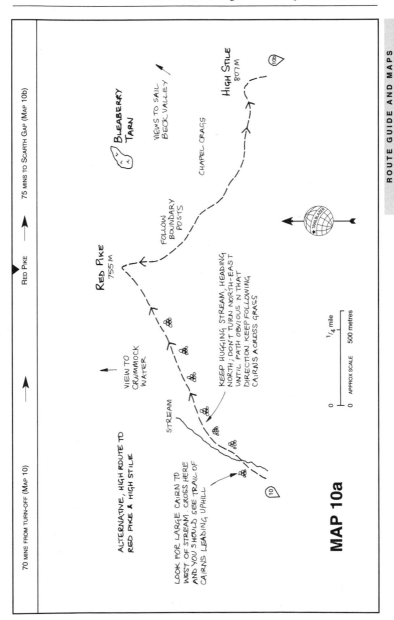

70 MINS FROM TURN-OFF (MAP 10)

RED PIKE

75 MINS TO SCARTH GAP (MAP 10b)

ALTERNATIVE, HIGH ROUTE TO
RED PIKE & HIGH STILE

VIEW TO
CRUMMOCK
WATER.

RED PIKE
755M

FOLLOW
BOUNDARY
POSTS

BLEABERRY
TARN

VIEWS TO SAIL
BECK VALLEY.

CHAPEL CRAGS

HIGH STILE
807M

10b

STREAM

KEEP HUGGING STREAM HEADING
NORTH; DON'T TURN NORTH-EAST
UNTIL PATH OBVIOUS IN THAT
DIRECTION. KEEP FOLLOWING
CAIRNS ACROSS GRASS

★ TRAILBLAZER

LOOK FOR LARGE CAIRN TO
WEST OF STREAM. CROSS HERE
AND YOU SHOULD SEE TRAIL OF
CAIRNS LEADING UPHILL

10

0   ¼ mile
0   APPROX SCALE   500 metres

MAP 10a

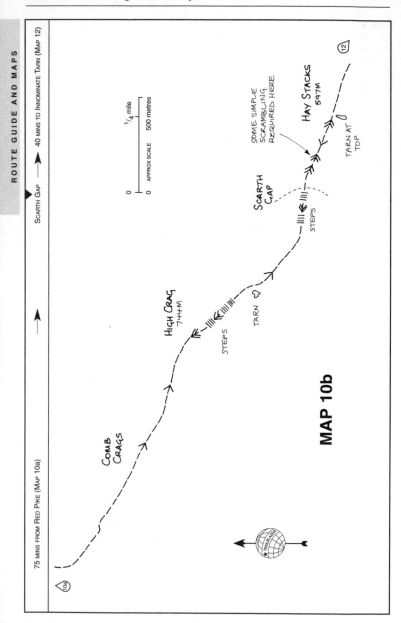

75 MINS FROM RED PIKE (MAP 10a) → | SCARTH GAP ▶ | 40 MINS TO INNOMINATE TARN (MAP 12)

COMB CRAGS

HIGH CRAG
744M

STEPS

TARN

STEPS

SCARTH CAP

SOME SIMPLE SCRAMBLING REQUIRED HERE

HAY STACKS
597M

TARN AT TOP

MAP 10b

¼ mile

0 ___ APPROX SCALE

0 ___ 500 metres

TRAILBLAZER

café, **hiking shop and agency** all occupying a house built in 1628. The kitchen here can rustle up some delightful dishes including Cumberland tattie pot (£7.75), a local dish containing minced lamb, potatoes and black pudding all set in layers and baked in the oven.

Sadly, the excellent information barn opposite the Yew Tree was closed at the time of writing, though the owners are confident of reopening by the summer of 2006.

As for **B&Bs**, Seatoller Farm and Seatoller House sit virtually opposite one another on the main road. *Seatoller House* (☎ 01768 777218; ⌨ www.seatoller house.co.uk; 1D/3D or T/6F) is a 300-year-old building that's been a guesthouse for over a century (previous guests have included the artist John Constable). They have ten rooms, all with their own bathroom (though only four are en suite) and charge from £40 per person for B&B, or £50 including a four-course dinner with coffee and homemade truffles (light supper only on Tuesdays). Single occupancy is subject to a £2 supplement.

Seatoller Farm (☎ 01768 777232; 2D/1T, all en suite) is a working National Trust hill farm that charges £27.50 per person. Their farmhouse breakfasts are said to be the perfect start to the day. Note that pets are not allowed here, though **camping** is allowed (£3.50 per person).

Finally, for a sneak preview of Seatoller visit their **webcam**, ⌨ www.bbc .co.uk/cumbria/webcams/seatoller.shtml.

BORROWDALE   MAP 14

These three charming settlements (Longthwaite, Rosthwaite and Stonethwaite) in Borrowdale are quintessential Lake District hamlets: small, picturesque, friendly and composed largely of slate-roofed, white-washed-stone farm cottages.

Longthwaite

Longthwaite contains a *Youth Hostel* (☎ 0870 770 5706; borrowdale@yha.org.uk; £15.50; 88 beds), a **campsite** (£5), and a fine B&B, *Gillercombe* (☎ 017687 77602; 1S/4D or T). The owner, Rachel Dunckley, currently works in the kitchens of the Langstrath (in Stonethwaite) and is happy to book a table at the Langstrath for hungry walkers. Rates are around £25 per person. This is also the place for campers to pitch.

Rosthwaite

The biggest of the three is Rosthwaite to the north, with a pub, a hotel, a couple of B&Bs, a camping barn and a shop. This last, the **General Store** (Mon-Sat 9am-5pm, Sun 9am-4pm), is decidedly walker-friendly, with maps, books and small items such as Camping Gaz and compasses for sale; they also sell sandwiches. Twenty metres down the road, *The Royal Oak* (☎ 017687 77214; ⌨ www.royaloakhotel.co .uk; 2S/7D or T/6F, singles with shared bathroom, the rest a mixture of en suite and

---

❏ **Borrowdale public transport (see also pp43-5)**
The No 79 bus, known as the **Borrowdale Rambler**, runs between Seatoller and Keswick (from where buses run to other destinations in Cumbria) via Rosthwaite. From Easter to late October there are 1-2 buses an hour Mon-Sat and 9/day on Sundays/Bank Holidays in each direction. From October to Easter there are 9/day (Mon-Sun). Buses generally run between 9am and 6pm in each direction though there may also be earlier/later services. The buses take two minutes to reach the junction with the road to Stonethwaite, five minutes to reach Rosthwaite (opposite the general store), and half an hour to reach Keswick. In addition, between Easter and late October, bus Nos 77/77A (the **Honister Rambler**) run in a loop (4/day) between Keswick, Seatoller, Buttermere and Honister youth hostels, taking 30 minutes on the 77A and an hour on the 77 from Keswick to Seatoller.

shared facilities) is a fine looking place with a long history. Once an 18th-century farmhouse, the hotel played host to the poet William Wordsworth (see p114) in 1812 and is said to be where he shared a bed (innocently, it should be added) with 'a Scotch pedlar'. Rates start at £42/38 sgl/dbl for DB&B in rooms with shared facilities, up to £48 per person for a room in the nearby converted barn annexe, Merrybreeches, with views over the river.

Next door is the *Scafell Hotel and Riverside Bar* (☎ 017687 77208; 💻 www. scafell.co.uk; 24 rooms all en suite), a large place which has served as a coaching inn since 1850. Some of the rooms have been decorated with antique furniture; rates start at £48.50 per person.

There are two National Trust farms that are worth checking out: *Nook Farm* (☎ 017687 77677; 💻 nookfarm1@aol.com; 1D/1T/1F, 1 double en suite) is a 16th-century farmhouse with lovely open fires – the perfect treat after a rainy day's walk. Dogs are positively welcome here (the owner has a couple of her own). Rates start at £27. Behind it, *Yew Tree Farm* (☎ 01768 777675; 3D or T), which dates from 1720, charges £30 for B&B in an en suite room. Nearby is the family-run self-styled 'walkers' tearoom', *The Flock In* (☎ 017687 77675, 💻 www.borrowdaleflockin.co.uk), where the produce from the farm, such as Herdwick sausages and 'Herdie-burgers', is also on sale.

On the path leading out of the village is the *Dinah Hoggus Camping Barn* (☎ 017687 77237), a very simple but attractively rustic place sleeping 12 people; £6 per person (bring your own sleeping bag and camping stove). Booking in advance is essential.

Stonethwaite

Just under a mile (about 1.5km) to the south, Stonethwaite is little more than a dead-end road running parallel to the beck that shares its name. But boy! What a dead end, a gorgeous string of farmhouses with views south to the menacing presence of Eagle Crag and Greenup Gill, which you'll be passing on the next stage. The hamlet is capped at the end by a small hotel and inn, *The Langstrath* (☎ 01768 777239; 💻 www .thelangstrath.com; 10 rooms), whose reputation for fine food extends well beyond Borrowdale (indeed, other than the Riverside Restaurant at Scafell Hotel in Rosthwaite, this is the only place for food in the evening in the 'thwaites'). Here you can sample some local trout or lamb, or a more exotic local dish such as wild boar (£8.90) and duck pie. Rates are £30 per person or £35-40 in an en suite room. They even have their own webcam. All in all, a fantastic place, though there is a problem in that the kitchen tends to close very early and sometimes refuses to serve non-guests altogether. To avoid disappointment, turn up as early as you can or, preferably, book a table in advance.

Besides the inn, Stonethwaite boasts a couple of other B&Bs including the former drovers' alehouse, *Knotts View* (☎ 01768 777604; 3D/2T), which charges £26. According to the owner the building is said to be 450 years old and, with its low ceilings, feels like it. The place is full of character but there are no en suite rooms. They don't offer evening meals so if you want to be sure of one book a table at the Langstrath.

Yet another National Trust place, *Stonethwaite Farm* (☎ 01768 777234; 3D or T) comes highly recommended. It sits adjacent to the phonebox by the path to the bridge across the beck. It's a pretty place with three bedrooms, and also offers **camping** in a field a short way up the valley (see map 15). The farm was to be under new management from March 2006 so rates were not available at the time of writing.

STAGE 3: BORROWDALE TO GRASMERE   MAPS 14-18

In good weather this **9½-mile (15km, 4½-5hr low/high routes)** stage is one of the loveliest, a reasonably straightforward climb up to Lining Crag and Greenup Edge followed by either a high-level ridge walk (see p100) or a simple stroll

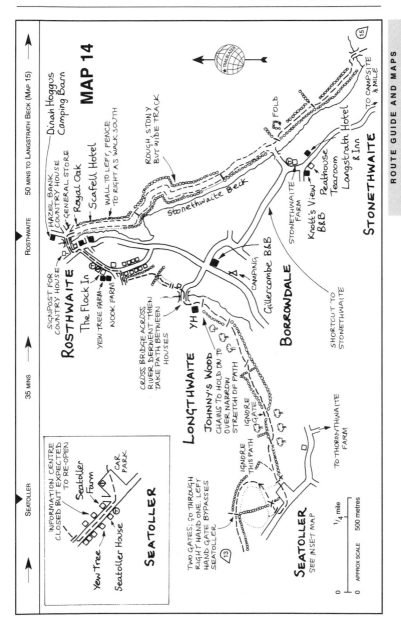

down the valley to Grasmere. A few people get lost on this section, usually just after Greenup Edge, but providing you're careful there's no reason why you should be one of them.

Wainwright combines this stage with the next one to Patterdale, and a few walkers do just that, completing the trek from Borrowdale to Patterdale in one long day. But we strongly recommend you don't: not only would that mean rushing through one of the prettiest and wildest parts of the whole walk, but it would also mean that you probably won't have time to attempt the wonderful high-level routes described on p100 and p109 and will have to keep to the valleys. Furthermore, to bypass Grasmere without stopping for at least one night is little short of criminal. So unless you're really pushed for time, keep the stages separate, take at least one of the high-level paths if conditions allow, and tackle these walks at a pace that will allow you to fully savour the beauty of the lakes and fells. You won't regret it.

The stage begins with a slightly strenuous amble through the fields alongside **Stonethwaite Beck** (Maps 14 and 15), with **Eagle Crag** a permanent, looming, malevolent presence across the water.

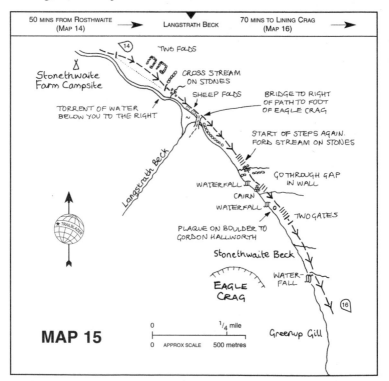

50 MINS FROM ROSTHWAITE (MAP 14) →   LANGSTRATH BECK   70 MINS TO LINING CRAG (MAP 16) →

TWO FOLDS

Stonethwaite Farm Campsite

CROSS STREAM ON STONES

SHEEP FOLDS

TORRENT OF WATER BELOW YOU TO THE RIGHT

BRIDGE TO RIGHT OF PATH TO FOOT OF EAGLE CRAG

START OF STEPS AGAIN. FORD STREAM ON STONES

Langstrath Beck

GO THROUGH GAP IN WALL

WATERFALL

CAIRN

WATERFALL

TWO GATES

PLAQUE ON BOULDER TO GORDON HALLWORTH

Stonethwaite Beck

EAGLE CRAG

WATER-FALL

TRAILBLAZER

MAP 15

0   1/4 mile
0   APPROX SCALE   500 metres

Greenup Gill

Climbing steadily higher alongside one of Stonethwaite Beck's tributaries, **Greenup Gill** (Map 15), with views back down to Borrowdale growing ever more impressive, the path bends slowly right and south round Eagle Crag to arrive, via various obstacles such as a basin of drumlins and a rock wall, at **Lining Crag** and, weather permitting, views towards Scafell Pike, England's highest summit at 3210ft (963m).

Look to the south and you'll also make out the beginning of the path to **Greenup Edge**. This next section is where most people get lost, the boggy ground and the occasional rocky surface helping to obscure the correct direction. The important things to look out for are the fence support posts, the remains of a fence that demarcated Greenup Edge and which clearly once stretched up and over the Low White Stones, the rocky outcrop up to your right as you look south.

If you've followed the right path and come to the right post, you'll see a few metres further on a **cairn** marking the correct way east and down into the head of **Wythburn Valley**. However, it's not Wythburn that we want, but its neighbour, Far Easedale, so you'll have to maintain your easterly direction for

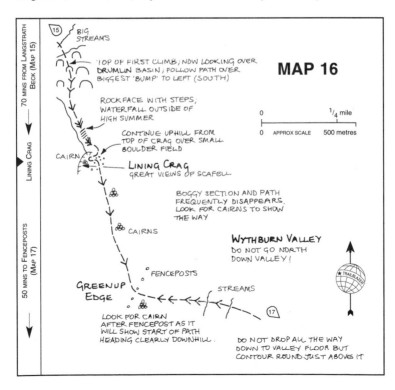

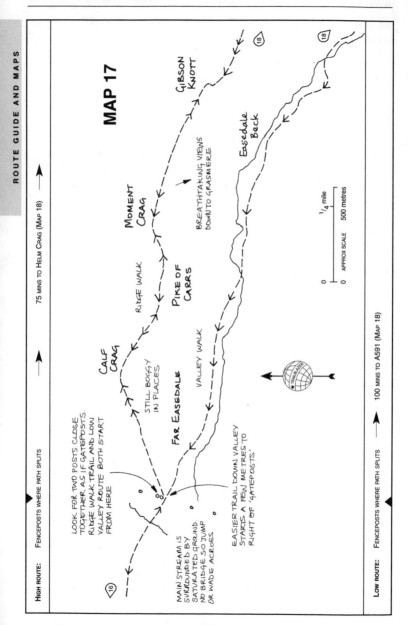

HIGH ROUTE: FENCEPOSTS WHERE PATH SPLITS → 75 MINS TO HELM CRAG (MAP 18) →

MAP 17

⟨16⟩

⟨18⟩

⟨18⟩

GIBSON KNOTT

MOMENT CRAG

PIKE OF CARRS

RIDGE WALK

CALF CRAG

STILL BOGGY IN PLACES

FAR EASEDALE

VALLEY WALK

Easedale Beck

BREATHTAKING VIEWS DOWN TO GRASMERE

LOOK FOR TWO POSTS CLOSE TOGETHER AS IF GATEPOSTS. RIDGE WALK TRAIL AND LOW VALLEY ROUTE BOTH START FROM HERE

MAIN STREAM IS SURROUNDED BY SATURATED GROUND ND BRIDGE SO JUMP OR WADE ACROSS

EASIER TRAIL DOWN VALLEY STARTS A FEW METRES TO RIGHT OF 'GATEPOSTS'

0   ¼ mile
0   APPROX SCALE   500 metres

TRAILBLAZER

LOW ROUTE: FENCEPOSTS WHERE PATH SPLITS → 100 MINS TO A591 (MAP 18) →

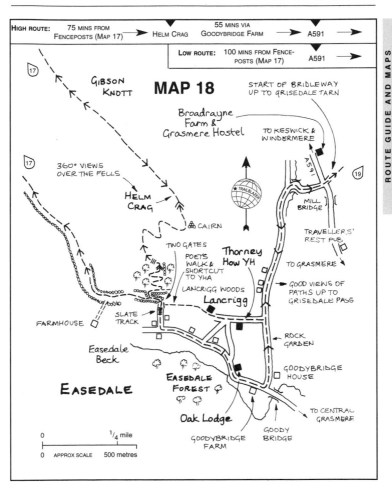

| HIGH ROUTE: | 75 MINS FROM FENCEPOSTS (MAP 17) | → | HELM CRAG | 55 MINS VIA GOODYBRIDGE FARM | → | A591 | → |

| LOW ROUTE: | 100 MINS FROM FENCE-POSTS (MAP 17) | A591 | → |

GIBSON KNOTT

MAP 18

START OF BRIDLEWAY UP TO GRISEDALE TARN

Broadrayne Farm & Grasmere Hostel

TO KESWICK & WINDERMERE

17

360° VIEWS OVER THE FELLS

A591

19

HELM CRAG

★ TRAILBLAZER

MILL BRIDGE

⚒ CAIRN

TRAVELLERS' REST PUB

TWO GATES

POET'S WALK & SHORTCUT TO YHA

Thorney How YH

TO GRASMERE

LANCRIGG WOODS

Lancrigg

GOOD VIEWS OF PATHS UP TO GRISEDALE PASS

FARMHOUSE

SLATE TRACK

ROCK GARDEN

Easedale Beck

GOODYBRIDGE HOUSE

EASEDALE

EASEDALE FOREST

Oak Lodge

TO CENTRAL GRASMERE

GOODYBRIDGE FARM

GOODY BRIDGE

0   1/4 mile

0   APPROX SCALE   500 metres

the next ten minutes and aim for the ridge opposite, the other side of the valley head. The easier path down the valley of Far Easedale to Grasmere now begins a few metres to the right of the 'gateposts' on Map 17. This **low-level route** is simplicity itself, the most gentle of ambles down the valley alongside Easedale Beck. It's a peaceful walk, too, as most hikers take the high route these days, attracted by the fact that it's the easiest of the high-level alternatives on the Coast to Coast. Indeed, sheep are likely to be your only company. At the bottom there are some pleasant riverside grassy patches which positively cry out for picnickers, before the first few farms on the outskirts of Grasmere are passed.

ROUTE GUIDE AND MAPS

The ridge-walk alternative to Grasmere via Helm Crag
Maps 17-18

For the more rewarding high-level route to **Calf Crag**, **Gibson Knott** and **Helm Crag** amongst other, lesser heights, having crossed the head of the Wythburn follow the path that contours round the hill ahead. The walking is not difficult, and though the ground is often saturated the climbs up to the various peaks from the ridge take little more than three or four minutes each time. It is a long walk, however, and despite the awesome views, with Castle, Land and Silver hows behind you to the south-west on one side and Helvellyn and Great Rigg to the north-east on the other, by the time you've conquered Helm Crag you'll be glad to see the path dropping sharply to the western outskirts of Grasmere. From the foot, it's just 20 minutes or so along the road to the heart of one of the Lake District's – and England's – prettiest villages.

GRASMERE

Wordsworth called this valley 'the fairest place on earth' and it is his association with Grasmere that has done so much to popularize the place over the years. Though Wordsworth lived here for only nine years, the period was a productive one and he wrote many of his best-known works here. His grave is in the grounds of St Oswald's Church, one of the more peaceful spots in Grasmere's busy centre. The village hasn't lost any of its charm since Wordsworth's day. It is the harmony of the natural and the man-made that makes Grasmere so enchanting. To the west of the village the large farmhouses and stately homes share the smooth, undulating land with forests of mature deciduous trees and flocks of dozy sheep; through the busy jumble of buildings in the centre flows the gentle River Rothay, a tranquil haven for ducks and other waterfowl; while to the south lies brooding Grasmere Lake, flanked by steep, forested hills and almost entirely undeveloped. Sure, more than a few Coast-to-Coasters of my acquaintance complain that they find it all a bit twee, with its cream-tea shops and folksy olde-worlde charm. But it's a hard-hearted trekker who doesn't appreciate the picture-postcard perfection of the place while even its critics will be pleased with the facilities on offer here, from hiking shops to a cash machine and even an internet connection.

If you're under no time constraints, consider stopping over for more than one night: there's enough here – from Wordsworth's Dove Cottage to a host of small private galleries and some lovely little walks around the surrounding countryside – to keep you contented for a couple of days.

Services

Grasmere's tourist information office closed in 2005; the nearest office is at Glenridding, see box p114.

The **post office** (Mon-Wed & Fri 9am-5pm, Thu & Sat 9am-12.30pm) is small but central and plays host to Grasmere's only **cash machine**.

If that's closed, the **Co-op** (Mon-Sat 8.30am-6pm; Sun 10am-6pm) provides a cashback service and is the best place to stock up on trekking provisions. Next to the Co-op is a **pharmacy**.

The **trekking shops**, Summitreks and Mountain Hi, are opposite the Methodist church on College St, with Stewart & Cunningham just round the corner on Broadgate, and Cotswold and Aktive8 near the post office. If you can't find what you need in one of these, a bus (£4.15 return; see Transport p104) leaves from the green every 20 minutes to Ambleside, where there are loads of trekking outlets.

Internet access is provided by Butharlyp Youth Hostel (an extortionate

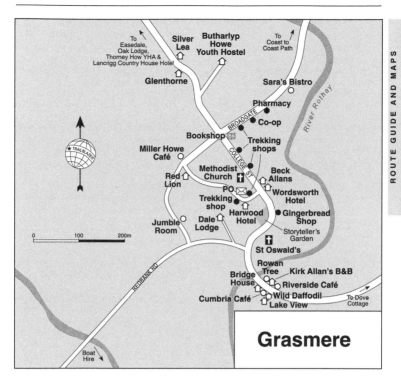

To
Easedale,
Oak Lodge,
Thorney How YHA &
Lancrigg Country House Hotel

Silver
Lea

Butharlyp
Howe
Youth Hostel

To
Coast to
Coast Path

Glenthorne

Sara's Bistro

River Rothay

Pharmacy

Co-op

BROADGATE

Bookshop

Trekking
shops

Miller Howe
Café

COLLEGE ST

Methodist
Church

Beck
Allans

Red
Lion

PO

Wordsworth
Hotel

Trekking
shop

Harwood
Hotel

Gingerbread
Shop

Jumble
Room

Dale
Lodge

Storyteller's
Garden

St Oswald's

Rowan
Tree

Kirk Allan's B&B

Bridge
House

Riverside Café

Cumbria Café

Wild Daffodil

Lake View

To Dove
Cottage

0   100   200m

TRAILBLAZER

Boat
Hire

Grasmere

50p for five minutes). There's a cheaper connection at Ambleside Library.

Where to stay

Hostels There are two YHA hostels (☎ 0870 770 5836; 🖥 grasmere@yha.org.uk) in Grasmere: *Thorney How* (53 beds; £13) and *Butharlyp Howe* (80 beds; £15.50). The former is right on the route, though a 15-minute walk from central Grasmere, while the latter is nearer to the centre but off the route a little way. Perhaps the pick of the two, Butharlyp is the larger and enjoys the advantages of a more central location, internet connection, a licence to sell alcohol, a smarter self-catering kitchen and more attractive grounds. The food is superior here too. Be warned, however, that because it is the larger it tends to attract more marauding school groups than

Thorney How, making its smaller rival, which sits bang slap on the trail, by far the more preferable on these days. The two share the same booking system, so if you fail to get into one they'll look for space at the other.

There's also the independent Grasmere Hostel at *Broadrayne Farm* (☎ 015394 35055; 🖥 www.grasmerehostel.co.uk, 24 beds) charging £15.50 per bed; see Map 18.

B&Bs Most B&Bs will be very reluctant to accept a one-night-only booking on summer weekends. Either stay for two nights or try to avoid the high-season weekends.

Oak Lodge (☎ 015394 35527 🖥 www.oaklodge-grasmere.co.uk; 2D/1T, all en suite) is the first place you see as you enter Grasmere on the Easedale Road. It's a very smart little establishment in a wonderful location next to tranquil Easedale Forest and charges £28 per person.

Silver Lea (☎ 015394 35657; 🖳 www .silverlea.com; 2T/2D all en suite) on Easedale Rd is a charming ivy-clad slate cottage, surprisingly bright inside, where each room has a TV and tea-/coffee-making facilities. Rates are from £39.50 per person for a twin or double, or £43.50 for a suite (with lounge). Dinner is £15.50 extra.

Back towards the centre, the large ***Glenthorne Guest House*** (☎ 015394 35389, 🖳 www.glenthorne.org; 8S/20D) is a Victorian, Quaker country house (though folk of any creed can stay) next to another of Wordsworth's old houses, Allan Bank. There's a wonderfully informal, convivial atmosphere to the place, though thankfully this doesn't come at the expense of any drop-in service. Across the lawn are comfortable self-catering apartments (not usually available for single-night bookings), which were previously joiners' cottages. Clothes-drying facilities are also available. Rates are £29/40 standard/en suite, or £20 in one of their three budget single rooms.

Beck Allans (☎ 015394 35563, free phone ☎ 0800 0744 766; 🖳 www.beck allans.com; 5D or T) is a non-smoking guesthouse with some self-catering apartments overlooking the Rothay. It lies in the heart of the village next to the Wordsworth Hotel, whose pool and gym facilities residents at Beck Allans are allowed to use. All rooms (£29-34 per person) are en suite with bath and shower, and come with TV, tea- and coffee-making facilities, hair dryer – and room No 2 has a four-poster bed (£37 per person). Note that no pets are allowed, and there's a single supplement of 50 per cent.

By the bridge is ***Kirk Allan's B&B*** (☎ 015394 35745, 2D en suite) with all en suite rooms for £27.50 per person (there is a £12.50 single person supplement). It's centrally located and convenient for exploring the nearby teashops and the lake shore.

Lake View (015394 35384, 🖳 www .lakeview-grasmere.com; 3D/1T) is, as its name suggests, one of the few hotels from where you can actually see the lake. It's a modern place near the centre of Grasmere,

quietly tucked away at the end of a lane. Rates vary from £38.50 to £47.

Hotels ***Red Lion Hotel*** (☎ 015394 35456; 🖳 www.hotelsgrasmere.co.uk; 47 en suite rooms) *is* the centre of town, a pleasant-enough place though one that lacks a little of the charm of some of the others around here. Nevertheless, it's a bit cheaper too, and all rooms are en suite, many with Jacuzzi baths. Rates are £53.50-61, though a single-night stay on a Saturday night attracts a £20 supplement. Dogs are welcome at a daily rate of £7.50 per day.

Wordsworth Hotel (☎ 015394 35592; 🖳 www.grasmere-hotels.co.uk; 4S/28D or T – three with four-poster beds – and two suites; all rooms en suite) is the smartest address in the centre of town, a large but attractive hotel with facilities including gym, pool, sauna, Jacuzzi and cocktail bar. They also offer fishing on the nearby Rothay. Rooms, all en suite, come with satellite TV, radio, phone and computer points. Rates are £75-110/£55-90 for sgl/dbl and £190-250 for a suite.

Bridge House Hotel (☎ 015394 35425; 🖳 www.bridgehousegrasmere.co .uk; 11D/8D or T) is another large non-smoking place and is also near the river, this one has no single rooms but 18 of the 19 rooms are en suite with a TV, telephone and tea-/coffee-making facilities. Unfortunately, they accept one-night bookings only if it's quiet which, in summer, it is unlikely to be. They also do not allow pets. Nevertheless, the hotel has two acres of gorgeous grounds, and if you buy a drink in their bar they will allow you to use them for a picnic with food brought in from outside. Rates, for one night with breakfast and dinner, are £57/64 standard/superior (ie larger) rooms.

Dale Lodge Hotel (☎ 015394 35300; 🖳 www.dalelodgehotel.co.uk; 2T/6D en suite) is a charming if slightly tired-looking old pile in the centre of Grasmere with some wonderful period features and three acres of sprawling gardens. Each bedroom, individually furnished and decorated, is en suite and has colour TV, tea- and coffee-making facilities and direct dial telephone.

The attached bar, Tweedies, is also recommended. No pets are allowed. Rates are £45/55 per person for en suite shower/bath, or £65 for the four-poster bed. Single occupancy is £65. Almost falling over the Dale Lodge is the *Harwood Hotel* (☎ 015394 35248; ☐ www.harwoodhotel.co.uk; 3D en suite/2S/1D/1T private bath) with rooms from £29.50 per person (less out of season).

Lancrigg Vegetarian Country House Hotel (Map 18; ☎ 015394 35317; ☐ www .lancrigg.co.uk; 10D/2T and a cottage) is probably the most attractive large hotel in Grasmere which, given the competition, is really saying something. Indeed, I can't think of a more splendid hotel on the walk. Lancrigg is a large country house, with parts dating back to the 17th century, a little way to the north-west of the village, very near Thorney How Youth Hostel. One of the previous occupants was Elizabeth Fletcher, a friend of Wordsworth (he found and helped her buy the house in 1839), and the house and adjoining woods became something of a meeting place for the Lakeland poets. All the rooms are individually furnished with many affording a magnificent view across Easedale Forest and the neighbouring fields. Some also have four-poster beds and whirlpool baths. If you don't eat meat and have got the money, this is the place to spend it. Rates are £60-100; add £27.50 for a four-course evening meal. Discounts are available at certain times of the year.

Where to eat

As you'd expect for a major tourist centre like Grasmere, tearooms are plentiful throughout the village. Best of all, however, is *Jumble Room* (daily 11.30am-3.30pm, 6pm 'till food runs out'). Aptly named, this is a quirky little place that resembles, from the outside, a cross between an art gallery and a toy shop. Don't be put off, however, for the food is some of the most imaginative in town, the menu changes daily and includes dishes from all four corners of the globe, including the locally inspired haddock in beer batter for £10.95.

Another place that's open for teas during the day is the *Rowan Tree*, overlooking the river. However, our advice is to save a visit until the evening (from 6pm), when they do a fine selection of pizzas from £6.75 and other Italian or English dishes. A number of other tea shops and cafés vie for position near the bridge including the contemporary *Riverside Café* with bacon butties for £2.95 and the *Cumbria Café* which does an excellent-value Yorkshire pudding for £3.50. The *Wild Daffodil* (daily 9.30am-9pm, except Wed 9.30am-5pm) also does evening meals such as lamb for £10.95 and sandwiches from £3.50.

The Red Lion offers four-course meals (£22.50) in either its *Garden Room* or *Courtyard* restaurants. Though the choices are limited in both (with only four or five main-course dishes) the food is good. The local fell-bred beef steak on a bed of garlic mash potato is popular. Opposite the Red Lion is a chic bistro, the *Miller Howe Café* (☎ 015394 35234; daily 9am-6pm) with further local specialities including Cumberland sausage for £6.95.

Moving north, *Sara's Bistro* (☎ 015394 35266; Tue-Sun 10.30am-4pm, 6-9pm) has been recommended for its exquisite French-influenced food (Mediterranean vegetarian lasagne £9.95), and the *Traveller's Rest Pub and Hotel* (see Map 18) at the very northern end of town serves hearty portions of mainly local dishes, including a very tasty rack of lamb (£9.95).

What to see

Dove Cottage William Wordsworth lived for less than ten years in beautiful Dove Cottage (☎ 015394 35544; ☐ www.words worthtrust.org.uk; daily 9.30am-5.30pm except early Jan to early Feb; £5.95/4.60 adults/YHA and student-card holders; children £3), yet its importance in both his development as a poet and his life is enormous. Many of his best loved and most powerful works were penned here (all together now: 'I wandered lonely as a cloud...'), and this is where he first lived with his wife Mary Hutchinson and where his first three children were born.

ROUTE GUIDE AND MAPS

Today all but the first room is furnished entirely with items owned, at one time or another, by the poet, though it should be added not all the pieces of furniture were originally part of Dove Cottage, but have come from other Wordsworth properties.

Guides show visitors around the cottage every hour on the half-hour, pointing out such items of interest as Wordsworth's **suitcase** (where he's sewn his name inside but didn't leave enough room and ended up embroidering 'Wordswort' on one line, with the final 'h' tucked up in the corner); a letter of introduction – a precursor to the modern-day passport – penned by the French authorities, and which has been stamped on the back by the border guards of a whole host of European countries that Wordsworth visited; and the **Royal Warrant** of 1843 in which he was bestowed with the honour of being Queen Victoria's poet laureate. It was an honour he accepted grudgingly, having already turned down the position twice, and one that he never truly fulfilled; indeed, from his acceptance of the post to his death in 1850, Wordsworth wrote precisely no official poems as poet laureate, the first (and so far only) poet laureate to do so.

The cottage is, by the standards of the Lake District, relatively large, containing eight rooms rather than the more typical three or four, thus betraying its origins as a 17th-century pub. It might interest you to know that one of Wordsworth's visitors at the cottage was that other well-known literary figure (and opium fiend) Thomas de Quincey. At the time of his visit de Quincey declared the house to be a fortuitous one for writers, and when the Wordsworths vacated the house in 1808 the de Quinceys moved in, thus extending the literary connections of the place still further.

The **museum** next door contains original manuscripts by both Wordsworth and de Quincey, as well as a whole host of other poetic paraphernalia.

Other sights Before you leave Grasmere, pay a visit to Wordsworth's family grave around the back of **St Oswald's**, a 13th-century church named after the 7th-century king of Northumbria who preached on this site. Wordsworth's prayer-book is on display in the church.

Standing by the side entrance to the church grounds is the 150-year-old **Gingerbread Shop** (☎ 015394 35428; ☐ www.grasmeregingerbread.co.uk; Mon-Sat 9.15am-5.30pm, Sun 12.30-5.30pm), a tiny 'factory' that, incredibly, used to be the local school. It is said that Wordsworth taught here occasionally.

Opposite is the **Storyteller's Garden** which plays host to several events throughout the year – ask at the tourist office for a schedule.

Around the village centre are a number of **galleries** displaying works by local artists, including the Heaton Cooper studio opposite the bus stop and the Slapestones Gallery on Pye Lane.

Make sure, too, that you check out Lancrigg Woods and the **Poet's Walk** (Map 18, p99), the start of which you walked past on your way into Grasmere. It's a tranquil delight and it comes as no surprise to find that the Lakeland poets enjoyed it too. Indeed, they planted many of the trees that grow in the woods. Along the way is an inscription, in Latin, describing how Wordsworth's sister Dorothy would sit at this spot while her brother walked up and down composing verses. The path finishes up going round the front of the very smart Lancrigg Hotel, where it joins the road to the youth hostel.

Finally, there's always **boating** on the lake. Walk south-west out of Grasmere along Redbank Rd and, after about five to ten minutes, you'll come to the tea shop which doubles as the boat-hire agency. It's open from about 10.15am to 4 or 5pm every day and charges £6/hour for one person, £3 for each additional person.

Transport (see also pp43-5)

From Easter to late August the open-top No 599 bus service travels every 20 minutes during the day via Ambleside (15 mins) and the train station and Bowness Pier at

Windermere, from where in the evening a few buses go on to Kendal. From late August to late October there are 2/hour. The No 555 goes from Keswick to Lancaster (hourly, Mon-Sat) via Ambleside, Windermere and Kendal (Grasmere to Lancaster takes 1hr 45min). The Sunday/ Public Holiday service for both the 599 and 555 operates only between Easter and October.

For other destinations, Grasmere **Taxis** can be reached on ☎ 015394 35506.

STAGE 4: GRASMERE TO PATTERDALE   MAPS 18-25

Ignoring the alternative routes on this stage for the moment, this is one of the shortest and easiest stages. Short, but no less sweet, for during this stage walkers can enjoy some great views both over the shoulder to Grasmere and, once over the pass, down Grisedale to Patterdale, another gorgeous valley with the lake of Ullswater hiding away to the north.

The most direct route is a mere **10 miles (16km, 3¹/₂hr)** and is a simple up and down, involving a crossing of **Grisedale Pass**. The stage can, however, be lengthened by attempting a conquest of one of the nearby peaks, Helvellyn or St Sunday. Both of these are described on pp109-10.

You can delay your choice on which path to take until Grisedale Tarn, where the three paths go their separate ways. But first of all you need to reach Grisedale Tarn, which involves a longish climb up a bridleway running off the A591 (Map 18, p99) reached by walking up the A591 to the bridleway from Grasmere or, more enjoyably, on the 'official' Coast to Coast path near Thorney How Youth Hostel.

The bridleway divides at the foot of **Great Tongue** (Map 19) and a choice must be made. The steeper route alongside **Little Tongue Gill** is harder on the calves but easy on the eye: this is the route to take for views back down to Grasmere. The 'easier path' to the east of Great Tongue along Tongue Gill is paved for much of its length; the gradients are slightly less on this trail, though, of course, at the end of the day you're still climbing to the same height and from the same starting point as the other trail.

At the top of the climb there's a wall and a great view of the entire **Grisedale Tarn** (Map 20). You will also note, behind it, the path up **Dollywaggon Pike** to Helvellyn etched into the grass (see Map 20). Keeping to the easier path down Grisedale, the descent is as uncomplicated as the ascent, a reasonably straight scamper down the valley. Just below the tarn is the **Brothers' Parting Stone** (so-called because it is said that this is the last time, 1800, Wordsworth saw his brother, John, who died at sea in 1805) and, just under a mile further on by rushing Ruthwaite Beck, **Ruthwaite Lodge**, a climbers' hut.

The path continues fairly straight down the valley and joins a tarmac road before leaving it to the right to bend left through the National Trust's **Glenamara Park** (Map 24), with some wonderful views over Patterdale and beyond to Ullswater (Norse for 'Water with a Bend'). All being well, you'll drop onto the road just below the post office and pub just over two hours (plus breaks) after leaving Grisedale Tarn.

ROUTE GUIDE AND MAPS

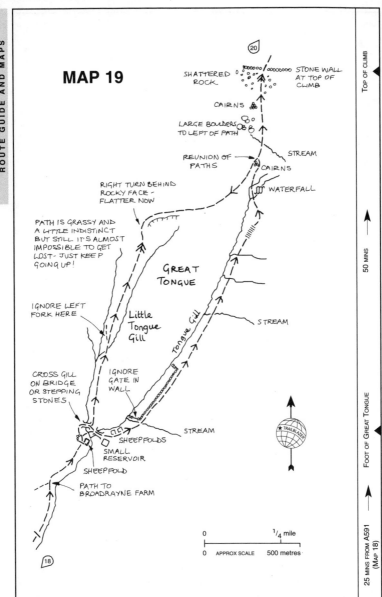

MAP 19

SHATTERED ROCK

STONE WALL AT TOP OF CLIMB

CAIRNS

LARGE BOULDERS TO LEFT OF PATH

REUNION OF PATHS

STREAM

CAIRNS

RIGHT TURN BEHIND ROCKY FACE - FLATTER NOW

WATERFALL

PATH IS GRASSY AND A LITTLE INDISTINCT BUT STILL IT'S ALMOST IMPOSSIBLE TO GET LOST - JUST KEEP GOING UP!

GREAT TONGUE

IGNORE LEFT FORK HERE

Little Tongue Gill

Tongue Gill

STREAM

CROSS GILL ON BRIDGE OR STEPPING STONES

IGNORE GATE IN WALL

SHEEPFOLDS

STREAM

SMALL RESERVOIR

SHEEPFOLD

PATH TO BROADRAYNE FARM

★ TRAILBLAZER

TOP OF CLIMB

50 MINS

FOOT OF GREAT TONGUE

25 MINS FROM A591 (MAP 18)

0   1/4 mile

0   APPROX SCALE   500 metres

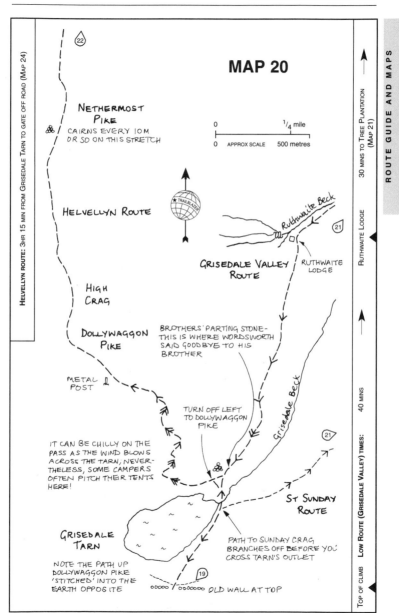

MAP 20

HELVELLYN ROUTE: 3HR 15 MIN FROM GRISEDALE TARN TO GATE OFF ROAD (MAP 24)

NETHERMOST PIKE

CAIRNS EVERY IOM OR SO ON THIS STRETCH

0   ¼ mile

0   APPROX SCALE   500 metres

★ TRAILBLAZER

HELVELLYN ROUTE

HIGH CRAG

DOLLYWAGGON PIKE

METAL POST

Ruthwaite Beck

GRISEDALE VALLEY ROUTE

RUTHWAITE LODGE

BROTHERS' PARTING STONE - THIS IS WHERE WORDSWORTH SAID GOODBYE TO HIS BROTHER

TURN OFF LEFT TO DOLLYWAGGON PIKE

Grisedale Beck

IT CAN BE CHILLY ON THE PASS AS THE WIND BLOWS ACROSS THE TARN; NEVERTHELESS, SOME CAMPERS OFTEN PITCH THEIR TENTS HERE!

GRISEDALE TARN

NOTE THE PATH UP DOLLYWAGGON PIKE 'STITCHED' INTO THE EARTH OPPOSITE

ST SUNDAY ROUTE

PATH TO SUNDAY CRAG BRANCHES OFF BEFORE YOU CROSS TARN'S OUTLET

OLD WALL AT TOP

30 MINS TO TREE PLANTATION (MAP 21)

RUTHWAITE LODGE

40 MINS

LOW ROUTE (GRISEDALE VALLEY) TIMES:

TOP OF CLIMB

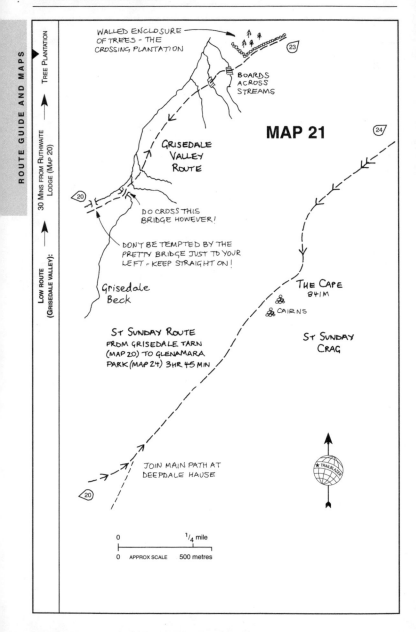

WALLED ENCLOSURE OF TREES - THE CROSSING PLANTATION

23

BOARDS ACROSS STREAMS

24

MAP 21

GRISEDALE VALLEY ROUTE

20

DO CROSS THIS BRIDGE HOWEVER!

DON'T BE TEMPTED BY THE PRETTY BRIDGE JUST TO YOUR LEFT - KEEP STRAIGHT ON!

Grisedale Beck

THE CAPE 841M

CAIRNS

ST SUNDAY ROUTE
FROM GRISEDALE TARN (MAP 20) TO GLENAMARA PARK (MAP 24) 3HR 45 MIN

ST SUNDAY CRAG

JOIN MAIN PATH AT DEEPDALE HAUSE

20

TRAILBLAZER

0   ¼ mile
0   APPROX SCALE   500 metres

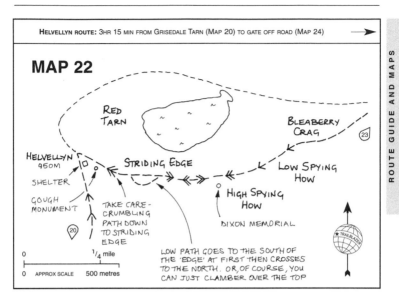

HELVELLYN ROUTE: 3HR 15 MIN FROM GRISEDALE TARN (MAP 20) TO GATE OFF ROAD (MAP 24) ➜

MAP 22

RED TARN

BLEABERRY CRAG ㉓

HELVELLYN 950M

STRIDING EDGE

Low SPYING How

SHELTER

GOUGH MONUMENT

TAKE CARE – CRUMBLING PATH DOWN TO STRIDING EDGE

㉑

High SPYING How

DIXON MEMORIAL

★ TRAILBLAZER

0   ¼ mile

0   APPROX SCALE   500 metres

LOW PATH GOES TO THE SOUTH OF THE 'EDGE' AT FIRST THEN CROSSES TO THE NORTH. OR, OF COURSE, YOU CAN JUST CLAMBER OVER THE TOP

The high-level alternatives: Helvellyn and Striding Edge (Maps 20, 22-24); St Sunday Crag (Maps 20, 21, 24)

If weather conditions allow, one of these two high-level options should be seriously considered instead of the simple trail down Grisedale. After all, it would be a shame on this, the penultimate stage in the Lake District, if you didn't try to climb as many peaks as possible.

Of the two, **Helvellyn** (950m), the third highest peak in England after Scafell Pike and Scafell, is perhaps the more popular. The climb is arduous and, having reached the top, you then face a nerve-tingling drop on a crumbing slope followed by a tightrope walk along Striding Edge to reach the onward trail to Patterdale; but the views and sense of achievement are ample reward for your efforts.

Wainwright himself waxes lyrical about this side trip, describing the famous/notorious Striding Edge as the 'best quarter mile between St Bees and Robin Hood's Bay'. You may feel less enamoured as you slide down on your backside to the start of Striding Edge, the scree tumbling down the sheer slope below you.

The route takes about 3hr 15 min from Grisedale Tarn, though that assumes you will take the lower route just below the summit of Striding Edge which could be completed in as little as 20 minutes. However, with the inevitable trips up to the summit and with all the waiting that needs to be done to let people coming the other way go by, expect it to take nearer an hour. You won't regret the extra time – it is truly exhilarating.

ROUTE GUIDE AND MAPS

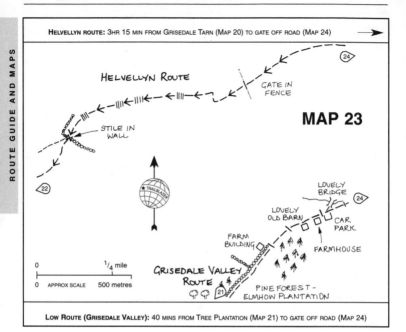

HELVELLYN ROUTE

GATE IN FENCE

STILE IN WALL

MAP 23

★ TRAILBLAZER

LOVELY BRIDGE

LOVELY OLD BARN

CAR PARK

FARM BUILDING

FARMHOUSE

0   ¼ mile

0   APPROX SCALE   500 metres

GRISEDALE VALLEY ROUTE

PINE FOREST – ELMHOW PLANTATION

LOW ROUTE (GRISEDALE VALLEY): 40 MINS FROM TREE PLANTATION (MAP 21) TO GATE OFF ROAD (MAP 24)

Wainwright visited Helvellyn on his first trip to the Lakes in 1930, and although the weather was such that the 'rain still sluiced down, making rivulets on our bellies', it was this first trip that inspired his passion for the Lakes. He approached the peak from the opposite direction to that described here, *from* Striding Edge, which he described as edging along 'in agonies of apprehension'.

Should you wish to avoid similar agonies, upon reaching the top of Helvellyn you can continue across the summit and take what is said to be an easier route down around Red Tarn (the name Helvellyn means, incidentally, 'The Hill Overlooking the Lake') clearly etched into the ground, which rejoins the main route at the end of Striding Edge. The scramble up **St Sunday Crag**, to the south of Grisedale, is more taxing on the joints, particularly the final descent into Patterdale, though less so on the nerves. For some reason, it is very often windier on this trail.

The path is fairly clear as it leaves Grisedale Tarn near its outlet, the narrowish trail aiming for Deepdale Hause between the peaks of Fairfield and St Sunday. Near the top follow the cairns and continue to do so up to St Sunday (841m), the summit of which is called The Cape, skirting below the ridge before dropping down to Glenamara Park, where you meet up with the low-level route to Patterdale.

ROUTE GUIDE AND MAPS

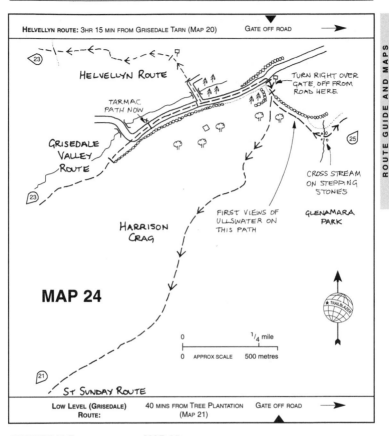

HELVELLYN ROUTE: 3HR 15 MIN FROM GRISEDALE TARN (MAP 20)   GATE OFF ROAD →

HELVELLYN ROUTE

TURN RIGHT OVER GATE, OFF FROM ROAD HERE

TARMAC PATH NOW

GRISEDALE VALLEY ROUTE

CROSS STREAM ON STEPPING STONES

FIRST VIEWS OF ULLSWATER ON THIS PATH

GLENAMARA PARK

HARRISON CRAG

MAP 24

0   ¼ mile
0   APPROX SCALE   500 metres

★ TRAILBLAZER

ST SUNDAY ROUTE

LOW LEVEL (GRISEDALE) ROUTE: 40 MINS FROM TREE PLANTATION (MAP 21)   GATE OFF ROAD →

PATTERDALE   MAP 25

Patterdale is little more than a meandering collection of houses strung along the A592. Nevertheless, it's a cracking place. Normally valleys this beautiful would be full of souvenir shops and tearooms. But Patterdale, while not exactly undiscovered if the huge volume of hikers walking through the village on a summer weekend is anything to go by, *is* mercifully free of the worst excesses of tourism.

It also has some cute touches. The **fountain of St Patrick** (Patterdale is a corruption of St Patrick's Dale) is an ornate Victorian construction set in a bank by the side of the road just outside Glenridding, and is said to mark the spot where the saint baptized the locals. The valley is also something of a wildlife haven, including a population of red squirrels – some of the last remaining in England – and badgers. And finally there's **Crookabeck Herdwicks** (ring first for an appointment on ☎ 017684 82742; 🖳 www.herdwickwool.com), a farm selling kits and rugs and other items made from wool sheared from the local Herdwick flocks.

For **information**, visit the **post office** (daily 8am-6pm), whose owners are Coast-to-Coast veterans and supply a reasonable selection of sandwiches (£2-3), call in at the youth hostel, which has a lot of information stuck on noticeboards, or take a walk down to Ullswater and Glenridding, where there's a tourist office (see box p114). Near this office is Kilner's Coffee House & Cybercafé (10am-6pm), where **internet connection** costs £2 for 30 minutes.

Where to stay and eat

There's a range of **accommodation** in Patterdale, though booking ahead is, as elsewhere, vital, else you could end up having to stay in Glenridding. Not that there's anything wrong with Glenridding, of course, and indeed its location by Ullswater is a delight – it's just a fair distance from the start of the next stage, which is one of the more wearying stretches and not one you'd want to extend if you can help it.

For **campers**, across the Goldrill Beck is *Side Farm* (☎ 017684 82337), open from Easter to November. The campsite is in a field protected by a dry-stone wall and a pitch costs £5 per adult. They have a tearoom, and breakfasts can be pre-ordered. Believe it or not, Wordsworth was a regular visitor to Side Farm.

At the other end of Patterdale, the *Youth Hostel* (☎ 0870 770 5986, 🖳 patterdale@yha .org.uk; 82 beds; £12.50) is on the main road. The hostel looks a bit like a comprehensive school, but inside it's comfortable and, unusually, is open all day. Facilities include TV and internet connection (£2 per half hour), and the current chef is said to be one of the best in the association. Though the building itself is only 30-or-so years old, it stands on the site of a previous one from the 1930s, making it one of the oldest hostels in Britain.

Just before the hostel, *Old Water View* (☎ 01768 482175; 🖳 www.oldwaterview .co.uk; 4D) is a pleasant place and a favourite of Wainwright's. Rates are £35 for single occupancy (Sun-Thu only), £25-27.50 for double occupancy. Opposite this is *Barco House* (☎ 017684 82474; 🖳 www .barcohouse.com; 2D/1T) an equally beautiful house built from local slate with B&B

for £28.50 per person. Nearer the centre of the village is *Glebe House* (☎ 017684 82339; 1D/1F), set back from the road and charging from £25.

Very close to the path and the focus of the village is the local pub, the 19th-century *White Lion* (☎ 017684 82214; 2S/2D/ 3T, all en suite or with private facilities). B&B starts at £29.50 and they do bar meals too. The extensive menu includes steaks, curry and fish & chips (12noon-9pm).

There are other B&Bs further south along the road beyond the youth hostel. A mile from the path, *Noran Bank Farm* (☎ 017684 82201; 2D/1F) is a whitewashed 16th-century farmhouse about half a mile from the centre of Patterdale. Rates are £23/20 sgl/dbl. Seventeenth-century *Greenbank Farm* (☎ 017684 82292; 1D/ 1T/1F) is nearby, a working sheep farm charging from £19.

The smartest and most expensive address in the village is the *Patterdale Hotel* (☎ 0845 458 4333; 🖳 www.pat terdalehotel.co.uk; 4S/50D or F), an enormous establishment by Patterdale's standards. Part of a chain, it's pleasant enough though not really memorable. The tariff is complex, but expect to pay around £65 for B&B. Bar meals are served from 10am to 8pm daily.

Finally, if everywhere else is full or you are determined to stay by the lake, **Glenridding** has a couple of places. Almost the first house you come to on the road from Patterdale is *Beech House* (☎ 017684 82037; 🖳 www.beechhouse.com; 2S/3D/3T, some en suite), charging from £25 for a standard room and £30 for en suite. Just a few yards away is *Glenridding Hotel* (☎ 017684 82228; 🖳 www.glenrid dinghotel.co.uk; 36D or T), part of the Best Western chain and the only hotel with a swimming pool in Patterdale. Rates are from £65 Sun-Thurs, £85 Fri & Sat.

Transport (see also pp43-5)

Bus No 517 (the Kirkstone Rambler; 3/day) travels daily between Windermere's Bowness Pier and Glenridding via Patterdale Hotel between mid-July and late

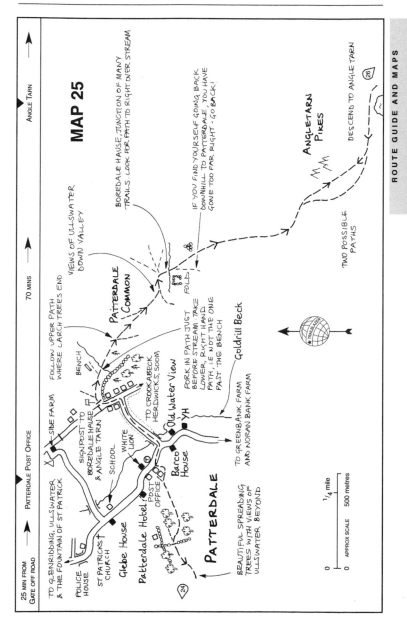

❏ Ullswater

I wandered lonely as a cloud,
That floats on high o'er vales and hills,
When all at once I saw a crowd,
A host of golden daffodils,
Beside the lake, beneath the trees,
Fluttering and dancing in the breeze.
William Wordsworth, *Daffodils*

It is said that Wordsworth was inspired to write these words after a trip to Ullswater. Certainly it's a beautiful lake and unlike neighbouring Grasmere and Haweswater there's plenty to do *on* the water too.

There is a **tourist information centre** in the main car park in Glenridding (☎ 017684-82414); it is open daily 9.30am-5.30pm in summer and weekends only the rest of the year. **Boats** can be hired from the café at the lake's southern corner. A motorboat costs £9 for 30 mins or £15 per hour for up to two people, or it's £10/17 for 30 mins/1hr for up to four people. These boats are fine, though don't try to emulate Donald Campbell, who broke the 200mph water speed record on Ullswater in 1955. For something more sedate, a rowing boat costs £4/6 for 30 mins/1hr for up to two people, £5/7.50 for three people, and £6/9 for four. Or you can take a cruise on a **steamer** (☎ 017684 82229; 🖳 www.ullswater-steamers.co.uk). There have been steamers on the lake since 1859 and two of the boats currently in service, *Lady of the Lake* and *Raven*, have been operating since the late 19th century. There are up to ten services daily to Howton, Pooley Bridge and back. Some Coast to Coasters have even recommended taking the trip to Pooley Bridge and continuing on from there as an alternative to the exhausting next stage to Shap – though how this is supposed to save time or effort I have yet to work out!

August; between Easter and mid-July and from late August to late October on Saturdays, Sundays and Bank Holidays only. The No 208 (the Ullswater Connexion; 5/day) travels between Patterdale and Keswick on a similar basis. The No 108 (Patterdale Bus; Mon-Sat, 4-5/day; Sunday only, 4/day, between late

March and late October) travels to/from Penrith railway station.

In addition there is a post bus service (🖳 www.royalmail.com/postbus) to and from Penrith bus and rail stations from Patterdale Hotel (Mon-Fri); the service waits for the steamer at Glenridding Steamer Pier.

STAGE 5: PATTERDALE TO SHAP   MAPS 25-34

Be prepared to feel very, very tired at the end of this **16-mile (26km, 6½hr)** stage from Patterdale to Shap. It's not the climb up to Angletarn and Kidsty pikes that makes most walkers feel weary, nor the long haul around the ups and downs of the western rim of the giant Haweswater Reservoir that has them begging for an end to the punishment. Rather, it's the gentle stretch over field and farmland at the very end of the day that, coming on top of all that has gone before, causes hikers to curse the name of Wainwright and regret the day they first donned a pair of walking boots.

Unfortunately, with no accommodation directly on the route (though a few walkers are now taking a one-mile detour to Bampton (see Map 31) to stay in the excellent *Mardale Inn* (☎ 01931 713244, 🖳 www.mardaleinn.co.uk; 2D or T/1F, 2 en suite; £33.50, £5 for dogs, non smoking), nor, indeed, any shops, tearooms or pubs. You have little choice but to grit your teeth, shoulder your back-

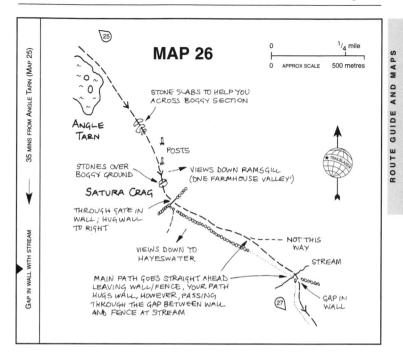

MAP 26

0 .... ¼ mile
0 .... 500 metres
APPROX SCALE

35 MINS FROM ANGLE TARN (MAP 25)

GAP IN WALL WITH STREAM

25

★ TRAILBLAZER

ROUTE GUIDE AND MAPS

ANGLE TARN

STONE SLABS TO HELP YOU ACROSS BOGGY SECTION

POSTS

STONES OVER BOGGY GROUND

VIEWS DOWN RAMSGILL ('ONE FARMHOUSE VALLEY')

SATURA CRAG

THROUGH GATE IN WALL; HUG WALL TO RIGHT

VIEWS DOWN TO HAYESWATER

MAIN PATH GOES STRAIGHT AHEAD LEAVING WALL/FENCE, YOUR PATH HUGS WALL, HOWEVER, PASSING THROUGH THE GAP BETWEEN WALL AND FENCE AT STREAM

NOT THIS WAY

STREAM

27

GAP IN WALL

pack and knuckle down to some serious long-haul trekking. Just don't forget to take a packed lunch!

There are, of course, plenty of positives about this stage: today is the day you leave the Lake District behind, and **Kidsty Pike** (Map 27) – at 780m the highest point, alternative routes excepted, on the Coast to Coast path – is the perfect summit from which to take a last, long look at the crags, knotts, pikes, fells and raises that have been your high-level companions for much of the past few days. From the top, looking west, you can see the Pillar, Scafell Pike, Helvellyn and St Sunday; to the south, the deep valley of Riggindale, while to the east, below, is Haweswater and, in the far distance, the grey, fuzzy form of the Pennines. Just near Kidsty, too, in the crags above Riggindale, is said to be the eyrie of England's last pair of **golden eagles**. However, it is thought that the female eagle may have died because she has not been seen for a while (see pp62-3), despite a concerted preservation campaign.

Furthermore, there is also the **Measand Forces** (Map 29), a small water-fall running into the Haweswater Reservoir and a wonderful place to stretch out your weary limbs and rest awhile; while the amble through the wooded glade along Haweswater Beck is an unequivocal delight. *(continued on p120)*

40 MINS FROM GAP IN WALL WITH STREAM (MAP 26)   →   The Knott   →   60 MINS TO BRIDGE OVER STREAM BY HAWESWATER (MAP 28)

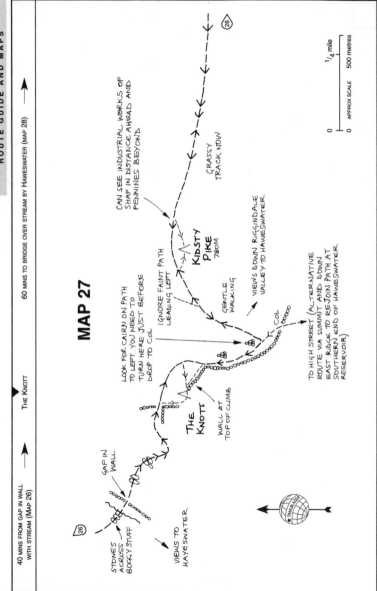

MAP 27

CAN SEE INDUSTRIAL WORKS OF SHAP IN DISTANCE AHEAD AND PENNINES BEYOND

GRASSY TRACK NOW

KIDSTY PIKE 780M

GENTLE WALKING

VIEWS DOWN RIGGINDALE VALLEY TO HAWESWATER

IGNORE FAINT PATH LEADING LEFT

LOOK FOR CAIRN ON PATH TO LEFT. YOU NEED TO TURN HERE JUST BEFORE DROP TO COL

COL

TO HIGH STREET (ALTERNATIVE ROUTE VIA SUMMIT AND DOWN EAST RIDGE TO REJOIN PATH AT SOUTHERN END OF HAWESWATER RESERVOIR)

THE KNOTT

WALL AT TOP OF CLIMB

GAP IN WALL

STONES ACROSS BOGGY STUFF

VIEWS TO HAYESWATER

TRAILBLAZER

0   APPROX SCALE   ¼ mile

0   500 metres

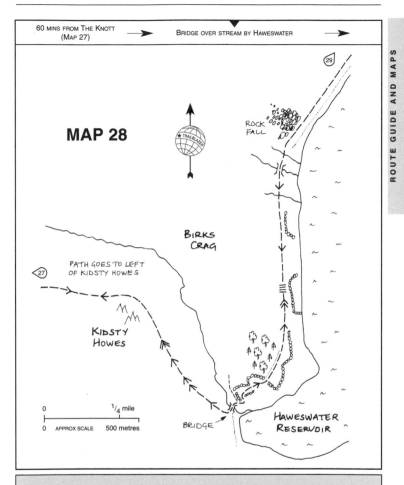

60 MINS FROM THE KNOTT (MAP 27) → BRIDGE OVER STREAM BY HAWESWATER →

29

MAP 28

★ TRAILBLAZER

ROCK FALL

BIRKS CRAG

27 PATH GOES TO LEFT OF KIDSTY HOWES

KIDSTY HOWES

0 ¼ mile
0 APPROX SCALE 500 metres

BRIDGE

HAWESWATER RESERVOIR

❏ Haweswater Reservoir

What is now one of Cumbria's largest bodies of water was once a small and fairly unassuming lake stuck on the eastern edge of the national park. In 1929, however, a bill was passed authorizing the use of Haweswater as a reservoir to serve the needs of the population of Manchester. A concrete dam, 470m wide and 35m high, was constructed at the northern edge of the lake, raising the depth of the lake by over 30m and increasing the surface area to four miles long by half a mile wide (6k by 1km).

This project was not without its opponents. In particular, many protested at the loss of the settlements that had existed on Haweswater's shore for centuries. The largest of these was Mardale Green on Haweswater's eastern *(continued on p118)*

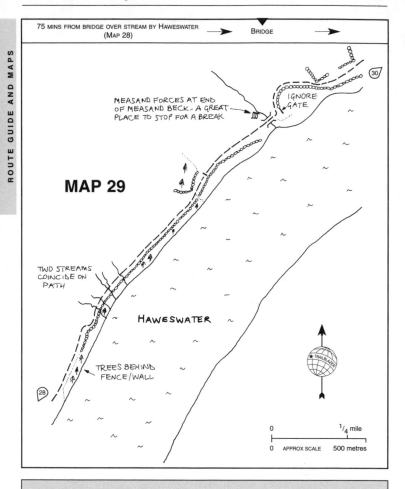

75 MINS FROM BRIDGE OVER STREAM BY HAWESWATER (MAP 28) → BRIDGE →

MEASAND FORCES AT END OF MEASAND BECK - A GREAT PLACE TO STOP FOR A BREAK

IGNORE GATE

30

MAP 29

TWO STREAMS COINCIDE ON PATH

HAWESWATER

TREES BEHIND FENCE/WALL

28

★ TRAILBLAZER

0   1/4 mile

0   APPROX SCALE   500 metres

❏ Haweswater Reservoir

(continued from p117) shore (near the pier). Before the village was flooded, coffins were removed from the graveyard and buried elsewhere and the 18th-century Holy Trinity Church was pulled down. Some of the windows from this church are now in the reservoir tower. Even today, during times of drought when the water level is low, the walls of Mardale emerge from the reservoir. This last happened in 2003. Despite man's interference the lake is still something of a wildlife haven. Swimming in the waters are wild brown trout, char, gwyniad and perch, while Riggindale is an RSPB haven, with wheatear, raven, ring ouzel and peregrine.

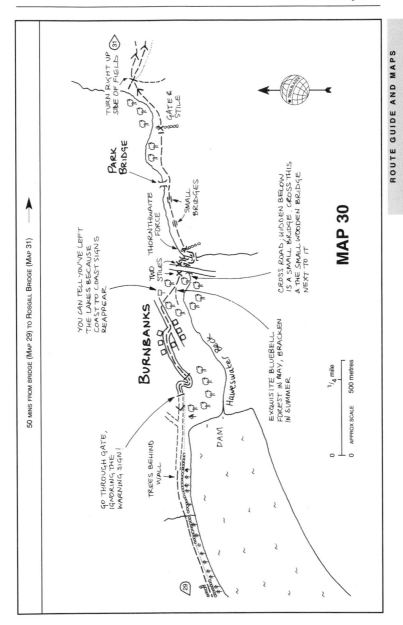

50 MINS FROM BRIDGE (MAP 29) TO ROSGILL BRIDGE (MAP 31)

MAP 30

YOU CAN TELL YOU'VE LEFT
THE LAKES BECAUSE THE
COAST TO COAST SIGNS
REAPPEAR

GO THROUGH GATE,
IGNORING THE
WARNING SIGN!

TREES BEHIND
WALL

BURNBANKS

DAM

Haweswater

EXQUISITE BLUEBELL
FOREST IN MAY, BRACKEN
IN SUMMER

TWO
STILES

THORNTHWAITE
FORCE

SMALL
BRIDGES

PARK
BRIDGE

TURN RIGHT UP
SIDE OF FIELD

GATE &
STILE

CROSS ROAD, HIDDEN BELOW
IS A SMALL BRIDGE. CROSS THIS
& THE SMALL WOODEN BRIDGE
NEXT TO IT

31

29

0   ¼ mile
0   500 metres
APPROX SCALE

ROUTE GUIDE AND MAPS

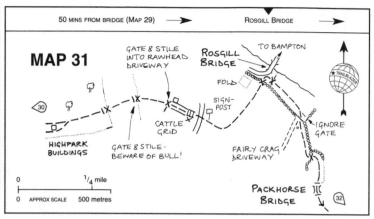

(continued from p115) The small village of **Burnbanks** at the head of the reservoir has nothing to offer the walker except for a very infrequent bus service to Bampton and Penrith (see public transport map p45).

And then, towards the end of the stage, there's **Shap Abbey** (see box below and Map 32), an atmospheric ruin set in a peaceful spot by the River Lowther. It's just unfortunate that, by the time you get there, you'll be in no mood to appreciate it, your thoughts having turned long ago from holy orders to hot showers. From the abbey, it's a straightforward trudge along roads to **Shap**.

And that's it: you've left the Lakes behind. Little of what you will encounter from here on in will be as wild – or as steep – as that which has gone before. But as much as you may be relieved now, it's those lakes and fells you'll be missing most when the walk is over.

❏ **Shap Abbey**
Shap Abbey (see Map 32 opposite) has the distinction of being the last abbey to be founded in England, in 1199. It was built by the French Premonstratensian order founded by St Norbert at Prémontré in Northern France, who were also known as the White Canons after the colour of their habits. The abbey also enjoys the distinction of being the last one dissolved by Henry VIII, in 1540. Presumably Henry's henchmen would have had plenty of practice in dissolving monasteries by this time, which is perhaps why the abbey is today in such a ruinous state. The best-preserved section is the **western belltower**, built around 1500. Information boards provide details of the layout of the abbey. Since its demise, the abbey has had to suffer the further indignity of having some of its best carved stonework purloined by the locals for use in their own buildings. The cottage by the abbey, for example, clearly used a couple of remnants of the abbey in its construction, albeit to good effect, while Shap's 17th-century market hall, just by the NatWest Bank, is built largely from abbey stone. Even some of the local stone walls contain abbey stones.

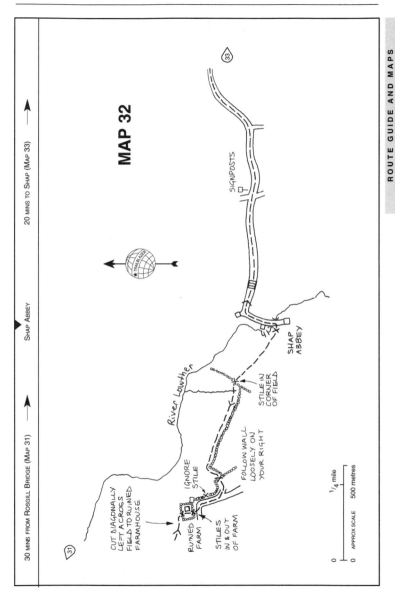

30 MINS FROM ROSGILL BRIDGE (MAP 31) ⟶   SHAP ABBEY ◀   ⟶   20 MINS TO SHAP (MAP 33) ⟶

MAP 32

SIGNPOSTS

33

River Lowther

SHAP ABBEY

STILE IN CORNER OF FIELD

FOLLOW WALL LOOSELY ON YOUR RIGHT

IGNORE STILE

RUINED FARM

STILES IN & OUT OF FARM

CUT DIAGONALLY LEFT ACROSS FIELD TO RUINED FARMHOUSE

31

0   ¼ mile
0   APPROX SCALE   500 metres

ROUTE GUIDE AND MAPS

SHAP   MAP 33

Shap is a thin, narrow village huddled around one long, wide street. That street is the A6, in former times one of the main routes north to Scotland and still the highest main road in the country.

The road used to supply Shap's traders with enough passing trade to make a living and the village grew on the proceeds. But then they built the M6, less than a mile to the east, and at a stroke in 1970 the lifeblood of traffic through Shap was siphoned away for good, and the village slipped into a gentle decline. Which is pretty much how you find it today.

There are some attractive features, including a 17th-century market hall built with masonry from the abbey, but overall the place is pretty plain. However, the fact that it lies at the end of a hard day's walk, offers the first accommodation since Patterdale, and has a chippy and a couple of pubs that offer platefuls of filling grub, are reasons enough to love this place.

Services

There isn't much in the way of services in Shap. By the **post office** (Mon-Thu 9am-12.30pm, 1.30-5.30pm; Fri 9am-12.30pm; Sun 9am-12 noon) is the **Co-op**, open late (Mon-Fri 8am-8pm, Sat 8am-6pm) and good for provisions; it also has a Link cash machine.

There's a NatWest **bank** (Mon & Fri only 10.45am-12.45pm) opposite the school and a **newsagent** (Mon-Sat 5am-5.30pm, Sun 7.30am-1pm) opposite the memorial park.

Further down is Fell House, an **off-licence/general store** (Map 34; Mon, Wed-Fri 9.30am-6.30pm, Sat 9am-1pm, Sun 10am-3pm, Tues closed) and B&B (see column opposite).

Where to stay

The **Bull's Head** (☎ 01931 716678) is a busy locals' pub with a small beer garden where you can **camp** for £5 (with a 25% discount off one of their filling bar meals).

Most popular of all, however, is the **Greyhound** (Map 34; ☎ 01931 716474; ▭ www.greyhoundshap.co.uk, 3S/7D or T/1F,

all en suite), right at the southern end of town, an excruciating walk to make at the end of the day. Your effort will be amply rewarded, however, for the owner and his staff are very welcoming and the rooms are very comfy. B&B starts at around £28 (£30 sgl). **Fell House** (Map 34; ☎ 01931 716343; ▭ www.fellhouse.com; 1S/5D or T/1F) is a general store with B&B accommodation on its upper floors. All rooms come with tea- and coffee-making facilities and some are en suite. Rates are from £24.

The **King's Arms** (Map 34; ☎ 01931 716277, 4D or T, shared facilities) charges £20 per person.

Built at the beginning of the 18th century, **New Ing Farm** (☎ 01931 716661; ▭ www.newingfarm.co.uk; 1S/3D/2T/1F, some en suite) continues to win plaudits from all who stay. Situated at the northern end of town, the farm is now a smallholding with fell ponies. Look for the pillar in reception which, the owners say, may have been salvaged from the abbey. The tariff of £25/20 sgl/dbl is terrific value.

Over the road, the smart **Hermitage** (☎ 01931 716671; ▭ www.thehermitageshap .co.uk; 1S/2D/3T/1F, some en suite) is just as good value and has also been recommended by readers. The house itself is over 300 years old yet the rooms come with all mod cons including TV, and tea- and coffee-making facilities. Rates start at £28.

Other places to stay include: **The Rockery** (☎ 01931 716106/716340; 1S/2D/1F, some en suite), which is the first place you come to on the way into Shap and where B&B costs from £18, and **Brookfield House** (☎ 01931 716397, ▭ www.brook fieldshap.co.uk; 2S/8D or T/3F, some en suite), where B&B is £26.50.

Where to eat

The **Greyhound** (Map 34, see p124) is reputed to cook the best grub in town and most trekkers are more than happy with their fare. The menu consists of mainly local dishes including a decent-sized plate of Cumberland sausage with mash or chips (£6.50). Unfortunately, the Greyhound's location at the very southern end of town is mightily inconvenient for those staying at the Hermitage or New Ing Farm B&B, for whom a walk of over a mile is necessary. More convenient is the **Bull's Head** which does traditional bar meals (daily 12 noon-2pm, 4.30-9pm) such as toad-in-the-hole as well as all-day breakfasts.

The third village pub is the **Crown Inn** (☎ 01931 716229) where you can fill up on sandwiches (from £3.75) or the more substantial beef, leek and mash dish for £6.50.

Nearer the centre, there's **Shap Chippy** (☎ 01931 716388) fish and chip shop (Mon-Sat 8.30am-1.30pm, 4-8pm; Sun 4-8pm) opposite the Bull's Head (isn't it curious that it is only now, a four- or five-day walk from the nearest sea, that we come across the first fish and chip shop on our route?) and a little further south stands the **Walkers' Café**, good for quiches and sandwiches but with limited opening times (Mon-Fri 4-6pm, Sat and Sun 2-6pm).

Transport (see also pp43-5)

Bus No 106 operates 3-5 times a day to Kendal via Orton (Mon-Sat; 45 mins) and 5-6/day (Mon-Sat; 30 mins) between here and Penrith. The buses leave from Shap's market square. The last service from Shap connects at Penrith with the No 563 to Kirkby Stephen.

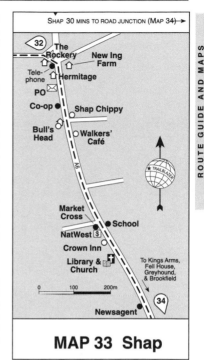

MAP 33 Shap

STAGE 6: SHAP TO KIRKBY STEPHEN   MAPS 34-43

Those who struggled to complete the previous stage will be less than delighted to hear that today's hike is, at **21 miles (33km, 7hr)**, even longer. Indeed, for many it will be the longest day on the entire route. Thankfully, there is again a chance to break this stage into two, this time by taking the short diversion into Orton, either to stay overnight or merely to rest awhile in one of the tearooms, indulging in the produce of the local chocolate factory as you do so. If you've got the time, we recommend you do.

This stage of the walk is also renowned for the **prehistoric sites** that crop up with reasonable regularity throughout the day. From stone circles to giants' graves and unearthed settlements, there's plenty to distract you from any nascent blisters and sore feet, though it's fair to say that none of the sites will make your jaw drop in amazement. The first of these sites occurs about an hour into the walk, just past the mysteriously isolated, walled village of **Oddendale** (Map 35) where, just five minutes off the path to the right (west), lie two **concentric stone circles**. As with just about every prehistoric site on the trail, both their age and purpose are unknown.

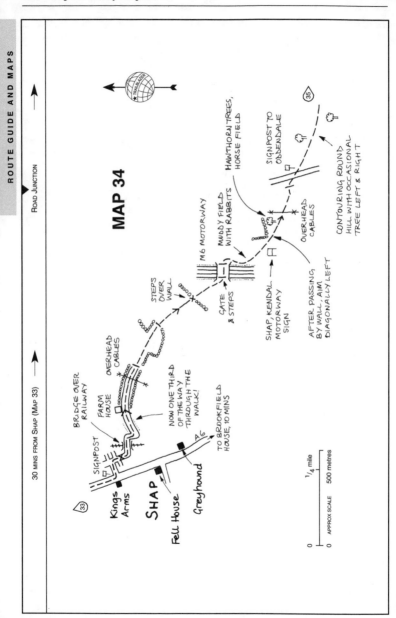

30 MINS FROM SHAP (MAP 33) ──►

ROAD JUNCTION

MAP 34

TRAIL BLAZER

33

Kings Arms

SHAP

Fell House

Greyhound

SIGNPOST

BRIDGE OVER RAILWAY

FARM HOUSE

OVERHEAD CABLES

NOW ONE THIRD OF THE WAY THROUGH THE WALK! 10 MINS

TO BROOKFIELD HOUSE, 10 MINS

A6

STEPS OVER WALL

GATE & STEPS

M6 MOTORWAY

SHAP, KENDAL MOTORWAY SIGN

AFTER PASSING BY WALL, AIM DIAGONALLY LEFT

MUDDY FIELD WITH RABBITS

HAWTHORN TREES, HORSE FIELD

SIGNPOST TO OSDENDALE

OVERHEAD CABLES

CONTOURING ROUND HILL WITH OCCASIONAL TREE LEFT & RIGHT

35

0 ————— ¼ mile
0 ————— 500 metres
APPROX SCALE

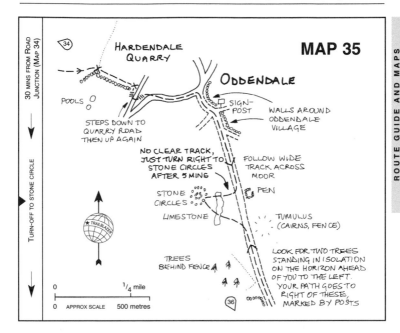

This stage's second prehistoric site, indicated by a signpost pointing off the path, is **Robin Hood's Grave** (Map 37), a large cairn in a shallow fold in the moor and not a grave at all (and certainly not the grave of the man who, on your walk so far, has already had a promontory named after him, and who gives his name to the bay that is our ultimate destination; both of which, as far as we know, also have nothing to do with him).

Eventually the trail drops down past a quarry and crosses the road, bending south to a junction with the B6260, leaving it to the left to drop down past a wonderfully preserved **limekiln** to Broadfell Farm. Those visiting Orton, whose church has been clearly visible since the brow of the hill, should continue down the hill through the farm from here; those who wish to carry on with their march should join the farm's driveway and continue east round Orton Scar. Incidentally, look up occasionally on this drop into Orton: more than one hiker has noted that the birdlife around here is surprisingly rich and varied.

ORTON see Map p128

Orton is typical of the quaint little villages in which the Coast to Coast specializes, but one with a couple of surprises in store for walkers who bother to make the short diversion off the trail. For one thing there's the church, built way back in 1293 though altered much since. Then there are the pillories below the church, used once upon a time (and who knows, maybe still today?) to restrain wrongdoers and teach them the error of their ways. Down the hill is a further surprise, Kennedy's, the chocolate factory (more of a kitchen really).

(continued on p128)

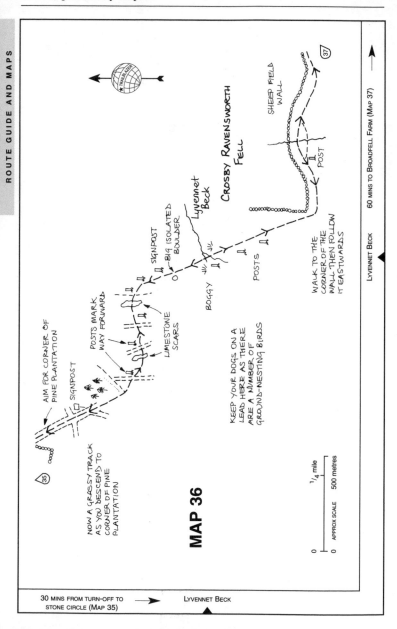

MAP 36

CROSBY RAVENSWORTH FELL

Lyvennet Beck

SHEEP FIELD WALL

POST

WALK TO THE CORNER OF THE WALL THEN FOLLOW IT EASTWARDS

SIGNPOST

BIG ISOLATED BOULDER

BOGGY

POSTS

KEEP YOUR DOGS ON A LEAD HERE AS THERE ARE A NUMBER OF GROUND-NESTING BIRDS

POSTS MARK WAY FORWARD

LIMESTONE SCARS

AIM FOR CORNER OF PINE PLANTATION

SIGNPOST

NOW A GRASSY TRACK AS YOU DESCEND TO CORNER OF PINE PLANTATION

35

37

TRAILBLAZER

¼ mile

APPROX SCALE   500 metres

0

0

60 MINS TO BROADFELL FARM (MAP 37)

LYVENNET BECK

30 MINS FROM TURN-OFF TO STONE CIRCLE (MAP 35)

LYVENNET BECK

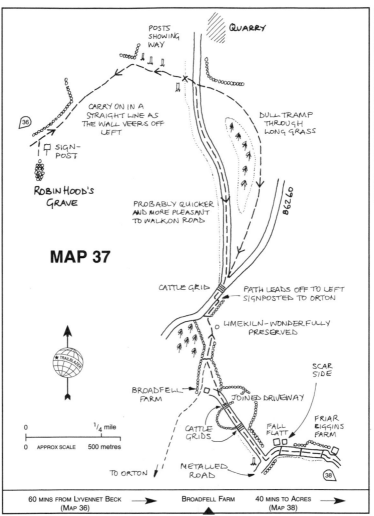

QUARRY

POSTS SHOWING WAY

CARRY ON IN A STRAIGHT LINE AS THE WALL VEERS OFF LEFT

DULL TRAMP THROUGH LONG GRASS

36

SIGN-POST

ROBIN HOOD'S GRAVE

PROBABLY QUICKER AND MORE PLEASANT TO WALK ON ROAD

MAP 37

B6260

TRAILBLAZER

CATTLE GRID

PATH LEADS OFF TO LEFT SIGNPOSTED TO ORTON

LIMEKILN – WONDERFULLY PRESERVED

0   ¼ mile

0   APPROX SCALE   500 metres

SCAR SIDE

BROADFELL FARM

JOINED DRIVEWAY

CATTLE GRIDS

FALL FLATT

FRIAR BIGGINS FARM

TO ORTON

METALLED ROAD

38

60 MINS FROM LYVENNET BECK → (MAP 36)   BROADFELL FARM   40 MINS TO ACRES → (MAP 38)

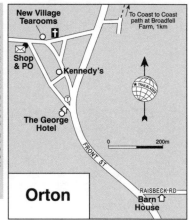

New Village Tearooms

Shop & PO

Kennedy's

To Coast to Coast path at Broadfell Farm, 1km

The George Hotel

Orton

FRONT ST

RAISBECK RD

Barn House

0   200m

three rooms, but each comes with TV and tea- and coffee-making facilities. Rates start at £28, or £25 for a single; this place is highly recommended by a number of trekkers.

The *George Hotel* (☎ 07765 402690; 🖥 www.georgehotel.net; 1S/6D) is in the centre of town. Rates start at £25 (£27.50 for single occupancy). One other place that is frequently recommended is *New House Farm* (☎ 015396 24324; 1D/2T) where **camping** (£4) is allowed and there's a static caravan for those with dogs to use. B&B starts at £22. Campers can also order breakfast and/or an evening meal (£13.50). New House Farm is best reached from Knott Lane (see map 38). Follow Knott Lane south to the T Junction. Turn west (right) and continue for five minutes. The farm is on the right-hand side.

You can sample *Kennedy's* (Mon-Sat 9am-5pm; Sun 11am-5pm) products in their attached coffee house and ice-cream parlour. For a chocoholic overdose, try their scrumptious chocolate cake and wash it down with a hot chocolate, made with pure chocolate and cocoa. *New Village Tearooms* (☎ 015396 24886; daily 10am-5pm, shorter hours outside summer) serve some lovely homemade biscuits and cakes. For pub grub, the *George* in the village centre serves lunches (12 noon-2pm) and dinner (6-9pm); the home-made lamb hotpot is £6.

(Cont'd from p125) The **post office** and **shop** (Mon, Tue, Thu, Fri 9am-1pm, 2-5pm; Wed 9am-1pm; Sat 9am-5.30pm; post office closes at 5pm Mon, Tue and Fri; 12noon Wed & Sat; closed Thu & Sun) are near by. Bus No 106 (Kendal to Penrith) stops in the square; see pp43-5 for details.

Where to stay and eat
Barn House (☎ 015396 24259; 🖥 www .barnhouse-orton.freeserve.co.uk; 1D/2T all en suite) on the Raisbeck Road has just

There's a second and more impressive **stone circle** (Map 38) a mile to the east of Orton on the Coast to Coast path. It can be reached, for those who didn't take the Orton detour, via a driveable track running east from Broadfell Farm. (Those who *did* visit Orton can rejoin this track at the stone circle by taking the Raisbeck road east and heading up Knott Lane).

After this, the trail continues east through yet more fields and on to **Tarn Moor** (Map 39). All being well, by continuing south-east you'll emerge from the moor at **Sunbiggin Tarn**, an important bird sanctuary.

There now follow three miles/5km of tedious road walking (Maps 39-40), perhaps the dullest section of the Coast to Coast, before you turn left at the third cattle grid on the second road and eventually come to *Bents Farm* (Map 41; ☎ 01768 371760; 🖥 www.bentscampingbarn.co.uk); they have a camping barn which sleeps 16 (bed £5) and permit camping (£3).

The next prehistoric site lies a short way past the farm where, having crossed a stile, a signpost urges you to stick to the recognized path running

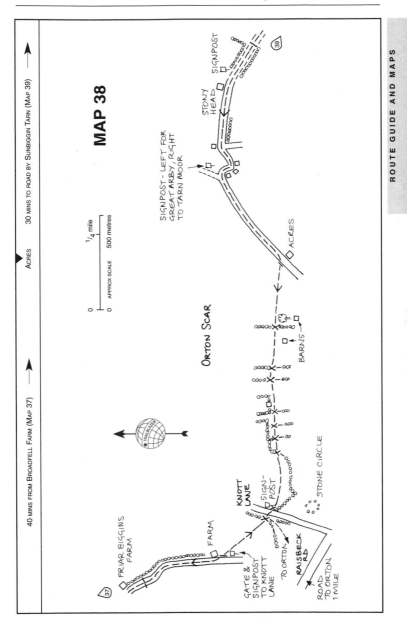

40 MINS FROM BROADFELL FARM (MAP 37) — ACRES — 30 MINS TO ROAD BY SUNBIGGIN TARN (MAP 39)

MAP 38

¼ mile
0 500 metres
APPROX SCALE

ORTON SCAR

FRIAR BIGGINS FARM

FARM

GATE & SIGNPOST TO KNOTT LANE

TO ORTON

RAISBECK RD

ROAD TO ORTON, 1 MILE

KNOTT LANE

SIGN-POST

STONE CIRCLE

BARNS

ACRES

SIGNPOST - LEFT FOR GREAT ARBY, RIGHT TO TARN MOOR

STONY HEAD

SIGNPOST

TRAILBLAZER

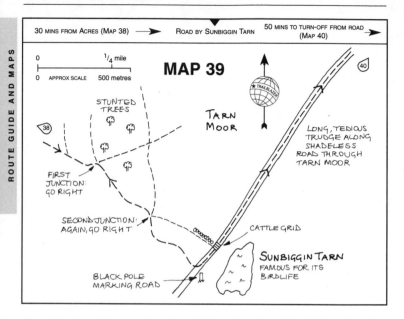

30 MINS FROM ACRES (MAP 38) ⟶ ROAD BY SUNBIGGIN TARN 50 MINS TO TURN-OFF FROM ROAD (MAP 40) ⟶

0   ¹/₄ mile

0   APPROX SCALE   500 metres

MAP 39

★ TRAILBLAZER

38

STUNTED TREES

TARN MOOR

LONG, TEDIOUS TRUDGE ALONG SHADELESS ROAD THROUGH TARN MOOR

FIRST JUNCTION: GO RIGHT

40

SECOND JUNCTION: AGAIN, GO RIGHT

CATTLE GRID

SUNBIGGIN TARN FAMOUS FOR ITS BIRDLIFE

BLACK POLE MARKING ROAD

alongside the wall so as not to disturb the archaeological site. This will probably come as something of a surprise, not least because, no matter how hard you look, there seems to be no archaeological site anywhere. However, this field plays host to the **Severals Village settlement** which, believe it or not, is considered to be one of the most important prehistoric sites in the whole of Britain. And the fact that it remains unexcavated does nothing to diminish this, or to quell the archaeologists' enthusiasm for the place. Without leaving the path, try to notice irregular or unnatural depressions and bumps in the land here; it is these undulations that have so excited the archaeologists.

On the opposite side of Scandal Beck lies the final ancient site on this stage, the so-called **Giants' Graves** (called pillow mounds on OS maps), a series of long narrow mounds which, some say, may have been prehistoric rabbit enclosures. Climbing to the crest of **Smardale Fell**, the Nine Standards now appears on the horizon for the first time – another prehistoric feature, but one for which you'll have to wait until the next stage.

By now, however, those who are attempting this walk from Shap in one go will not be thinking of such distant prospects, but will be concentrating more on the delights that await them in the valley below – a valley, appropriately enough, that goes by the name of Eden.

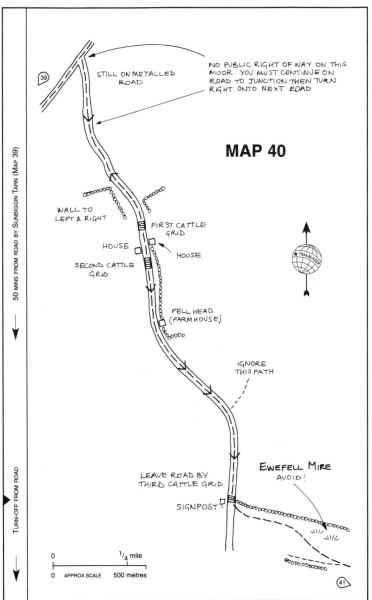

(39)

STILL ON METALLED ROAD

NO PUBLIC RIGHT OF WAY ON THIS MOOR. YOU MUST CONTINUE ON ROAD TO JUNCTION THEN TURN RIGHT ONTO NEXT ROAD

MAP 40

50 MINS FROM ROAD BY SUNBIGGIN TARN (MAP 39)

WALL TO LEFT & RIGHT

FIRST CATTLE GRID

HOUSE

HOUSE

SECOND CATTLE GRID

FELL HEAD (FARMHOUSE)

IGNORE THIS PATH

TURN-OFF FROM ROAD

LEAVE ROAD BY THIRD CATTLE GRID

EWEFELL MIRE AVOID!

SIGNPOST

0   1/4 mile

0   APPROX SCALE   500 metres

(41)

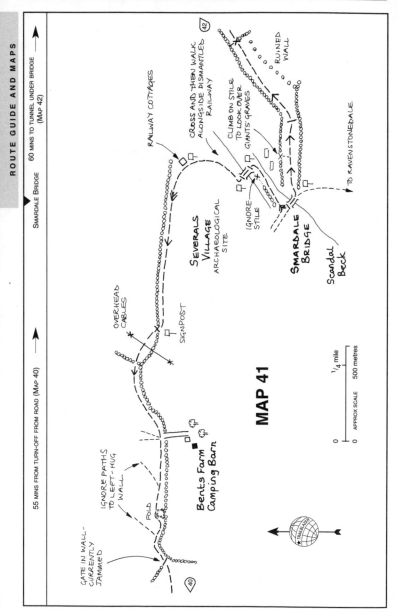

MAP 41

55 MINS FROM TURN-OFF FROM ROAD (MAP 40)

SMARDALE BRIDGE

60 MINS TO TUNNEL UNDER BRIDGE (MAP 42)

GATE IN WALL - CURRENTLY JAMMED

IGNORE PATHS TO LEFT - HUG WALL

FOLD

Bents Farm Camping Barn

OVERHEAD CABLES

SIGNPOST

RAILWAY COTTAGES

CROSS AND THEN WALK ALONGSIDE DISMANTLED RAILWAY

CLIMB ON STILE TO LOOK OVER GIANT'S GRAVES

RUINED WALL

SEVERALS VILLAGE ARCHAEOLOGICAL SITE

IGNORE STILE

SMARDALE BRIDGE

Scandal Beck

TO RAVENSTONEDALE

APPROX SCALE

0   ¼ mile

0   500 metres

42

40

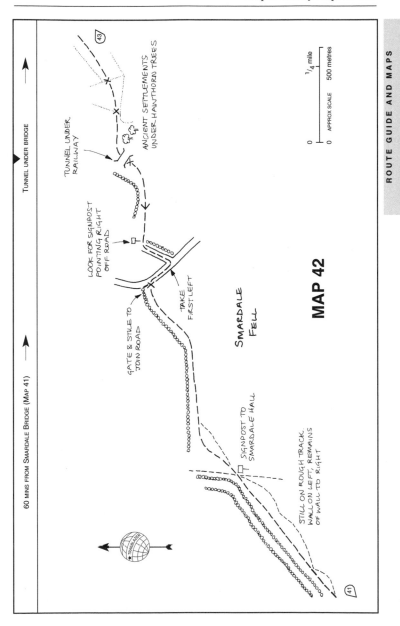

60 MINS FROM SMARDALE BRIDGE (MAP 41)

TUNNEL UNDER BRIDGE

TUNNEL UNDER RAILWAY

LOOK FOR SIGNPOST POINTING RIGHT OFF ROAD

GATE & STILE TO JOIN ROAD

TAKE FIRST LEFT

ANCIENT SETTLEMENTS UNDER HAWTHORN TREES

SMARDALE FELL

MAP 42

SIGNPOST TO SMARDALE HALL

STILE ON ROUGH TRACK. WALL ON LEFT, REMAINS OF WALL TO RIGHT

43

41

0 APPROX SCALE
0 500 metres
¼ mile

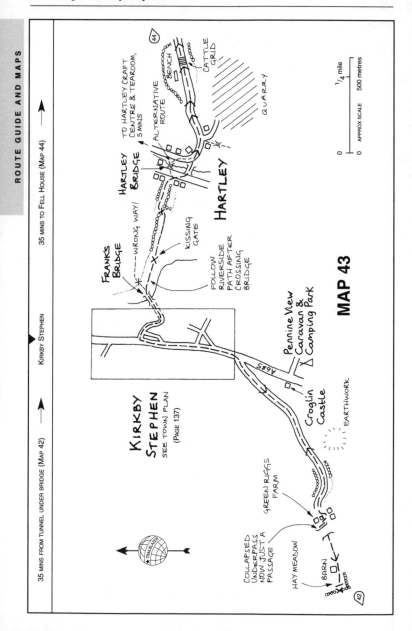

35 MINS FROM TUNNEL UNDER BRIDGE (MAP 42)   KIRKBY STEPHEN   35 MINS TO FELL HOUSE (MAP 44)

TRAILBLAZER

KIRKBY STEPHEN
SEE TOWN PLAN
(PAGE 137)

FRANKS BRIDGE

WRONG WAY!

HARTLEY BRIDGE

TO HARTLEY CRAFT CENTRE & TEAROOM, 5 MINS

ALTERNATIVE ROUTE

BENCH

CATTLE GRID

44

QUARRY

HARTLEY

KISSING GATE

FOLLOW RIVERSIDE PATH AFTER CROSSING BRIDGE

Pennine View Caravan & Camping Park

A685

Croglin Castle

EARTHWORK

MAP 43

GREEN RIGGS FARM

COLLAPSED UNDERPASS NOW JUST A PASSAGE

HAY MEADOW

BARN

42

0   ¼ mile
APPROX SCALE
0   500 metres

KIRKBY STEPHEN

Kirkby Stephen (usually pronounced 'Kirby Stephen' without the second 'k') vies with Richmond as the biggest town on the route, though don't let that fool you into thinking that this place is a metropolis. In fact, Kirkby Stephen is a pleasant market town built along the A685 with a population of 1600, a figure that's swollen considerably during the summer months by walkers, runners, cyclists and other holidaymakers.

The focus of the town is its market square. There have been markets in Kirkby Stephen since at least 1361 when it was granted a market charter. Note the cobbled outline on the square's floor: it marks the outer limits of the old bull-baiting area, a popular pastime in the town up until 1820 when a bull broke free and ran amok, killing a number of bystanders.

The main tourist attraction in Kirkby Stephen is the 13th-century **St Hedda church**, (see box below).

Other sites of note include the old and much-photographed **signpost** at the top end of town, where the distances are given in miles and furlongs (see p42); and the curious but attractive **stone seats** in the form of sheep, that stand by the door of the tourist office. Carved by artist Keith Alexander, they are reputed to increase the fertility of any who sit upon them. **Frank's Bridge** is a pretty double-arched stone footbridge, a quiet place to sit by the grassy riverbank and feed the ducks. It is thought to be named after a local brewer called Frank Birkbeck who lived in the 19th century.

One other item of note is the **flock of parrots** that have taken up residence by the Eden river below the town. If you've got time to kill, there are worse places to spend it than on the banks looking for these exotic aliens. There are a number of stories as to how they got there, with a break-out from a nearby collector's house the most likely.

❏ St Hedda Church

The church is separated from the market square by the peaceful lawn of the **cloisters**. On entering the main gate, on your right is the **Trupp Stone**, resembling a stone tomb or table, where until 1836 the locals' tithes were collected. Take half an hour or so to wander around inside the church, which is known locally as the Cathedral of the Dales. It is built on the site of a Saxon church, though the earliest feature (the nave) of the present structure dates only to 1220. Features to look out for include the 17th-century **font**, a great stone lump at the rear of the church, and the nearby **bread shelves**, used for distributing bread to the poor. There's also a **Norman coffin** by the north wall, unearthed in 1980 during restoration work, and a glass display cabinet, also by the north wall, housing 16th- and 17th-century Bibles and, curiously, a **boar's tusk**, said to belong to the last wild boar shot in England. It was killed by the first Sir Richard Musgrave (died 1464), who was buried with the tusk in Hartley Chapel, to the south of the chancel. (The place where Sir Richard shot the boar, by the way, lies to the south of Kirkby Stephen.)

The church's most interesting feature, however, is the 8th-century **Loki Stone** facing the main door, a metre-high block carved by the Vikings with the horned figure of the Norse god Loki. A bit of a prankster, one of Loki's tricks backfired and resulted in the death of Odin's son, which led to Loki being bound in chains and thrown into a subterranean dungeon. When the church was built the locals interpreted the carving as a representation of a demon. The stone was thus placed in the church to remind parishioners of the terrifying creatures that awaited non-believers in the afterlife.

Indeed, demons still play a big part in the folklore of Kirkby Stephen. At 8pm step outside to hear if they are still ringing the **Taggy Bell**, a warning to those who are still on the streets that Taggy, the local demon, now stalks the town looking for prey.

Services

Kirkby Stephen has become the spiritual (though not geographical) heart of the Coast to Coast path. A couple of the baggage courier services operate out of the town, and those who opt to take advantage of their taxi service will spend the night in Kirkby Stephen before heading to St Bees the next morning.

The **tourist office** (☎ 017683 71199, Mon-Sat 9.30am-5.30pm, Sun 10am-4pm) is crammed with brochures and leaflets and the staff seem knowledgeable. There's also a **website**, 🖳 www.kirkby-stephen.com.

Just down Market St a little way is the library with **internet** connection (£1 for 30 minutes; Mon-Wed & Fri 10am-12.30pm; also Mon 5-7pm, Tue 4-6pm, Wed 1.30-4pm, Fri 1.30-6pm, Sat 10am-1pm). There are two **banks** with **cash machines** while on the other side of the road is the **post office** (Mon-Sat 9am-5.30pm), and opposite is the best **supermarket** in town, Co-op (Mon-Sat 8am-10pm, Sun 9am-10pm). There's also a Spar (daily 8am-10.30pm) further up the street and a second, larger, Co-op at the north end of town.

Eden Outdoors (☎ 017683 72431; Mon-Fri 9am-5.30pm; Sat 9.30am-4.30pm; Sun 11am-5pm) is currently the only **hiking shop**, and it's a pretty good one, with plenty of cheap army surplus gear as well as regular trekking stuff. The owners say that, for emergencies, they will open up out-of-hours if you call them at home (Mark ☎ 017683 72599, David ☎ 017683 71424). Blister kits are also on sale at the **chemist** (Mon-Fri 9am-5.30pm; Sat 9am-1pm).

Near the bottom of North Rd (the continuation of Market St), at No 37, is a **holistic health centre** (☎ 017683 72482), with a sauna, Jacuzzi and treatments such as Indian-heated massage, perfect for sore muscles.

Where to stay

The Pennine View Caravan and Camping Park (☎ 017683 71717) is a smart spot for campers just outside town near the Croglin Castle pub, with laundry room, sinks for washing up and a clean shower and toilet block (complete with piped music). It costs £6 per person with free showers.

Kirkby Stephen Youth Hostel (☎ 0870 7705904; 🖳 kirkbystephen@yha.org.uk; 40 beds; £11) is housed in a converted Methodist chapel in the centre of town. Unfortunately, it's closing in late 2006. It is hoped that a new owner will soon be found and it will reopen as a backpacker hostel.

Of the B&Bs, I've received more recommendations for the *Old Croft House* (☎ 017683 71638; 🖳 www.oldcrofthouse. co.uk; 1S with private bathroom, 1D en suite/2D or T), than any other place on the walk. It is a lovely old cottage, made all the better by the extraordinary warmth and generosity of the owners who advertise their establishment as a B&B run by walkers for walkers. And they seem to know what trekkers want, welcoming guests with freshly baked scones and even supplying foot spas! The breakfasts are great and overall this place scores top marks in every area. Rates start at £24.

Redmayne House (☎/🖳 017683 71441; 1S/1D/1T/1F) is highly recommended. It's a comfortable Georgian house with large rooms and a warm welcome. Rates are £22 per person and it's the same for single occupancy which is refreshingly unusual. There are no en suite rooms but that means that anyone can use the wonderful Victorian loo, probably the oldest throne you'll ever sit on!

Next to the youth hostel, *Fletcher House* (☎ 017683 71013; 🖳 www.fletcher housecumbria.co.uk; 1S/2D/1T/1F all en suite or with private bathroom) is another Georgian house, with TV in every room, that charges from £25, while further up the street is the very pleasant *Lockholme* (☎ 017683 71321; 🖳 www.lockholme.co.uk; 1S/1D/1T/1F some en suite), a large house made of Brockram stone; B&B costs £22-5.

At 63 High St the *Jolly Farmers Guest House* (☎ 017683 71063; 🖳 www.jolly farmers.co.uk; 8 en suite rooms) has the added attraction of hydro-spa baths, which should help take those aches away. Rates start at £26 per person.

Back in the centre near the square, the *Kings Arms* (☎ 017683 71378; 🖳 www. kingsarmskirkbystephen.co.uk; 1S/8D) is a 17th-century former posting inn with many antiques in the rooms. Rates are £25/22.50

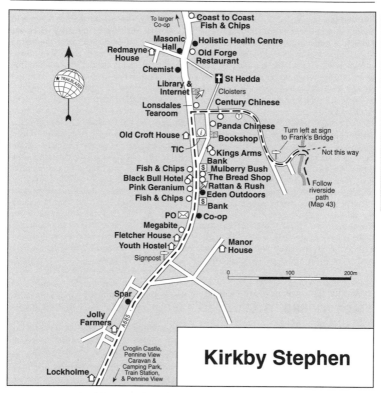

To larger Co-op

Coast to Coast Fish & Chips

Masonic Hall

Holistic Health Centre

Redmayne House

Old Forge Restaurant

Chemist

St Hedda

Library & Internet

Cloisters

Lonsdales Tearoom

Century Chinese

Old Croft House

Panda Chinese

Bookshop

Turn left at sign to Frank's Bridge

TIC

Not this way

Kings Arms

Bank

Fish & Chips

Mulberry Bush

Black Bull Hotel

The Bread Shop

Follow riverside path (Map 43)

Pink Geranium

Rattan & Rush

Fish & Chips

Eden Outdoors

Bank

PO

Co-op

Megabite

Fletcher House

Manor House

Youth Hostel

Signpost

0   100   200m

Spar

Jolly Farmers

A685

Croglin Castle,
Pennine View
Caravan &
Camping Park,
Train Station,
& Pennine View

Lockholme

Kirkby Stephen

sgl/dbl, £32.50/26.25 en suite. To the east of the main road, on a back route down to Frank's Bridge, is the grand 17th-century *Manor House* (☎ 017683 72757; 🖳 www .manorhouse.netfirms.com; 2D/1F all en suite) with exposed beams in the rooms. Rates are £23, £28 single occupancy.

Other places to stay include *The Black Bull Hotel* (☎ 017683 71237, 🖳 www .blackbullkirkbystephen.co.uk; 2S/10D/2F, all en suite), 38 Market Sq, which charges £25 sgl/£25 dbl (single occupancy £30) and £65 for a family room (1D/1S) and *Croglin Castle* (☎ 017683 71389; 1S/4D/1F), South Rd. B&B costs from £20.

Where to eat
On the main street there are no fewer than three chippies including the *Coast to Coast*

that features in Wainwright's video. However, they close early (7pm) and don't open on Tuesday or Wednesday.

As for tearooms, our favourite is the *Pink Geranium* (☎ 017683 71586) which gives you a great big pot of tea, and whose food is some of the most imaginative and generous around. *Lonsdale's* (daily 11.30am-4pm) is by the church. Though a more refined place, it also serves dishes like sausage and chips (£2.90). The *Rattan & Rush* (Tue-Sat 9am-4pm; Sun 12 noon-4pm) is particularly popular during the regular live folk music sessions. If it's too busy try next door at *The Mulberry Bush*.

For a picnic lunch to eat by the river, call in at *The Bread Shop* or try *Megabite*, an unpretentious takeaway specializing in baguettes (from £2) with wonderful fillings.

For evening meals, many hikers rave about the simple but exquisite food at the *Croglin Castle* (daily 12 noon-2pm, 6-9pm); unless you're staying at the campsite or the pub itself, it's a bit of a trek but it is worth it. The ploughman's (£4.95) is filling enough while the steak is so big it hangs off the side of a plate heaped with chips and fried onions. In the centre the *Kings Arms* (daily 12 noon-2pm, 7-9pm) has a fine reputation and a fair vegetarian selection; the moussaka (£5.75) here is tasty, while the rack of Lakeland lamb is good value at £9.25. Of the other pubs the *Black Bull* does locally inspired meals including the ubiquitous Cumberland sausage for £6.50.

The most exclusive evening meals are at the intimate, some might say tiny, *Old Forge Restaurant* (☎ 017683 71832; Tue-Sun 6.30pm-late) which has a reputation for excellent food; the spicy beans and mushrooms are £9.50 and there are steaks from £12.50. For something more exotic, both the *Panda Chinese Takeaway* (☎ 017683 71283;

Sun-Thu 5.30-11.30pm; Fri-Sat 5.30pm-12 midnight) and the *Century Chinese Restaurant* (☎ 017683 72828; Tue-Sat 12 noon-2pm, 5-11.30pm; Sun 5-11.30pm) serve up the usual array of Oriental fare. The latter also has a sit-in restaurant.

Transport (see also pp43-5)

The **train** station – the only one, apart from St Bees, on the Coast to Coast path – lies over a mile to the south of the town centre. Kirkby Stephen is on the Carlisle to Leeds Line, with 5-6 trains in each direction Mon-Sat, including one from Glasgow Central, and 3/day on Sunday.

As for **buses**, the No 563 runs to Penrith and back from the Market Square, while the No 564 runs from both the Market Square and the railway station to Kendal, a journey of just over an hour.

Finally, for a **taxi** Steady Eddie's Taxis (☎ 017683 72036) are said to be reliable, or call Prima **taxis** on ☎ 017683 72557.

STAGE 7: KIRKBY STEPHEN TO KELD   MAPS 43-50

This **13-mile (21km, 4^1/$_2$-5^1/$_2$hr)** stage is something of a red-letter day, full of major landmarks. Not only do you cross the mighty **Pennines** – the backbone of the British Isles – but in doing so you cross the watershed; from now on, all rivers flow eastwards, where before they flowed west to the Irish Sea. This is also the stage where you pass from the county of Cumbria, your home for the past week or so, to **Yorkshire**, your home for the rest of the trek. And finally, by the end of this stage you are virtually at the halfway point, completing more than 95 miles out of approximately 192 (153km out of 307).

Yet in spite of the importance of today, the one thing that most walkers remember about this stage is not the number of landmarks they achieve but the bogs they have to negotiate along the way. If you've heard the stories about Coast-to-Coasters falling into waist-deep mud it is during this stage that they probably did it. The maps point out where the boggiest sections are. If you do succumb to one of the deeper mires, cheer yourself up with the thought that, at the end of the stage, you'll be spending the night in the gentle pastoral scenery of Swaledale, Yorkshire's most northerly dale, and perhaps its loveliest.

Note that, due to severe trail erosion, there are now **three paths** across the Pennines to Keld, your choice depending upon what time of year you are walking. These three paths are marked on Maps 45a, 46 and 47 as well as on modern OS maps, and are colour coded. All are about the same length, but walking times vary due to terrain. Briefly: the **green route** is for those walking in winter (December to April) and does not actually take you up to the Nine Standards.

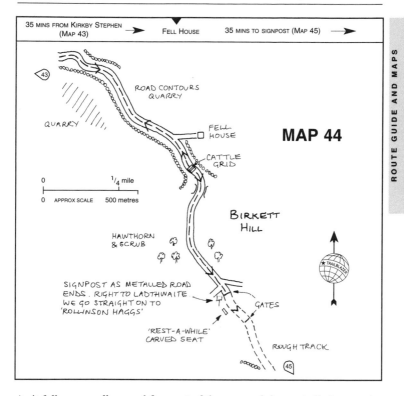

ROUTE GUIDE AND MAPS

43

ROAD CONTOURS QUARRY

QUARRY

FELL HOUSE

MAP 44

CATTLE GRID

0   ¼ mile

0   APPROX SCALE   500 metres

BIRKETT HILL

HAWTHORN & SCRUB

★ TRAILBLAZER

SIGNPOST AS METALLED ROAD ENDS. RIGHT TO LADTHWAITE WE GO STRAIGHT ON TO 'ROLLINSON HAGGS'

GATES

'REST-A-WHILE' CARVED SEAT

ROUGH TRACK

45

As it follows a wall or road for most of the way and does not climb up to the same altitude as the others, this is also the route to take if weather conditions are particularly poor. The other two routes, **red** (May to July) and **blue** (August to November) both climb up to Nine Standards before going their separate ways down on the other side.

To begin, from Kirkby Stephen you cross Frank's Bridge (Map 43) up to **Hartley** where, at the northern end of the village the Hartley Craft Centre and Tearoom used to display the works of local wood- and stone-carvers and there were tearooms in renovated stables. However, at the time of writing the centre had closed though it is possible that it will be taken over and re-opened.

Back at the southern end of Hartley, the path climbs the hill and skirts around a working quarry on a fairly steep metalled road. At the end lies a wide dirt track up Hartley Fell, where the path splits (Map 45): the red and blue routes head up the hill to Nine Standards, while the green route continues to hug the stone wall that has accompanied you for most of your walk up Hartley Fell so far. The three routes are described on pp141-4.

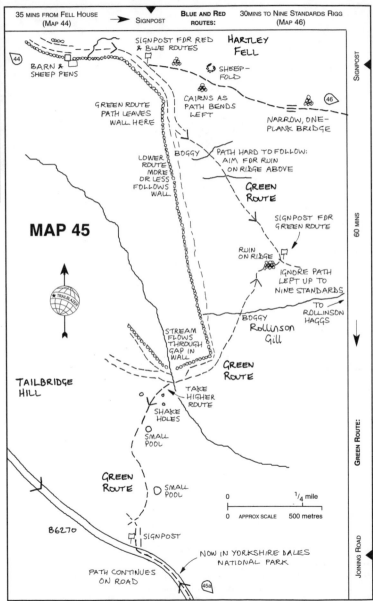

MAP 45

35 MINS FROM FELL HOUSE (MAP 44) → SIGNPOST   BLUE AND RED ROUTES: 30 MINS TO NINE STANDARDS RIGG (MAP 46)

HARTLEY FELL

SIGNPOST FOR RED & BLUE ROUTES

BARN & SHEEP PENS

44

SHEEP-FOLD

GREEN ROUTE PATH LEAVES WALL HERE

CAIRNS AS PATH BENDS LEFT

NARROW, ONE-PLANK BRIDGE

46

BOGGY

PATH HARD TO FOLLOW: AIM FOR RUIN ON RIDGE ABOVE

LOWER ROUTE MORE OR LESS FOLLOWS WALL

GREEN ROUTE

SIGNPOST FOR GREEN ROUTE

60 MINS

RUIN ON RIDGE

IGNORE PATH LEFT UP TO NINE STANDARDS

TO ROLLINSON HAGGS

STREAM FLOWS THROUGH GAP IN WALL

BOGGY Rollinson Gill

GREEN ROUTE

TAILBRIDGE HILL

TRAILBLAZER

TAKE HIGHER ROUTE

SHAKE HOLES

SMALL POOL

GREEN ROUTE

SMALL POOL

0   ¼ mile
0 APPROX SCALE 500 metres

GREEN ROUTE:

B6270

SIGNPOST

NOW IN YORKSHIRE DALES NATIONAL PARK

PATH CONTINUES ON ROAD

45a

JOINING ROAD

SIGNPOST

ROUTE GUIDE AND MAPS

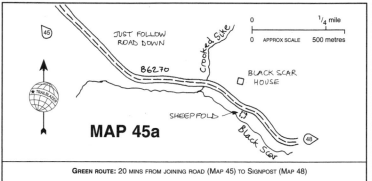

GREEN ROUTE: 20 MINS FROM JOINING ROAD (MAP 45) TO SIGNPOST (MAP 48)

The three routes to Keld

● **Green Route (Maps 45, 45a, 48-49; 5hr)** This is the simplest route and perhaps in very inclement weather the best one, regardless of season. The disadvantage is that it doesn't actually visit the Nine Standards, instead continuing south along the farm wall towards Rollinson Haggs and on to the B6270, before diverting east to Ravenseat. All in all, a little dreary.

● **Red Route (Maps 45-49; 5¹/₂hr)** You will already have seen glimpses since Kirkby Stephen of the 3m-high piles of slate and stones that are the **Nine Standards**. Though they continue to disappear temporarily behind the curves and folds of Hartley Fell as you head uphill, the path itself is straightforward enough and, all being well, you should reach the Standards just 30 minutes after leaving the junction with the green route.

At the top enjoy sumptuous views west over the Eden Valley to the Lakeland fells. Take your time. From now on, things get a little muddy as the route continues south up to the crest of **White Mossy Hill**. There, all being well, you should be able to make out a

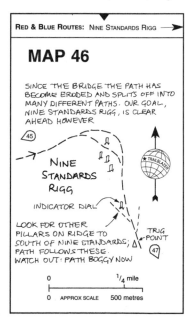

RED & BLUE ROUTES: NINE STANDARDS RIGG ⟶

MAP 46

SINCE THE BRIDGE THE PATH HAS BECOME ERODED AND SPLITS OFF INTO MANY DIFFERENT PATHS. OUR GOAL, NINE STANDARDS RIGG, IS CLEAR AHEAD HOWEVER

NINE STANDARDS RIGG

INDICATOR DIAL

LOOK FOR OTHER PILLARS ON RIDGE TO SOUTH OF NINE STANDARDS; PATH FOLLOWS THESE. WATCH OUT: PATH BOGGY NOW

TRIG POINT

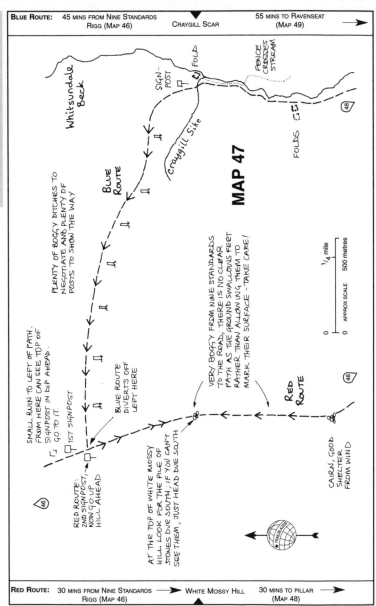

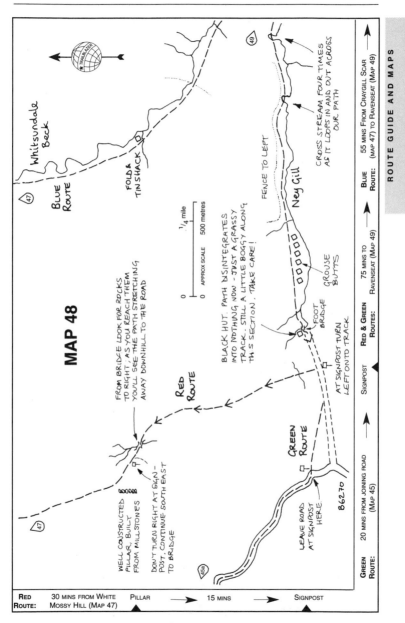

MAP 48

WHITSUNDALE BECK

47 BLUE ROUTE

FOLD & TIN SHACK

FROM BRIDGE LOOK FOR ROCKS TO RIGHT, AS YOU REACH THEM YOU'LL SEE THE PATH STRETCHING AWAY DOWNHILL TO THE ROAD

0 APPROX SCALE 500 metres
0 ¼ mile

47

WELL CONSTRUCTED PILLAR, BUILT FROM MILLSTONES

DON'T TURN RIGHT AT SIGN-POST, CONTINUE SOUTH EAST TO BRIDGE

RED ROUTE

BLACK HUT. PATH DISINTEGRATES INTO NOTHING NOW - JUST A GRASSY TRACK. STILL A LITTLE BOGGY ALONG THIS SECTION, TAKE CARE!

FENCE TO LEFT

NEY GILL

GROUSE BUTTS

CROSS STREAM FOUR TIMES AS IT LOOPS IN AND OUT ACROSS OUR PATH

49

FOOT BRIDGE

AT SIGNPOST TURN LEFT ONTO TRACK

SIGNPOST

GREEN ROUTE

B6270

LEAVE ROAD AT SIGNPOST HERE

45a

| GREEN ROUTE: | 20 MINS FROM JOINING ROAD (Map 45) | ► | | | | | | 75 MINS TO RAVENSEAT (MAP 49) | ► |

| RED & GREEN ROUTES: | SIGNPOST | ► | | | | | |

| BLUE ROUTE: | 55 MINS FROM CRAYGILL SCAR (MAP 47) TO RAVENSEAT (MAP 49) | ► |

| RED ROUTE: | 30 MINS FROM WHITE MOSSY HILL (MAP 47) | PILLAR | ► | 15 MINS | ► | SIGNPOST |

ROUTE GUIDE AND MAPS

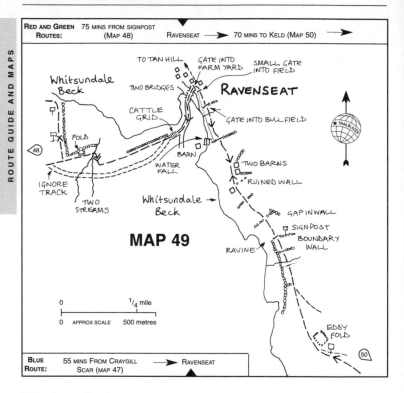

RED AND GREEN 75 MINS FROM SIGNPOST
ROUTES: (MAP 48) RAVENSEAT ⟶ 70 MINS TO KELD (MAP 50) ⟶

TO TAN HILL   GATE INTO   SMALL GATE
FARM YARD   INTO FIELD
Whitsundale
Beck   TWO BRIDGES   RAVENSEAT
CATTLE
GRID   GATE INTO BULL FIELD
FOLD
⟨48⟩   BARN
WATER   TWO BARNS
FALL   RUINED WALL
IGNORE
TRACK   Whitsundale
TWO   Beck   GAP IN WALL
STREAMS
MAP 49   SIGNPOST
BOUNDARY
RAVINE   WALL

★ TRAILBLAZER

0   ¹/₄ mile
0   APPROX SCALE   500 metres

EDDY
FOLD
⟨50⟩

BLUE   55 MINS FROM CRAYGILL   ⟶ RAVENSEAT
ROUTE: SCAR (MAP 47)

large **pile of stones** (resembling a ruin) in the distance due south of you; once there you should be able to see a well-constructed **pillar** standing among millstones to the south-south-east. From here you drop to the road and, turning left, walk on to the farm at **Ravenseat**, situated by a weir.

● **Blue Route (Maps 45-49; 4¹/₂hr)** Up to Nine Standards this route is identical to the red route, but near the ruin at the end of the ridge this route takes an eastern course *around*, rather than over, White Mossy Hill. Regular posts (often every 30m or so) ensure that you can't get lost as you make your way to Whitsundale Beck, which you follow south to a reunion with the other two paths.

(Opposite): Looking down Greenup, on the trail between Borrowdale and Grasmere; Skiddaw in the distance. (Photo © Henry Stedman).

From Ravenseat the path drops south through farms lining **Whitsundale Beck**, a picturesque little river punctuated with some fairly impressive waterfalls and ravines. Passing the farmhouse of **Smithy Holme** (Map 50), you can join the B6270 immediately by crossing the bridge, or take the path above **Cotterby Scar**. (For once we recommend the road, as it allows you to visit Wainwath Force.) The two paths reunite by the bridge before ***Park House*** (☎ 01748 886549; a campsite charging £4 per person) from where it's a gentle stroll to Keld, virtually the halfway point on the Coast to Coast.

KELD   MAP 50

Keld sits at the head of Swaledale, its houses huddled together against the often inclement weather. It's tiny today, at first sight merely a pretty village of little consequence save that it marks, almost, the halfway point on our trek and is also the only place on both the Coast to Coast and Pennine Way walks. However, in common with the rest of Swaledale, in the mid-19th century Keld stood at the heart of the lead-mining industry in the area. Many of the buildings were constructed at this time, as a quick survey of the construction dates written above the doors of the houses will confirm.

The village's two Methodist chapels (one next to the YHA, the second in the heart of the village) were also built then. Keld is more about water than lead today. The name means 'spring' in Norse and the Swale River (dyed brown by the peat) rushes through town. Do take the opportunity to visit some of the small nearby waterfalls – more accurately called cascades or, locally, **forces** – including Catrake Force, just above the village, and East Gill Force below it.

There are few places to stay in Keld but don't be too hard on yourself if you fail to book in time and as a consequence can't find a room. Further down the valley are Thwaite and Muker, both with some accommodation, and the walk down to both is wonderful. Indeed, such are the sumptuous charms of Swaledale's gentle rolling scenery, dotted here and there with the valley's distinctive, cubic laithes – stone barns for housing hay and livestock – that many

hikers are persuaded to forego the 'official' Coast to Coast path via Swinner and Gunnerside gills (see p150) in favour of a gentle stroll down the valley, joining up with the path again only towards the end of Swaledale at Reeth. And even if you *are* staying in Keld, do take the time to stroll (or take a **bus**) down to these villages. (However, check when the last bus goes back to Keld from Muker as it's a fairly long uphill walk.)

For more details on Keld and the rest of Swaledale visit the **website**, 🖳 www .swaledale.net.

Where to stay and eat in Upper Swaledale

It seems almost ironic that **Keld**, virtually the halfway point on the walk and thus a place where you'd want to celebrate, is the only village at the end of a stage with no pub (the nearest is the Farmers Arms in Muker (see p154), a 50-minute walk away.

A couple of the places to stay, however, do have licences to sell alcohol, including the **youth hostel** (☎ 0870 770 5888; 38 beds, £11), formerly a shooting lodge. One of the smallest hostels on the route, it's a pleasant place with a lot of books about the area. Sadly it's on the list of hostels earmarked for closure over the next three years.

Butt House (☎ 01748 886374; 🖳 www .coasttocoastguides.co.uk; 3D/1F en suite), run by the formidable Doreen Whitehead, author of an accommodation guide to the Coast to Coast (see p37), is another place with a licence to serve alcohol. People rave about the dinners here. Rates are around £38 for B&B and an evening meal.

There are **campsites** in Keld, both with showers and both charging £3 per camper: *Park House* (see p145) and *Park Lodge* (☎ 01748 886274; 🖳 www.rukins-keld.co.uk). The latter incorporates a lovely little **tearoom** (daily 10.30am-5pm) in the farmhouse with tables and chairs in the garden out front. There are bacon rolls for £2.50 and they have a limited selection of supplies for sale but it does include beer and wine, which can be a godsend for drinkers who are only too aware of the lack of a pub in the village.

Further down the hill from Keld on the way to Thwaite are the friendly, licensed *Green Lands* (☎ 01748 886778; 🖳 greenlands@keld.uk.net; 1D/1T en suite) which caters specifically for the walker including

washing and drying facilities. They charge £27 per person, with a three-course evening meal an extra £13.

In **Thwaite** itself, *Kearton Country Hotel* (☎ 01748 886277; 🖳 www kearton countryhotel.co.uk; 6D/5T/1F, most en suite) is a good-looking place, though some people have complained about the noise in some of the rooms from the water pipes. Rates are £38 (standard room) and £39 (en suite) for one night's dinner, bed and breakfast; rates are reduced for longer stays. Their smart restaurant is open to non-residents. Local specialities such as Yorkshire Pudding are prominent on the menu; dinner is served 6.30-7.30pm.

Bus No 30 goes from Keld to Richmond via Thwaite (see pp43-5) for details.

STAGE 8: KELD TO REETH   MAPS 50-56

The walk from Keld begins at the foot of the village – a bit of a pain to those who have spent the night at Thwaite or Muker and who must now return uphill to Keld to rejoin the path. There are two ways around this problem: the first is the valley walk alternative to Reeth as described on pp154-7; the second is to catch the bus back up to Keld. There is one morning service (No 30) a day Monday to Saturday from Muker to Keld via Thwaite. Note that on this high-level route there is nowhere to buy any food or drink: come prepared.

The wildlife along this **11-mile (17.5km, 4¹/₂hr)** walk is abundant, so try to set off as early as possible to increase your chances of seeing deer, rabbits and pheasants. However, as with the walk from Shap to Kirkby Stephen, this high-level route is mainly about archaeology and the evidence of man's existence in the far north of England. But, unlike that stage where we encountered a number of prehistoric sites, the precise purposes of which remain the subject of much speculation to the present day, this stage is all about uncovering the region's well-documented recent history, and the evidence on the ground is easy to interpret. For today's walk takes us through a part of Yorkshire that has been forever altered and scarred by the activities of the lead-mining industry.

The first evidence of this is **Crackpot Hall** (Map 51), 30 minutes from Keld along a gloriously pretty trail high above the Swale. Though there has been a house here since the 16th century, the ruin you see today actually dates from the 18th century and, while not directly connected to the mining industry, the farmhouse was once owned by one of the mine's managers. Quiet and ruined now, the location, with views down the valley, is perfect. As a plaque poignantly puts it, remember that this hall used to echo to the sound of children laughing. 'Crackpot', by the way, means 'Deep hole or chasm that is the haunt

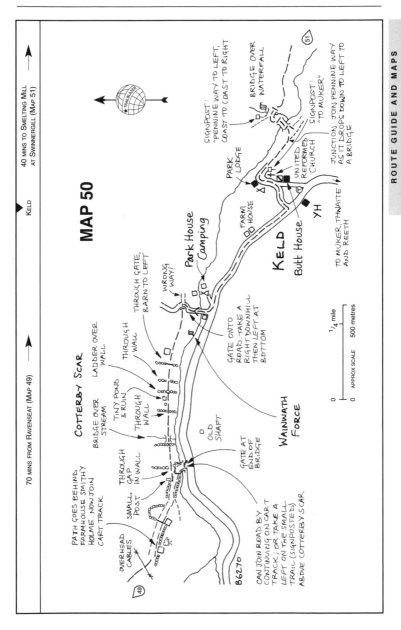

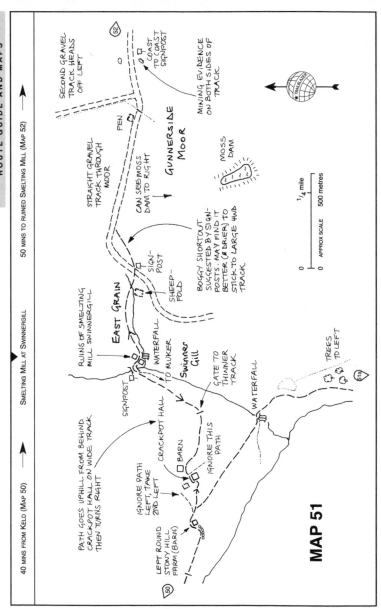

MAP 51

40 MINS FROM KELD (Map 50) →

SMELTING MILL AT SWINNERGILL →

50 MINS TO RUINED SMELTING MILL (MAP 52) →

52

COAST TO COAST SIGNPOST

MINING EVIDENCE ON BOTH SIDES OF TRACK

SECOND GRAVEL TRACK HEADS OFF LEFT

PEN

STRAIGHT GRAVEL TRACK THROUGH MOOR

GUNNERSIDE MOOR

CAN SEE MOSS DAM TO RIGHT

MOSS DAM

SIGN-POST

SHEEP-FOLD

BOGGY SHORTCUT SUGGESTED BY SIGNPOSTS. MAY FIND IT BETTER (& DRIER) TO STICK TO LARGE HAND TRACK

EAST GRAIN

RUINS OF SMELTING MILL SWINNERGILL

WATERFALL

SIGNPOST

PATH GOES UPHILL FROM BEHIND CRACKPOT HALL ON WIDE TRACK THEN TURNS RIGHT

CRACKPOT HALL

PATH TO MUKER

Swinner Gill

GATE TO THINNER TRACK

IGNORE PATH LEFT, TAKE 2ND LEFT

BARN

IGNORE THIS PATH

WATERFALL

LEFT ROUND STONY HILL FARM (BARN)

TREES TO LEFT

51a

50

APPROX SCALE

0 ¼ mile

0 500 metres

TRAIL BLAZER

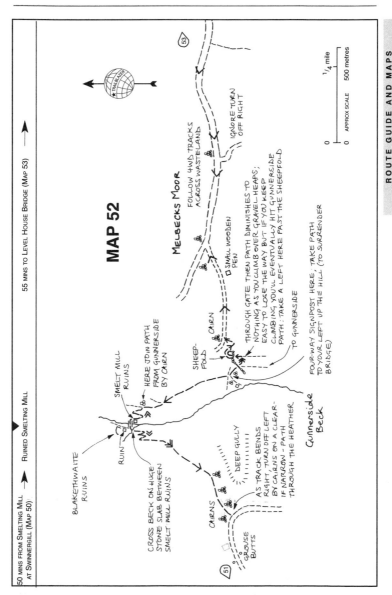

50 MINS FROM SMELTING MILL AT SWINNERGILL (MAP 50) ➤ RUINED SMELTING MILL ➤ 55 MINS TO LEVEL HOUSE BRIDGE (MAP 53) ➤

MAP 52

MELBECKS MOOR

FOLLOW 4WD TRACKS ACROSS WASTELANDS

IGNORE TURN OFF RIGHT

53

★ TRAILBLAZER

SMELT MILL RUINS

BLAKETHWAITE RUINS

RUIN

CROSS BECK ON HUGE STONE SLAB BETWEEN SMELT MILL RUINS

HERE JOIN PATH FROM GUNNERSIDE BY CAIRN

SHEEP-FOLD

CAIRN

SMALL WOODEN PEN

THROUGH GATE THEN PATH DIMINISHES TO NOTHING AS YOU CLIMB OVER GRAVEL HEAPS; EASY TO LOSE THE WAY BUT IF YOU KEEP CLIMBING YOU'LL EVENTUALLY HIT GUNNERSIDE PATH: TAKE A LEFT HERE PAST THE SHEEPFOLD

TO GUNNERSIDE

FOUR-WAY SIGNPOST HERE, TAKE PATH TO YOUR LEFT UP THE HILL (TO SURRENDER BRIDGE)

GUNNERSIDE BECK

DEEP GULLY

AS TRACK BENDS RIGHT, TURN OFF LEFT BY CAIRNS ON A CLEAR IF NARROW PATH THROUGH THE HEATHER

CAIRNS

GROUSE BUTTS

51

0 APPROX SCALE ¼ mile

0 500 metres

❏ **Lead mining in Swaledale**

According to the best estimates, lead has been mined in Swaledale since at least Roman times, and very possibly there was some small-scale mining back in the Bronze Age. A couple of pigs (ingots) of lead, including one discovered in Swaledale with the Roman name 'Hadrian' marked upon it, have been found. A versatile metal, lead is used in plumbing (indeed the word 'plumbing' comes from the Latin for lead), ship-building, roofing as well as in the manufacture of glass, pottery and paint. During medieval times lead was much in demand by the great churches and castles that were being built at that time.

The onset of the Industrial Revolution caused mining in Swaledale to become more organized and developed from the end of the 17th century. The innovation of gunpowder blasting, too, led to a sizeable increase in production, and the Yorkshire mines were at the centre of the British mining industry. Indeed, during the mid-19th century Britain was producing over half the world's lead, and the mines in Yorkshire were producing 10 per cent of that.

But while some of the mine owners grew fabulously wealthy on the proceeds, the workers themselves suffered appalling conditions, often staying for a week or more at the mine, spending every daylight hour inside it. Deaths were common as the mines were rarely built with safety in mind, and as the mines grew ever deeper as technology progressed, so conditions became ever more hazardous. Illnesses from the cramped, damp and insanitary conditions were rife. As if to rub salt into the wounds, many of the workers did not even own their own tools, but instead hired them from an agent.

The industry continued to prosper throughout much of the 19th century until the opening of mines in South America lead to an influx of cheaper imports and a fall in price, sending many British mines into bankruptcy. Many workers drifted away, usually to the coal mines around Durham, or to London and North America, in search of better prospects. By the early 20th century many of the villages were struggling to survive. Indeed, in the words of one resident of Reeth, when the mines closed the village became a 'City of the Dead'. Thankfully, tourism today has gone some way to securing the future of these attractive mining villages, and with the establishment of the Yorkshire Dales National Park, the future looks a lot brighter for the villages of Swaledale.

of crows', and is not a comment on the mental stability of the people who once lived here.

The path bends north now from behind the Hall to the remains of **Swinnergill mines**, including the ruins of a smelt mill, and on over **Gunnerside Moor**. Passing Moss Dam (a small body of water to your right) and various mineshafts and spoil heaps to left and right, you then continue down to the next extensive set of ruins at **Blakethwaite** (Map 52) in the valley of Gunnerside Beck, a good place to stop for a picnic lunch. While sitting on the grassy bank behind the large ruin with the arched windows, look for the flue coming down from the hill opposite, finishing near the kiln on the western banks.

From here the path continues east up to the top of **Melbecks Moor**. Most people lose their way on this ascent, but not to worry: everybody eventually hits the path to Gunnerside, and by following it north the trail across the moor is joined once more. The landscape at the top is a bit of a shock. Whereas the mining relics you have encountered thus far have been rather neat and charming,

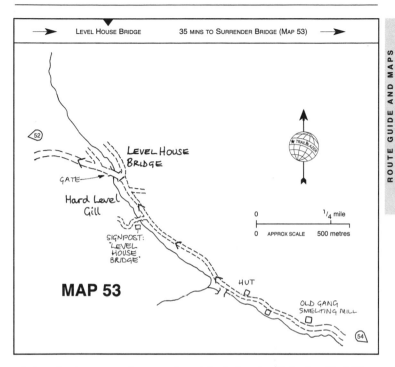

ROUTE GUIDE AND MAPS

what confronts you now is a gravel wasteland almost entirely devoid of life; a landscape that more or less exactly conforms to the definition of the word 'desolate'. This devastation is, it won't surprise you to discover, the work of man. The area was artificially stripped of any vegetation by water which would be dammed up above the site, then released by the miners to reveal the minerals underneath. This stripped land is known as a *hush*. While few will fall in love with the tedious monotony of the place, it does at least have its own intrinsic interest, showing how easily man can alter the landscape for good – or rather, for bad. It also serves to remind Coast to Coast trekkers, jaded, perhaps, by a week or more of incredible scenery, just what ugliness looks like. Furthermore, though you may feel melancholy walking through such lifeless terrain, you'll probably be pleased to know that during it you pass the trek's hundred-mile mark.

At the end of your 'moon walk' lies **Level House Bridge** (Map 53), where you cross Hard Level Gill before following it down to the ruined Old Gang Smelting Mill, the most extensive set of ruins yet and one now protected by a preservation order. At **Surrender Bridge** (Map 54) you cross the road and continue past another smelt-mill ruin, traversing the excellently named Cringley Bottom and a great deal of farmland on your way to Reeth.

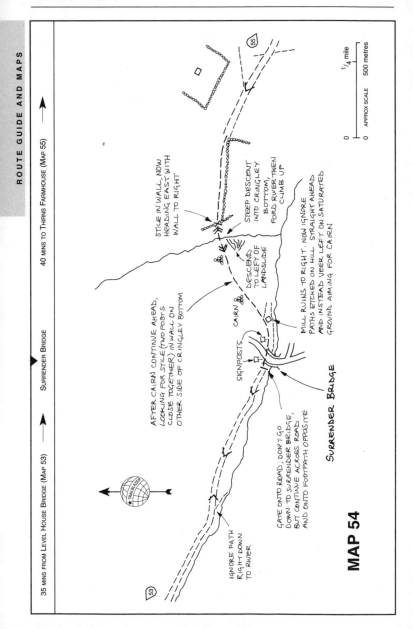

35 MINS FROM LEVEL HOUSE BRIDGE (MAP 53) ——▶   SURRENDER BRIDGE   ——▶   40 MINS TO THIRNS FARMHOUSE (MAP 55) ——▶

STILE IN WALL NOW HEADING EAST WITH WALL ON RIGHT

STEEP DESCENT INTO CRINGLEY BOTTOM, FORD RIVER THEN CLIMB UP

DESCEND TO LEFT OF LANDSLIDE

AFTER CAIRN CONTINUE AHEAD, LOOKING FOR STILE (TWO POSTS CLOSE TOGETHER) IN WALL ON OTHER SIDE OF CRINGLEY BOTTOM

CAIRN

MILL RUINS TO RIGHT. NOW IGNORE PATHS ETCHED ON HILL STRAIGHT AHEAD AND INSTEAD VEER LEFT ON SATURATED GROUND AIMING FOR CAIRN

SIGNPOSTS

SURRENDER BRIDGE

GATE ONTO ROAD; DON'T GO DOWN TO SURRENDER BRIDGE, BUT CONTINUE ACROSS ROAD AND ONTO FOOTPATH OPPOSITE

IGNORE PATH RIGHT DOWN TO RIVER

TRAIL BLAZER

MAP 54

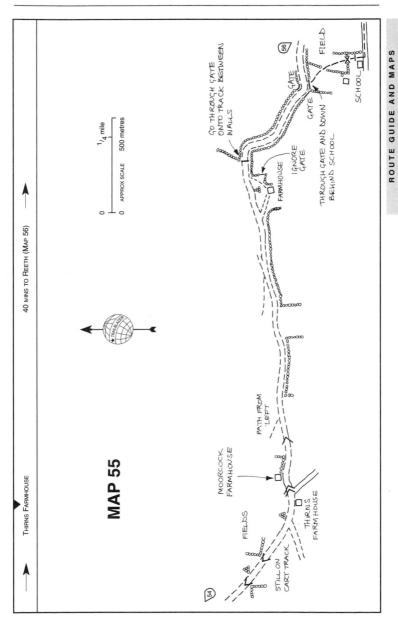

THIRNS FARMHOUSE

40 MINS TO REETH (MAP 56)

MAP 55

0 ¼ mile

APPROX SCALE

0 500 metres

TRAILBLAZER

FIELDS

STILL ON CART TRACK

54

THIRNS FARM HOUSE

MOORCOCK FARMHOUSE

PATH FROM LEFT

GO THROUGH GATE ONTO TRACK BETWEEN WALLS

FARMHOUSE

IGNORE GATE

THROUGH GATE AND DOWN BEHIND SCHOOL

GATE

GATE

56

FIELD

SCHOOL

The Swaledale Valley alternative · Maps 51a-e, 52

The disadvantage with this walk is that it does make this stage rather short (about 4½hrs) and simple, and you may well end up in Reeth at lunchtime. You could, if time is pressing, walk on to Richmond, though that would be an awful lot to tackle in one day and it would be a shame to bypass Reeth and all its pubs without spending at least one night there. Our advice? Enjoy the walk at a leisurely pace, stop frequently to admire the valley, take the diversion to Muker – and silence the voices in your head that insist that you haven't done enough today with a pint or two of Old Peculier in one of Reeth's hostelries.

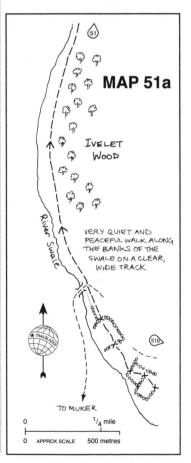

The advantage of this walk is that it is beautiful, particularly in the early morning before the crowds arrive. The path is so easy and unstrenuous that you can fully appreciate your surroundings without distraction and spend time looking for riparian wildlife such as herons, ducks and, so it is said, otters.

The villages passed on the way are a joy too. **Muker** (actually slightly off the route) is a very pleasant little place and one of James Herriot's (see p157) favourites. It has a church and a pub, the *Farmers Arms* (☎ 01748 886297, 🖳 www.mukervillage.co.uk), which serves food 12 noon-2.15pm and 6.30-8.45pm. It has also been the home for 30 years of **Swaledale Woollens** (🖳 www.swaledalewoollens.co.uk), its products made from the wool of Swaledale sheep, a hardy breed whose tough wool is considered ideal for carpets. The shop boasts that it actually saved the village following the depression caused by the collapse of the mining industry. Following a meeting in the local pub, a decision was made to set up a local cottage industry producing knitwear, and

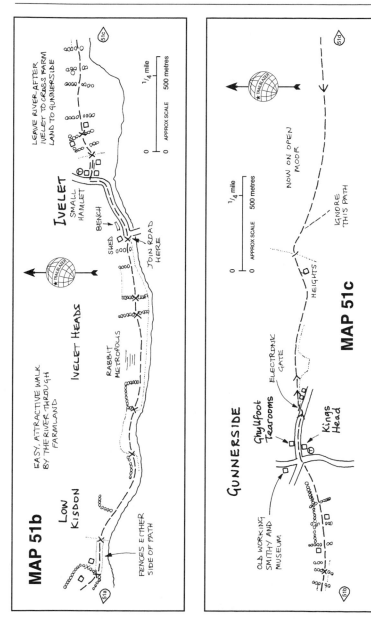

MAP 51b

EASY, ATTRACTIVE WALK BY THE RIVER THROUGH FARMLAND

LEAVE RIVER AFTER IVELET TO CROSS FARM LAND TO GUNNERSIDE

51c

0   APPROX SCALE
0   500 metres   1/4 mile

IVELET

SMALL HAMLET

BENCH

SHED

JOIN ROAD HERE

IVELET HEADS

RABBIT METROPOLIS

LOW KISDON

FENCES EITHER SIDE OF PATH

51a

MAP 51c

51d

NOW ON OPEN MOOR

IGNORE THIS PATH

0   APPROX SCALE
0   500 metres   1/4 mile

HEIGHTS

ELECTRONIC GATE

GUNNERSIDE

GHYLLFOOT TEAROOMS

KINGS HEAD

OLD WORKING SMITHY AND MUSEUM

51b

MAP 51d

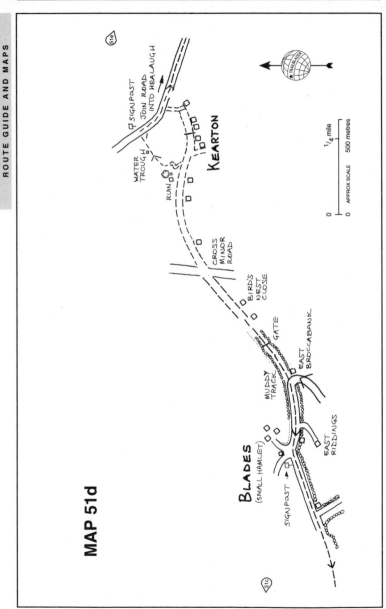

SIGNPOST
JOIN ROAD
INTO HEALAUGH

WATER
TROUGH

RUN OFF

KEARTON

CROSS
MINOR
ROAD

BIRD'S
NEST
CLOSE

GATE

MUDDY
TRACK

EAST
BROGABANK

EAST
RIDDINGS

BLADES
(SMALL HAMLET)

SIGNPOST

¼ mile

APPROX SCALE   500 metres

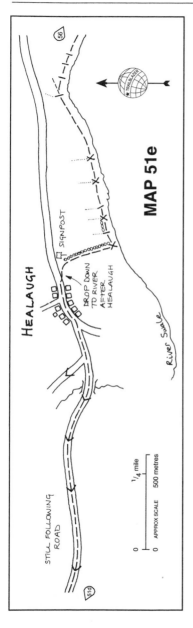

MAP 51e

HEALAUGH

SIGNPOST

DROP DOWN TO RIVER AFTER HEALAUGH

River Swale

STILL FOLLOWING ROAD

¼ mile

500 metres

APPROX SCALE

0

0

56

51b

today nearly 40 home workers are employed in knitting the jumpers, hats and many other items available in the store.

Then there's **Gunnerside** (Map 51c) which has a post office, the excellent *Ghyllfoot Tearooms* (☎ 01748 886239; 10.30am-5pm, closed Tues), a pleasant pub, the *King's Head* (☎ 01748 886261), which serves pub grub 12noon-3pm and 7-9pm, and even an old **smithy** with attached museum (11am-5pm, closed Mon; £2.50).

From Gunnerside the path crosses moor and farmland, eventually dropping down to fair **Healaugh** (Map 51e), from where it returns to the river to continue to Reeth, which it enters via the raised pavement of the Quaker Road.

REETH   see Map p159

Reeth, the 'capital' of Swaledale, is the archetypal Yorkshire dale village: flanked to north and south by mine-scarred valley walls, at its heart lies a village green surrounded on all sides with examples of those twin institutions of Yorkshire hospitality: the **tearoom** (of which it has five), and the **pub** (three at the last count). As if to underline its Yorkshire credentials still further, it also has a renowned brass band. Hardly surprising, therefore, that the village was used as a location for many of the episodes of the quintessential Yorkshire series *All Creatures Great and Small* by James Herriot.

Mentioned in the Domesday survey of 1086, the village grew in prominence, as did everywhere else in Swaledale, on the profits of the mining industry, though unlike other villages it could always claim a second string to its bow as the main market town for Swaledale (the market is held on the Green on Fridays). Thankfully, after the mines had closed tourism gave Reeth a new lease of life and today the town is host to a number of B&Bs and hotels, as well as some good **gift shops** and a small **museum**.

Services

The **tourist office** (☎ 01748 884059; daily 10am-5pm) is to the west of the Green in Hudson House. On the other side of the Green is the **post office** (Mon-Sat 9am-5.30pm) whose **general store** is open Mon-Fri 9am-5.30pm, Sat 9am-12 noon. As well as getting cash from the post counter you can also get cashback from the store if you spend £10 or more. Or there are **cash machines** in both the Black Bull, and the newsagents (Mon-Fri 7am-7.30pm, Sat 7.30am-7pm, Sun 8am-4pm) at the bottom of the hill on the way out of town.

For **souvenir shopping**, Garden House deals largely with pottery and handiworks made of wood, cloth, paper and clay, while nearby Pots 'n' Presents (🖳 www.jewellery tree.co.uk) specializes in handsome hand-made jewellery including earrings, necklaces and cufflinks.

Several **buses** pass through Reeth; see pp43-5 for details.

Where to stay

The nearest **youth hostel** is at Grinton (☎ 0870 770 5844; 69 beds; £12.50), an exhausting 1¼ miles (about 2km) further along the road (and off the trail). We recommend that you take a **B&B** here tonight. Alternatively, you could **camp** at *The Orchard Caravan Park* (☎ 01748 884475; £5 per person; check in at the house signed 'Warden Enquiries'), open April-Oct; book in advance in peak season. One reader wrote to say that you'll get a warmer reception as a camper if you continue to The Lodge at Marrick, although it's another hour away.

Of the B&Bs, *Hackney House* (Bridge Terrace; ☎ 01748 884302; 2S/2D/1T/1F) at the bottom of town is the most highly praised in Reeth. From the outside it's just an unassuming terrace, though guests wax lyrical about the friendliness and consideration of the hosts and the huge breakfasts. With rates starting at just £20/24 sgl/dbl, this is great value. Another place to try is *Walpardo* (☎ 01748 884626; 🖳 walpar

doreeth@aol.com; 1S/1T), just off the Green, where B&B is £19. *Hillary House* (☎ 01748 884171, 1D/1T), 4 Hillary Terrace, offers B&B for £18.50 per person and comes recommended. *The Olde Temperance* (☎ 01748 884401, 1S/1F) charges £20 for a one-night stay (£18 for two nights or more) and is situated above an old bookshop.

The Black Bull (☎ 01748 884213; 3D/3T/1F all en suite) dates back to 1680 and has rooms overlooking the Green and down Swaledale. Prices start at £30. The Kings Arms, next door, is 50 years' younger, the stone above the door testifying to a construction date of 1734. However, at the time of writing, this had closed though it is possible it will re-open.

Off the north-east corner of the Green, *Arkleside Hotel* (☎ 01748 884200; 🖳 www .arklesidehotel.co.uk) with B&B from £60/45 sgl/dbl.

The smartest place in town, *The Burgoyne Hotel* (☎ 01748 884292; 🖳 www .theburgoyne.co.uk; 5D/3T all en suite), dominates the north side of the Green, though you may feel a little out of place in such salubrious surroundings. Rates start at £112.50 for a twin or double room or £165 for four-poster extravagance.

Where to eat

Reeth Bakery (🖳 www.reethbakery.co.uk), on Silver St on the way into Reeth, is a little treasure. All the breads are home-baked with organic flour from the water mill at Little Salkeld; in addition they have a great selection of Swaledale cheeses and chutneys, as well as shortbreads, flapjacks and other cakes: if you stop for only one cup of tea in Reeth, make sure it's here.

On the village green, *The Cobbles Tearoom* (☎ 01748 884332, open Wed-Mon) has a decent selection of cakes, though by the afternoon many have sold out. The *White House Tea Shop* (☎ 01748 884763; open Mar-Jan, Fri-Tue) on the corner of Anvil Square sells ice cream and filling lunches; the ploughmans is £5.75.

There are two further tea shops on the Green; the *Copper Kettle* (☎ 01748 884748) with takeaway sandwiches from

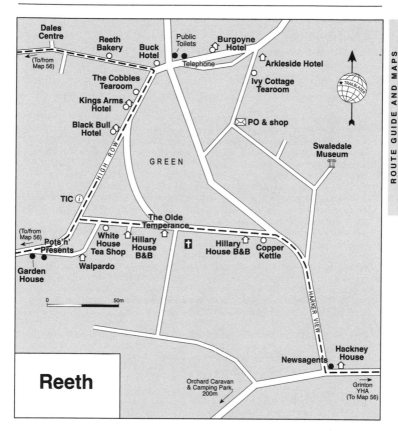

Reeth

Map labels:
Dales Centre
(To/from Map 56)
Reeth Bakery
Buck Hotel
Public Toilets
Burgoyne Hotel
Telephone
Arkleside Hotel
The Cobbles Tearoom
Ivy Cottage Tearoom
Kings Arms Hotel
Black Bull Hotel
HIGH ROW
PO & shop
GREEN
Swaledale Museum
TIC
The Olde Temperance
(To/from Map 56)
Pots 'n' Presents
White House Tea Shop
Hillary House B&B
Hillary House B&B
Copper Kettle
Garden House
Walpardo
HARKER VIEW
Newsagents
Hackney House
Orchard Caravan & Camping Park, 200m
Grinton YHA (To Map 56)
0   50m

£1.25 and *Ivy Cottage Tearoom* (☎ 01748 884418; 🖳 www.ivycottagereeth.co.uk, open Tue-Sun) where you can try a plate-sized Yorkshire pudding for £5.50.

For an evening meal (6-9pm), the *Buck Hotel* does Dale lamb cutlets for £8.25. The *Black Bull* is known for its homemade pies (from £6.95) and serves food between noon and 2.30pm and 6-9.30pm. Turn up early and you should be able to get a seat at the Old Draper's Shop at the centre of the pub, which is a quieter sectioned-off area for non-smokers. The smartest place to eat, with lamb and Whitby crab on the menu, is the *Burgoyne* but at £27.50 per person for dinner it's a little pricey.

What to see

Swaledale Folk Museum (☎ 01748 884373), open daily (10.30am-5.30pm and Sat 2-5pm) from Good Friday to the end of October (£1.25/50p, family ticket £3) holds some surprisingly good exhibits and is well worth an hour or so of anyone's time, particularly if you want to learn more about the local mining and farming industries. The drystone wallers' craft (see box p160) is examined, and the museum also looks at the social history of the area in some detail, attempting through its exhibits to show how the locals used to live a hundred or more years ago.

❑ **Drystone walls**

I am a Dry Stone Waller
All day I Dry Stone Wall
Of all appalling callings
Dry Stone Walling's worst of all
Pam Ayres, 1978

Along the Coast to Coast path you'll pass hundreds of drystone walls. Beautiful and photogenic, particularly when covered in a layer of velvety green moss, they are probably the most ubiquitous feature of northern England's landscape. That said, few walkers give much thought to who built them, nor have any idea just how much skill and effort goes into making these walls.

Drystone walls, so called because they are built without mortar, have been around since Elizabethan times when, as now, they were used to demarcate the boundaries between one farmer's land and another. Many others were built during the Enclosure Acts between 1720 and 1840, when previously large fields shared between a number of farmers were divided into strips of land. A very few of these 18th-century walls are still standing: those nearest to a village tend to be the oldest, as it was this land that was divided and enclosed first. The fact that the walls have lasted so long is largely due to the care that goes into building each one.

The first step to building a drystone wall is to dig some deep, secure foundations. That done, the next step is to build the wall itself, or rather walls, for a typical drystone wall is actually made up of two thinner walls built back to back. This design helps to make the wall as sturdy as possible. Every so often, a row of 'through-stones' are built into the wall that serve to bind the two halves together. It is estimated that one tonne of stone is required for one square yard of wall. Each stone is chosen carefully to fit exactly: a bad choice can upset the pressure loading, leading to an early collapse. Smaller chippings are used to fill the gaps.

Despite the walls' longevity, or perhaps because of it, drystone walling is becoming something of a lost art. The wire fence is a cheaper, simpler and just as effective way of dividing land, and while the existing drystone walls have to be repaired occasionally, more often than not the farmer would rather do it himself than call in a professional. As a result, the industry is in decline. In Swaledale there is said to be only one full-time drystone waller left.

STAGE 9: REETH TO RICHMOND   MAPS 56-61

There are a couple of lovely tracts of woodland on this **10¹/₂-mile (17km, 3¹/₂hr)** stage, a simple and short one that should, if you set off early enough, allow you time to enjoy the sights of Richmond at the end of it. A couple of charming villages are passed on the way too, as well as the remains of an old priory. Overall, not a spectacular day but, if the weather's OK, an exceedingly pleasant one.

The priory is **Marrick Priory** (Map 57) and its ruins lie just 40 minutes outside Reeth; it is reached by taking the turn-off on the main road by the ***Broadlands B&B*** (☎ 01748 884297, 1S/1T/1D), a very grand 17th-century building with rooms from £24 per person, signposted towards Marrick, Marske and Hurst. Though it's visible from a distance away, casual visitors are not now

(**Opposite**) **Top**: Looking down on Marske (see p164). **Bottom**: Ewe with adolescent lambs. (Photos © Jim Manthorpe).

ROUTE GUIDE AND MAPS

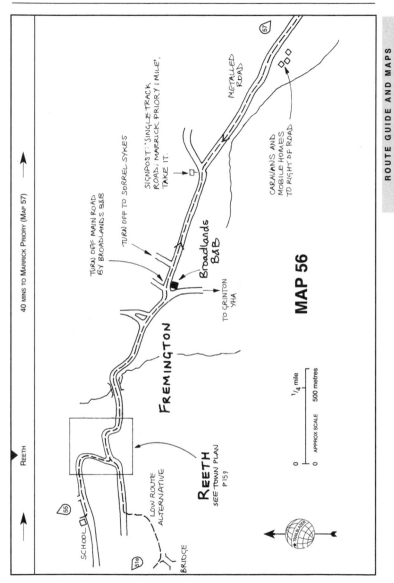

40 MINS TO MARRICK PRIORY (MAP 57) →

← REETH

REETH →

TURN OFF MAIN ROAD BY BROADLANDS B&B

TURN OFF TO SORREL-SYKES

SIGNPOST: "SINGLE-TRACK ROAD, MARRICK PRIORY 1 MILE", TAKE IT.

METALLED ROAD

57

CARAVANS AND MOBILE HOMES TO RIGHT OF ROAD

Broadlands B&B

TO GRINTON YHA

FREMINGTON

REETH
SEE TOWN PLAN P159

MAP 56

¼ mile

500 metres

APPROX SCALE

0

0

LOW ROUTE ALTERNATIVE

SCHOOL

55

51b

BRIDGE

TRAILBLAZER

(Opposite) Top: The Nine Standards (see p141) mark the end of the climb up the Pennines. (Photo © Jim Manthorpe). **Bottom**: Richmond's market square (see p167), viewed from the top of the castle. (Photo © Henry Stedman).

allowed to visit the ruins which have been incorporated within Marrick Priory Outdoor Education and Residential Centre. Nevertheless, workers there are pretty used to seeing people walking down the drive to inspect the exterior of the place and seem pretty relaxed about it. The abbey was founded by local noble, Roger de Aske, for Benedictine nuns who numbered 17 at the priory's dissolution in 1540. There are a couple of tomb slabs in the grounds, including one by the entrance belonging to a Thomas Peacock who died in 1762 at the grand old age of 102.

Those disappointed with not being able to explore the ruins thoroughly will find some consolation in the walk up to Marrick village, an incredibly pretty uphill amble through the first of this stage's woods, known as **Steps Wood**. The path you are walking on is known as the **Nuns' Steps**, so-called because the nuns are said to have constructed the 375 steps as a walkway to the abbey. At the top, through a couple of fields, lies the village that gave Marrick Priory its name.

MARRICK   MAP 57

Mentioned in *The Domesday Book* as Mange and Marig, the derivation of the name Marrick is something of a mystery. According to one school of thought it has something to do with marshes; according to another, it means something like 'The Habitation of Mary'. Still others believe it to mean Horse or Boundary Ridge from old Norse.

There are no pubs or shops here, in fact very little save for some 25 houses and a village institute, but there is a delightful B&B, *The Lodge* (☎ 01748 884477; 🖥 http ://members.aol.com/marricklodge/marrick lodge.html; 1D/1T), tucked down a drive-way. The owners are a wonderfully welcoming couple who'll ply you with tea and flapjacks as soon as you walk in; the house itself is a country-cottage delight filled with interesting knick-knacks and furniture. They also have a small lawn for **camping** (£5) nearby. All in all, highly recommended. Rates are from £22.50, the three-course dinner is £12.50.

From Marrick the trail begins a long north-easterly march up to Marske through farmland punctuated by any number of stiles and gates. Look out for *Elaine's Teas*, a farmhouse serving snacks and drinks. At the end of this march through the pastures the road to **Marske**, with impressive Marske Hall (Map 58) on the right, is joined. Continuing up through Marske past the 11th-century crenellated **Church of St Edmund the Martyr**, half a mile out of the village the road is once again forsaken in favour of pasture as the trail continues its relentless march north-east, bending east only when the farm track to West Applegarth (Map 59), below **Applegarth Scar**, is reached.

The farms High and Low Applegarth are passed before the trail reaches a third farm at East Applegarth where, high above the wooded valley, there is *Richmond Camping Barn* (☎ 01748 822940; the nearest camping option to Richmond), a beautifully rustic place open April to October. There are 12 beds (£6 per person) and a small grassy patch for **camping** (£3). Facilities are limited, but there is a kitchen and at the time of writing they were installing a shower.

The trail continues into enchanting **Whitecliffe Wood**, emerging 15 minutes later at High Leases Farm with its free-range chickens. A road walk follows before you eventually pass through the suburbs and into Richmond.

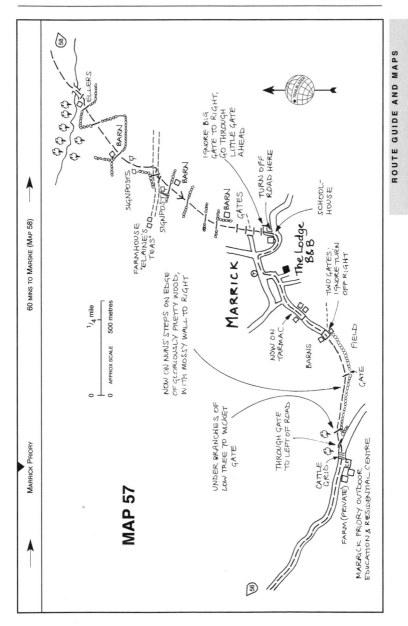

MARRICK PRIORY

60 MINS TO MARSKE (MAP 58)

MAP 57

APPROX SCALE
0 — ¼ mile
0 — 500 metres

ELLERS

BARN

SIGNPOSTS

FARMHOUSE 'ELAINE'S TEAS'

SIGNPOSTS

BARN

IGNORE BIG GATE TO RIGHT, GO THROUGH LITTLE GATE AHEAD

BARN

GATES

TURN OFF ROAD HERE

SCHOOL-HOUSE

NOW ON NUNS' STEPS ON EDGE OF GLORIOUSLY PRETTY WOOD, WITH MOSSY WALL TO RIGHT

MARRICK

The Lodge B&B

NOW ON TARMAC

BARNS

TWO GATES: IGNORE TURN OFF RIGHT

FIELD

UNDER BRANCHES OF LOW TREE TO WICKET GATE

THROUGH GATE TO LEFT OF ROAD

GATE

CATTLE GRID

FARM (PRIVATE)

MARRICK PRIORY OUTDOOR EDUCATION & RESIDENTIAL CENTRE

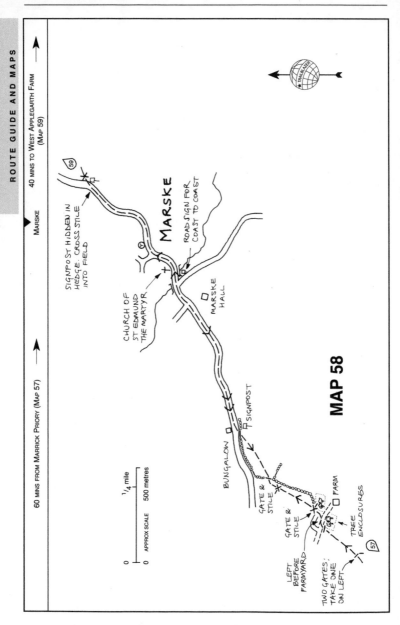

60 MINS FROM MARRICK PRIORY (MAP 57)

MARSKE

40 MINS TO WEST APPLEGARTH FARM (MAP 59)

0 APPROX SCALE
0 ¼ mile
500 metres

SIGNPOST HIDDEN IN HEDGE. CROSS STILE INTO FIELD

MARSKE

ROADSIGN FOR COAST TO COAST

CHURCH OF ST EDMUND THE MARTYR

MARSKE HALL

MAP 58

BUNGALOW

SIGNPOST

GATE & STILE

GATE & STILE

FARM

TREE ENCLOSURES

LEFT BEFORE FARMYARD

TWO GATES; TAKE ONE ON LEFT

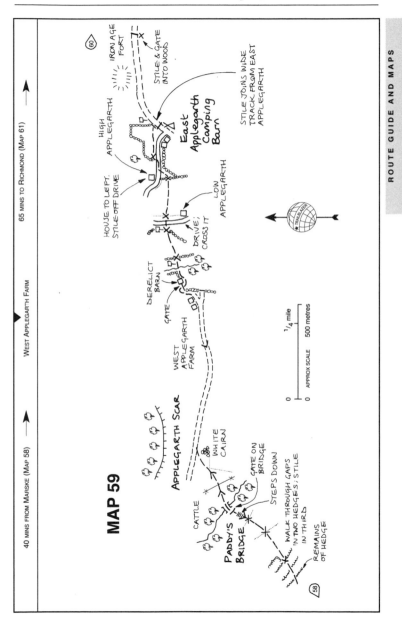

40 MINS FROM MARSKE (MAP 58)

WEST APPLEGARTH FARM

65 MINS TO RICHMOND (MAP 61)

MAP 59

IRON AGE FORT

STILE & GATE INTO WOOD

HIGH APPLEGARTH

East Applegarth Camping Barn

STILE JOINS WIDE TRACK FROM EAST APPLEGARTH

HOUSE TO LEFT; STILE OFF DRIVE

LOW APPLEGARTH

DRIVE; CROSS IT

DERELICT BARN

GATE

WEST APPLEGARTH FARM

APPLEGARTH SCAR

CATTLE

WHITE CAIRN

GATE ON BRIDGE

STEPS DOWN

WALK THROUGH GAPS IN TWO HEDGES; STILE IN THIRD

PADDY'S BRIDGE

REMAINS OF HEDGE

¼ mile

APPROX SCALE   500 metres

ROUTE GUIDE AND MAPS

65 MINS FROM WEST APPLEGARTH FARM (MAP 59) TO RICHMONDSHIRE CRICKET CLUB (MAP 61)

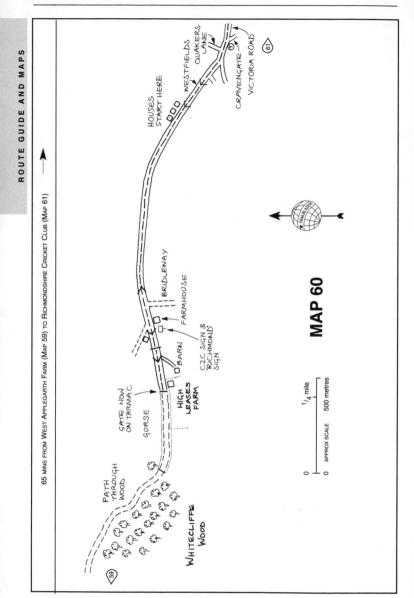

MAP 60

1/4 mile

0 ——— APPROX SCALE
0 ——— 500 metres

WESTFIELDS
QUAKERS LANE
VICTORIA ROAD
CRAVENGATE
61
HOUSES START HERE
BRIDLEWAY
FARMHOUSE
C2C SIGN & 'RICHMOND' SIGN
BARN
GATE NOW ON TARMAC
HIGH LEASES FARM
GORSE
PATH THROUGH WOOD
WHITECLIFFE WOOD
59

RICHMOND   MAP 61

Up above a castle! Down below a stream!
Up above a ruin! Down below a dream!
Man made the castle, rude, forbidding, bare.
God made the river, swift, eternal, fair.
From the recollections of **Mr M Wise** as
recorded in *Richmond Yorkshire in 1830s*
(Wenham Publishers 1977).

This is the largest settlement on the Coast
to Coast and feels like it too. Richmond is a
busy market town that grew parasitically
around the **castle**, built by one Alan the Red
in the 11th century.

As the castle fell into disrepair over
time some of its stones were pillaged to
build the surrounding houses, giving the
entire town the same sombre hue as the castle. As that castle, and the reason for the
town's existence, disintegrated still further,
Richmond discovered a new source of pros-
perity as, curiously, the foremost cabinet-
making town in the country during the
Georgian era at the end of the 18th century.
Many of the buildings leading off the main
market-place date back to this era (indeed,
the town museum is housed in a former
cabinet-maker's workshop), and in addition
there's a **Georgian theatre**, said to be the
finest in the country, particularly following
its restoration in 2003.

Dominating the centre of the town is
its large cobbled **market-place**, while off it
run small winding alleys, known as *wynds*.
Most of the town's attractions can be found
on or near this market-place, though a couple of the ruins nearby also warrant further
investigation. The size and scale of the
town – to say nothing of the noise, the bus-
tle and the traffic – may come as something
of a shock to Coast to Coasters used to
smaller and more genteel settlements. But
Richmond does have its advantages too,
particularly in terms of the facilities it provides, as well as enough sights to keep
amused those who decide to rest for a day
in the town.

Services

The **tourist office** (☎ 01748 850252; 🖳 www
.yorkshiredales.org, open daily in summer
9.30am-5.30pm), on the junction of Victoria

and Queens roads, is extremely helpful and
stocks all manner of souvenirs, books and
brochures about nearby attractions. There's
also a Richmond **website** (🖳 www.rich
mond.org.uk/), that's worth checking out
before you arrive in town.

On the subject of the internet, the
library (Mon, Tue, Fri 9.30am-7pm, Thu
9.30am-5pm, Sat 9.30am-4pm; Wed and
Sun closed) has a **free internet** service and
ten terminals, making this the best place on
the trail to check email.

The **post office** (Mon-Fri 9am-
5.30pm, Sat 9am-12.30pm) does foreign
exchange and all the major **banks** are rep-
resented on the main square, including
HSBC, NatWest and Barclays. All have
cashpoints. Having got your money you'll
then want something to spend it on. The
trekking shop, Yeoman's, on Finkle St is
worth checking out for replacement equipment. It also stocks Camping Gaz. Studio 5
on Bargate is Richmond's **camera shop**;
Boots the Chemist on the main square also
stocks film and a few cameras. A second
pharmacy, Richmond Pharmacy, can be
found on King St.

Castle Hill **Bookshop**, below the castle, has a good selection on local history.
For **food shopping** there's a Somerfield
between the Kings Head and Castle Tavern
on the main square, and a Co-op superstore
(Mon-Fri 8am-10pm, Sat 8am-8pm, Sun
11am-5pm) to the north of Grey Friars
Tower.

Where to stay

There are no hostels in Richmond, and the
nearest campsite is the **camping barn** at
Applegarth (see p162). The only realistic
option, therefore, is to take a room at a B&B
or hotel. If you haven't pre-booked a place,
your best bet is the tourist office which runs
a free accommodation-booking service.

There's a good chance you'll end up
staying on Frenchgate, which has plenty of
B&Bs. *Willance House* (☎ 01748 824467;
🖳 www.willancehouse.com; 1S/2D/1F) at
No 24 is an oak-beamed house dating back
to the 17th century. It's named after the first
alderman of Richmond and stands just a

ROUTE GUIDE AND MAPS

few yards off the main square. All rooms are en suite and rates start at £30/27.50 sgl/dbl. Further up this road, away from the square is *Frenchgate Guesthouse* (☎ 01748 823421; 2D/1T), 66 Frenchgate, which, like the others, has superb views down to and across the Swale; rates start at £65 per room.

Almost opposite Willance House is the smart *Frenchgate Restaurant & Hotel* (59-61 Frenchgate; ☎ 01748 822087; ⌨ www .frenchgatehotel.com; 2S/4D/4T/1F) where all the rooms are en suite, come with all mod cons and start at £58/49 sgl/dbl.

Across town from Frenchgate, two other great options stand near each other close to the bridge. *Restaurant on the Green* (5-7 Bridge St; ☎ 01748 826229; 1D/1T) is a handsome Grade II William and Mary house that was rebuilt in 1689 and which has some wonderful features, including two magnificent 18th-century sundials. Rates here start at £25.

On the other side of the small Green is *The Old Brewery Guesthouse* (☎ 01748 822460; ⌨ www.oldbreweryguesthouse .com; 1S/3D/2T), another Grade II Georgian building. Most rooms are en suite and rates start at £25 for a single (not en suite) and £29 for a double.

On the square itself is the *Kings Head* (☎ 01748 850220; ⌨ www.kingsheadrich mond.co.uk; 30 rooms), part of the Best Western chain and probably the smartest hotel in town, though it doesn't look much on the outside. All rooms are en suite and start at £78/54 sgl/dbl for B&B.

Another excellent choice is *Nuns Cottage* (☎ 01748 822809; ⌨ www.nuns cottage.co.uk; 2D/1T), 5 Hurgill Rd, which is actually three cottages converted into one Grade II listed house. The house is lovely and filled with antiques and guests are welcomed with a sherry and find fresh fruit in the room and a video recorder (with videos); nevertheless, the favourite part for most trekkers is the enclosed garden surrounded by high stone walls, a wonderfully tranquil sanctuary from the hubbub outside. B&B here starts at £35 for one night or £32.50 for two nights or longer.

Other places to stay include: *Windsor House* (☎ 01748 823285; 9 Castle Hill; 1S/5D/4T all with shared facilities, from £18/25 sgl/dbl); *Pottergate Guesthouse* (4 Pottergate; ☎ 01748 823826; 1S/2D/2T/1F, £27.50 en suite, £22 shared bathroom); and *Emmanuel Guesthouse* (☎ 01748 823584; 41 Maison Dieu; 2S/3T/1F some rooms en suite; from £22 per person).

Where to eat

Our favourite tearoom is *Mary's*, overlooking the town square from its first-floor location just down from the entrance to the Green Howards Museum. The menu is large and changes regularly and the walls here are decorated with original works of art that also change frequently. Another recommended eatery is the *New Frenchgate* (☎ 01748 824949; ⌨ www.frenchgatecafe .co.uk), on Frenchgate, open 11am to 5pm and 6pm to late, with the menu offering tapas for £3.50 during the day and changing to à la carte after 6pm. It's a good place for a coffee during the day and does a fine tomato and onion salad with Swaledale goats' cheese (£4.50). In our opinion it's also the best place for vegetarians. Of the many other tea shops that decorate Richmond's streets, the *Richmond Tearooms* (daily 10am-4pm) on Queens Rd and *Harvey's Café* on Rosemary Lane are probably the best places for a full English breakfast (£4.95 and £4.35 respectively). Across the street from Harvey's is the more contemporary *Kat's Café* (daily 11am-1am) where the quiche is a very affordable £3.50.

Richmond is well-served by fish and chip shops, the most popular of which is probably *Richmond Fisheries*, just off the main square at 4 Newbiggin and open daily. All manner of food is served here, including the unfussy nosh boxes, where for £1.80 you get a plastic carton filled with chips and kebab meat. There is another chippie in the centre of the market-place.

For a quick bite of a different kind there are pizzas to takeaway at *Pizza Figaro* (☎ 01748 825995; daily 4pm-late) on Rosemary Lane and an excellent sandwich shop, *Tasty Macs*, with a menu the

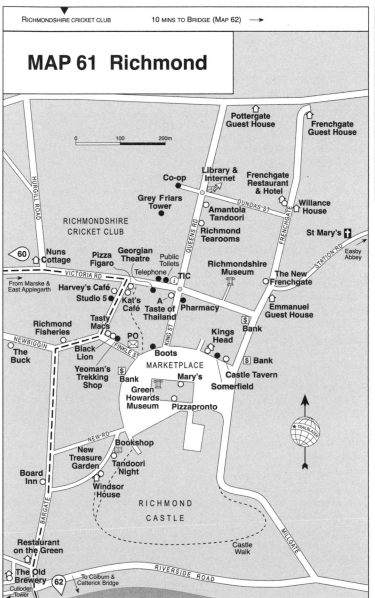

RICHMONDSHIRE CRICKET CLUB   10 MINS TO BRIDGE (MAP 62) ⟶

MAP 61 Richmond

0   100   200m

Pottergate Guest House

Frenchgate Guest House

Co-op

Library & Internet

Frenchgate Restaurant & Hotel

Willance House

Grey Friars Tower

Amantola Tandoori

DUNDAS ST

RICHMONDSHIRE CRICKET CLUB

Richmond Tearooms

St Mary's

60 Nuns Cottage

Pizza Figaro

Georgian Theatre

Public Toilets

Richmondshire Museum

FRENCHGATE

STATION RD

Easby Abbey

HURGILL ROAD

VICTORIA RD

Telephone

TIC

The New Frenchgate

From Marske & East Applegarth

Harvey's Café

Studio 5

Kat's Café

A Taste of Thailand

Pharmacy

Emmanuel Guest House

QUEENS RD

Richmond Fisheries

Tasty Mac's

PO

Kings Head

Bank

NEWBIGGIN

The Buck

Black Lion

Yeoman's Trekking Shop

Bank

Boots

MARKETPLACE

Mary's

Green Howards Museum

Pizzapronto

Bank

Castle Tavern

Somerfield

KING ST

FINKLE ST

Board Inn

NEW RD

New Treasure Garden

Bookshop

Tandoori Night

Windsor House

RICHMOND CASTLE

BARGATE

Restaurant on the Green

The Old Brewery

62

Culloden Tower

To Colburn & Catterick Bridge

RIVERSIDE ROAD

Castle Walk

MILLGATE

TRAILBLAZER

size of a wall, on Finkle St. Prices start at a bargain £1.30. Food is served up in the *Black Lion* (5.30-9pm), on the market square.

For more exotic flavours, there's an Indian restaurant, *Amantola Tandoori* (☎ 01748 826070; Sun-Thu 5.30-11.45pm, Fri-Sat 5.30pm-12 midnight), on Queen's Rd, and another, *Tandoori Night* (☎ 01748 826677) on Castle Hill, while *New Treasure Garden* (☎ 01748 826085/ 825827; Wed-Mon 6-11pm), 7 Castle Hill, is a good Cantonese restaurant with an interesting Szechuan selection; if you're unfamiliar with this spicy Chinese fare, you may care to try the Szechuan House special, which has a sample of every dish (including dishes made from chicken, squid, bean curd, duck and pork), much of it covered with a special sauce made with chillies, garlic, 'five spicy powder' and yellow bean sauce. *A Taste of Thailand* (☎ 01748 829696, daily 5-11pm) on King St has been recommended and has everybody's favourite Thai dish, green curry, for around £8.

The smartest place to eat is said to be the *Kings Head*, and with dishes such as the exquisite gin-marinated venison steak with camargue rice, grape mustard jus and red onion marmalade, it's hard to disagree. However, for a more intimate experience visit the five-table candle-lit *Restaurant on the Green*, with its enormous 17th-century inglenook fireplace. The wine list here, full of Bordeaux and Rhone reds, is particularly impressive.

The *Frenchgate Restaurant and Hotel* (12noon-2pm, 7-9pm, Tue-Sun) is another good, if expensive, choice for a relaxed evening's dining with venison at £14.95 and duck for £12.95.

For drinking, there are plenty of pubs lining the main square, though often they are extremely noisy and a couple seem to cater largely to groups of local youths looking for a fight. Nevertheless the Castle Tavern is quieter during the day and does cheap pub grub from £3.50. A more pleasant option is *The Buck* on Newbiggin which, though it still has loud music playing, is a lot more friendly and relaxed and has great views across the river. Further

down on Bargate is the *Board Inn*, a quiet freehouse.

What to see

The following sites of interest are all listed at 🖳 www.richmond.org.uk.
● **Richmond Castle** (☎ 01748 822493) Without Richmond Castle it is arguable that there would be no Richmond and while it ceased performing the proper duties of a castle years ago, in the middle of the 18th century it found alternative employment as a tourist attraction and has been welcoming visitors ever since. The castle is open daily from April to September, 10am-6pm (Oct-Mar, Thu-Mon, 10am-4pm), and charges £3.60 adult, £2.70 with concessions, £1.80 children, under 5s free, family ticket £9.

Visitors are advised not to rush headlong to the ruins, but instead should take time to visit the **exhibition** in the reception building first; it gives a thorough account of the history of the castle and the town – and how historians have pieced this history together – as well as a display on how the castle was built. There's also an interesting section on conscientious objectors (absolutists) who refused to fight and were held captive here during the First World War. Their poignant graffiti still exists on the cell walls, though for protection these cells are today kept locked; copies of the graffiti, however, have been made and can be seen in the exhibition.

Advancing to the ruins themselves, you may be a little disappointed at first by the lack of surviving structures within the castle walls, though by being patient and reading thoroughly the information boards dotted around, you should get a reasonable idea of how the castle once looked. Scholars will be excited by the ruins of **Scolland Hall**, the finest ruins left from Alan the Red's time; most visitors, however, will find the views from the **keep** overlooking the town far more engrossing.
● **Richmondshire Museum** (☎ 01748 825611) Another surprisingly absorbing local museum, similar in terms of content to Reeth Museum though bigger and with even more impressive exhibits, the Richmondshire Museum is open daily from

Good Friday to 31 October (closed the rest of the year) 10.30am to 4.30pm and has an entrance fee of £2/1. Highlights include Cruck House, a 15th-century building moved wholesale from Ravensworth in 1985, an exhibition tracing the history of transport (including an original penny farthing), and, most popular of all, the set of the surgery of the TV version of James Herriot's *All Creatures Great and Small*.

● **Green Howards Museum** (☎ 01748 826561; 🖳 www.greenhowards.org.uk) Richmond has a long military association and is the garrison town of Catterick (now, surprisingly, larger than Richmond itself!). The town's regiment, the Green Howards, have their own museum and headquarters in the heart of the town (open Feb-Nov, Mon-Sat 9.30am-4.30pm, Sun 2-4.30pm; £3/2.50, children free) in the former Holy Trinity Church, right in the middle of the market-place. The top floor is the most interesting for those with no specific connection to the regiment, explaining the history of the regiment, though the 3500-strong medal collection on the second floor is little short of staggering, and the display by the entrance on POWs is interesting. At the time of writing the museum was expecting to close temporarily towards the end of 2006 for refurbishment.

● **Easby Abbey** Formerly and more properly known as **St Agatha's Monastery**, Easby Abbey, lies about a mile to the east of Richmond Castle. You get a distant view of it from across the Swale during the next stage's walk, but if you've got the time we strongly advise you to pay a proper visit. Like those at Shap, the ruins at Easby were once part of a Premonstratensian Abbey, this one built in 1152, just 31 years after the founding of the order by St Norbert in Prémontré. The monastery served the community for almost 400 years (unlike many other orders who deliberately cut themselves off from the outside world, the Premonstratensians saw it as their duty to administer and serve the laity) until the reign of Henry VIII and the dissolution. Unwilling to bow to Henry's demands that the monastery be closed, the monks joined the Pilgrimage of Grace in 1536, the most popular rebellion against Henry. Many monasteries were briefly restored by the rebels – St Agatha's at Easby among them – though after they were defeated, Henry set about exacting a chilling revenge on those monasteries who had dared to defy his orders, instructing his forces in the north to

'cause such dreadful execution upon a good number of inhabitants, hanging them on trees, quartering them and setting their heads and quarters in every town, as shall be a fearful warning'.

While visiting, be sure to check out the parish church here at Easby, which has survived in remarkable condition and plays host to some wonderful 13th-century **wall paintings**. Look out, too, for the 12th-century **panel of glass** depicting St John.

Other sights There are a couple of magnificent ruined towers. The first you'll come across is **Grey Friars Tower**, in the gardens behind the tourist office. This was once part of a Franciscan monastery, founded in 1258, though the tower itself wasn't built until sometime around 1500. The second, clearly visible to the west of town from Richmond Castle, is **Culloden Tower**, a folly dating back to 1746. Amazingly, it is now a novelty holiday cottage let out by the Landmark Trust.

Transport (see also pp43-5)
The nearest **railway station** is in Darlington, but there are plenty of **buses** from the market-place. Bus Nos 29, 34 and X59 run to Darlington, taking around 45 mins. Bus No 30 runs back up the Swaledale Monday to Friday, calling at Reeth (5-7/day), Gunnerside (4-6/day) and Keld (2-3/day). On Saturday there are 3/day all the way through to Keld plus the 30A runs 2/day to Reeth. Cheaters who wish to skip some of the next section can catch one of the many buses to Catterick Bridge or Brompton-on-Swale.

There are plenty of other services to nearby villages and towns; ask at the tourist

ROUTE GUIDE AND MAPS

office for details. **National Express** do not operate to Richmond, though coaches go from Darlington to a number of cities in Britain including Edinburgh, Liverpool, Newcastle and London; you can book tickets at Richmond tourist office. For a **taxi** call Amalgamated Taxis (☎ 01748 822269) or Top Taxis (☎ 01748 821414).

STAGE 10: RICHMOND TO INGLEBY CROSS   MAPS 61-72

This is another long stage, so long that we strongly advise you break it up with a night at Danby Wiske. True, there is something to be said for completing the walk across the **Vale of Mowbray** that separates Swaledale from the Cleveland Hills as quickly as possible. It is, after all, a fairly uneventful trudge by the lofty standards of the Coast to Coast, much of it conducted on roads. Indeed tackling it all in one go is what Wainwright recommends. It's true, too, that the terrain is largely flat and though **23 miles (37km, 8¾hr)**, the distance between Richmond and Ingleby Cross, sounds a long way, it's actually very achievable.

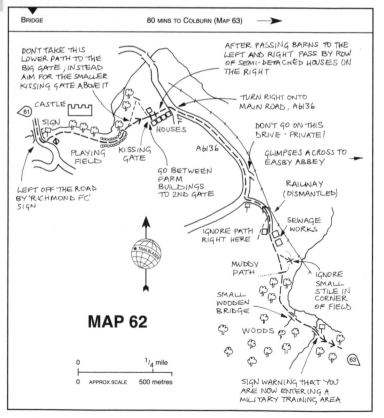

BRIDGE   80 MINS TO COLBURN (MAP 63) ⟶

DON'T TAKE THIS LOWER PATH TO THE BIG GATE; INSTEAD AIM FOR THE SMALLER KISSING GATE ABOVE IT

AFTER PASSING BARNS TO THE LEFT AND RIGHT PASS BY ROW OF SEMI-DETACHED HOUSES ON THE RIGHT

CASTLE

61

SIGN

PLAYING FIELD

KISSING GATE

HOUSES

GO BETWEEN FARM BUILDINGS TO 2ND GATE

TURN RIGHT ONTO MAIN ROAD, A6136

DON'T GO ON THIS DRIVE - PRIVATE!

GLIMPSES ACROSS TO EASBY ABBEY ⟶

A6136

LEFT OFF THE ROAD BY 'RICHMOND FC' SIGN

RAILWAY (DISMANTLED)

SEWAGE WORKS

IGNORE PATH RIGHT HERE

MUDDY PATH

IGNORE SMALL STILE IN CORNER OF FIELD

SMALL WOODEN BRIDGE

WOODS

★ TRAILBLAZER

MAP 62

0   ¼ mile
0   APPROX SCALE   500 metres

63

SIGN WARNING THAT YOU ARE NOW ENTERING A MILITARY TRAINING AREA

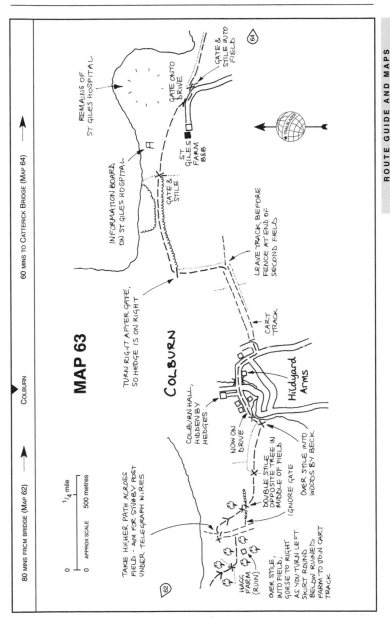

80 MINS FROM BRIDGE (MAP 62) — COLBURN — 60 MINS TO CATTERICK BRIDGE (MAP 64) —

MAP 63

0 ¼ mile
0 APPROX SCALE 500 metres

TAKE HIGHER PATH ACROSS FIELD - AIM FOR STUBBY POST UNDER TELEGRAPH WIRES

62

OVER STILE, INTO FIELD; GORSE TO RIGHT AS YOU TURN LEFT SKIRT ROUND BELOW RUINED FARM TO JOIN CART TRACK

HAGG FARM (RUIN)

DOUBLE STILE OPPOSITE TREE IN MIDDLE OF FIELD

IGNORE GATE

OVER STILE INTO WOODS BY BECK

NOW ON DRIVE

COLBURN HALL, HIDDEN BY HEDGES

COLBURN

Hildyard Arms

CART TRACK

TURN RIGHT AFTER GATE, SO HEDGE IS ON RIGHT

LEAVE TRACK BEFORE FENCE AT END OF SECOND FIELD

INFORMATION BOARD ON ST GILES HOSPITAL

REMAINS OF ST GILES HOSPITAL

GATE & STILE

ST GILES FARM B&B

GATE ONTO DRIVE

GATE & STILE INTO FIELD

64

TRAIL BLAZER

But when Wainwright was researching his book, facilities in Danby Wiske were scarce; in his own words, '*you might, with luck, get a bag of crisps at the inn but certainly not a meal or a sandwich*'. Things have obviously changed for the better, however, and now there are not only two great B&Bs but the pub is an absolute treat. So if you have time, in our opinion there's a lot to be said for spending a morning ticking off a couple more sights in Richmond, before heading on to Danby Wiske in the afternoon.

Starting off with a quick riverside stroll from the southern side of Richmond Bridge, you join the A6136, leaving it by following a lane to the left that leads to the sewage works and then into a gorgeous stretch of riparian woodland. At the top of the woods are the ruins of **Hagg Farm** and, a little way further on, the village of **Colburn** (Map 63). Saxon for 'Cold Brook', Colburn's two dozen houses – plus one enormous stately home, Colburn Hall – are all built, literally, within a stone's throw of the river. This, so the story goes, is because the location of each house was determined by a man throwing stones from the river: where each stone landed, a house was built.

This interesting if implausible story aside, Colburn has little of fascination to the average hiker, though it does play host to the *Hildyard Arms* (☎ 01748 832353) which permits **camping** on their lawn free of charge but there are no facilities except the toilets in the pub (and they are only open in the evenings). Also, the pub does not serve food.

From Colburn the path skirts the eastern side of the last cottage, crosses two fields and then heads towards and follows the course of the Swale. At one point there's an information board in a field recounting the history of the **St Giles Hospital** that 800 years ago used to stand by the river below the board. Across the field from the hospital site is *St Giles Farm* (☎ 01748 811372; 1T/1D) which does B&B for £25, an evening meal for £15 (£18 with wine) and **camping** for £5 per person.

From here the path continues above the river past *Thornborough Farm* (Map 64; ☎ 01748 811421) where **camping** is possible but very basic (£2 per person, toilet block but no shower, hot water available from the farmhouse), and under the A1 to **Catterick Bridge**. Famous now for its giant racecourse, the name Catterick comes from the Roman name *Cataracta*, meaning waterfall, and a Roman town lies buried underneath the modern settlement. By the bridge is the *Bridge House Hotel* (☎ 01748 818331; 🖥 www.bridgehousehotelcatterick.com; 15 rooms, £50/42.50/95 sgl/dbl/fam).

Further evidence of the Romans can be seen across the bridge where, having taken the riverside path to the right after crossing the Swale, you walk by an ancient wall that many believe was once some kind of Roman embankment. The hamlet of **Bolton-on-Swale** (Map 65) is the next place of note. Don't look for refreshments here – you'll do so in vain – but do visit the churchyard, famous for the **monument to Henry Jenkins**, a local man who lived an unremarkable life; unremarkable that is, except for its length: he was 169 when he died.

More unexceptional field-walking ensues on your way to *Laylands Farm* (Map 65; ☎ 01748 811491, camping possible), followed by the *(cont'd on p180)*

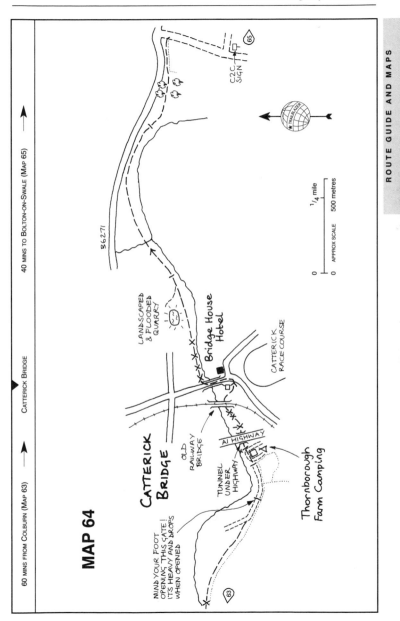

MAP 64

60 MINS FROM COLBURN (MAP 63) →   CATTERICK BRIDGE   40 MINS TO BOLTON-ON-SWALE (MAP 65) →

CATTERICK BRIDGE

MIND YOUR FOOT OPENING THIS GATE! ITS HEAVY AND DROPS WHEN OPENED

Thornborough Farm Camping

TUNNEL UNDER HIGHWAY

A1 HIGHWAY

OLD RAILWAY BRIDGE

Bridge House Hotel

CATTERICK RACE COURSE

LANDSCAPED & FLOODED QUARRY

B6271

C2C SIGN

65

63

0   ¼ mile
0   500 metres
APPROX SCALE

TRAILBLAZER

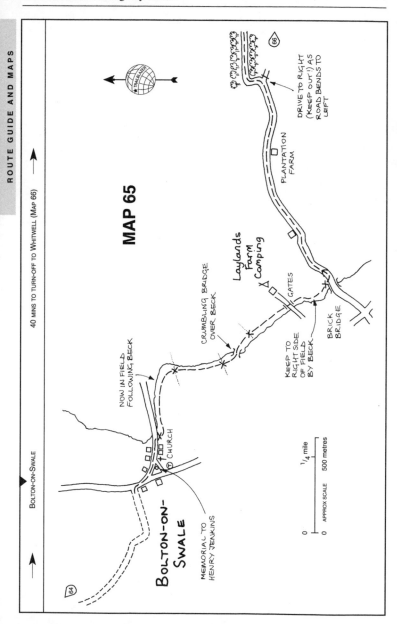

MAP 65

BOLTON-ON-SWALE

40 MINS TO TURN-OFF TO WHITWELL (MAP 66)

★ TRAILBLAZER

BOLTON-ON-SWALE

MEMORIAL TO HENRY JENKINS

CHURCH

NOW IN FIELD FOLLOWING BECK

CRUMBLING BRIDGE OVER BECK

Laylands Farm Camping

GATES

KEEP TO RIGHT SIDE OF FIELD BY BECK

BRICK BRIDGE

PLANTATION FARM

DRIVE TO RIGHT (KEEP OUT!) AS ROAD BENDS TO LEFT

66

64

0   ¼ mile
0   500 metres
APPROX SCALE

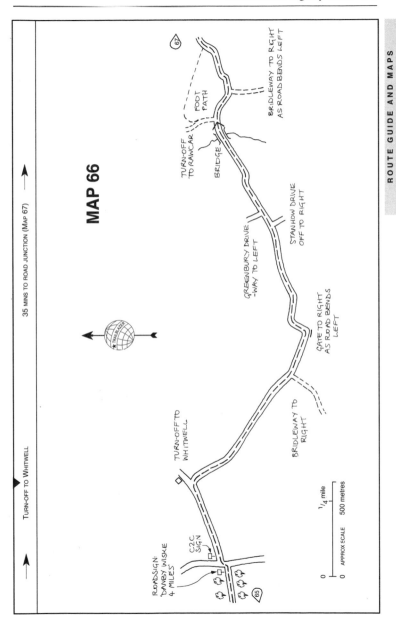

← TURN-OFF TO WHITWELL

35 MINS TO ROAD JUNCTION (MAP 67) →

MAP 66

67

BRIDLEWAY TO RIGHT AS ROAD BENDS LEFT

FOOT PATH

TURN-OFF TO RAWCAR

BRIDGE

STANHOW DRIVE OFF TO RIGHT

GREENBURY DRIVE -WAY TO LEFT

GATE TO RIGHT AS ROAD BENDS LEFT

TRAIN IN RAIN

TURN-OFF TO WHITWELL

BRIDLEWAY TO RIGHT

ROADSIGN: 'DANBY WISKE 4 MILES'

C2C SIGN

65

0 ¼ mile

0 500 metres

0 APPROX SCALE

ROUTE GUIDE AND MAPS

← ROAD JUNCTION

40 MINS TO DANBY WISKE (MAP 68) →

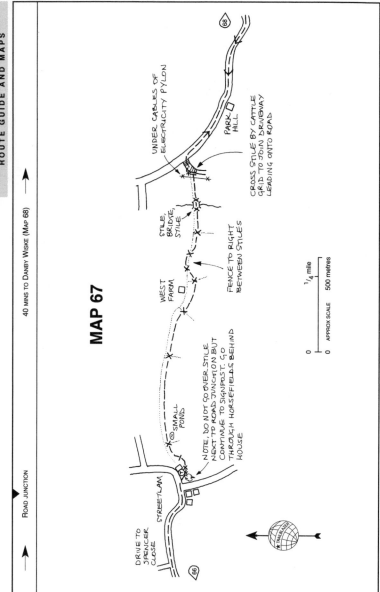

MAP 67

68

UNDER CABLES OF
ELECTRICITY PYLON

PARK
HILL

CROSS STILE BY CATTLE
GRID TO JOIN DRIVEWAY
LEADING ONTO ROAD

STILE,
BRIDGE,
STILE

FENCE TO RIGHT
BETWEEN STILES

WEST
FARM

NOTE. DO NOT GO OVER STILE
NEXT TO ROAD JUNCTION BUT
CONTINUE TO SIGNPOST. GO
THROUGH HORSEFIELDS BEHIND
HOUSE

SMALL
POND

STREETLAM

DRIVE TO
SPENCER
CLOSE

66

0   APPROX SCALE   500 metres
0   ¼ mile

TRAILBLAZER

DANBY WISKE

100 MINS TO RAILWAY (MAP 69)

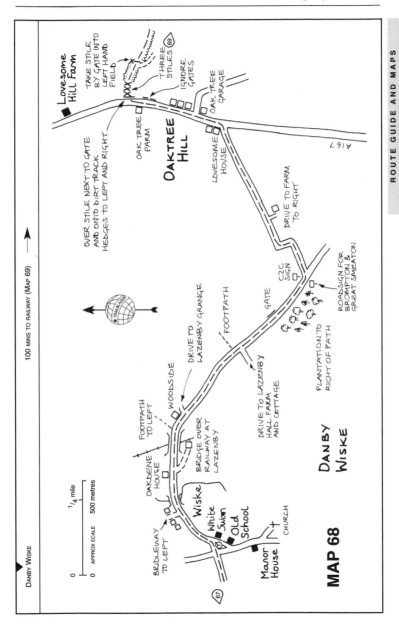

MAP 68

(cont'd from p174) longest stretch of road-walking on the entire trail (Maps 65-8). Though the roads are quiet and the flanking hedges alive with birdsong, you'd be forgiven for dreaming of public transport to help you along this section. Dream on: there is no public transport around here. At **Streetlam** (Map 67) there is an opportunity to leave the road for more fields of pasture and livestock. Negotiate these and rejoin the road leading into Danby Wiske.

DANBY WISKE   MAP 68

It may be only a small place with little to see save for a small but sturdy 11th-century Norman church, but the quality of the accommodation alone justifies spending a night in Danby Wiske.

The pub, *The White Swan* (☎ 01609 770122; 1S/2D/2T/1F), is both the geographic and social heart of the place and has done an awful lot to put the village on the map since Wainwright was rather sniffy about it 30 years ago. The Swan has one en suite room and five others with shared facilities, all with TV, coffee- and tea-making facilities. Rates are £30 in the en suite, £27 otherwise. Note, however, that they do not allow pets.

They also offer **camping** (£5 per person) on the lawn out back in one of the best dedicated campsites on the route, complete with its own separate shower and toilet facilities. The bar is home to an **internet** terminal (£1 for 30 mins) and a useful pinboard for Coast to Coasters to leave messages for their wayward fellow walkers. Food is served in the bar from 12noon to 3pm and 6-9pm.

Stiff competition is provided by *The Old School* (☎ 01609 774227; 1S/1D/2T), a 19th-century schoolhouse 20m away and run by the former owners of the pub. B&B here is £27; all the rooms are en suite apart from one twin. *The Manor House* (☎ 01609 774662; 2S/1D/1T) is on the way to the church, also with B&B from £22.

As for the **church** – one of the very few in England that has no known dedication – only the solid oak door and the font are 11th-century originals, though much of the north aisle is only slightly younger. Look above the main door at the tympanum and you should be able to make out the outlines of three badly weathered figures. They have been interpreted as follows: the central figure is the Angel of Judgement who weighs the soul of the figure on the right using the scales that he holds in his other hand. Though the evil deeds in one of the scale's pans outweigh the good ones in the other, the third figure, the Angel of Mercy (Jesus Christ), has slipped his fingers under the pan containing the bad deeds, thus causing the good deeds to seem heavier.

From the bridge crossing the Wiske outside the village you can see the outline of the Cleveland Hills – our next destination – in the distance. Unfortunately, you still have half the Vale of Mowbray to cross before you get there, much of it, as before, on roads, including this first section to **Oaktree Hill**, a string of houses lining the A167.

Despite the noise of the highway, *Lovesome Hill Farm* (☎ 01609 772311; 🖳 www.lovesomehillfarm.co.uk; 1S/4D/1F) has been highly praised by some walkers for the quality of its accommodation and the opportunity it offers to stay on a 165-acre working farm complete with pigs, cattle and sheep. As well as the **B&B**, with rates starting at £28 per night, the farm also has a **bunkhouse barn** (the farm can supply you with duvets and pillows) that sleeps 10 people for just £6.50 per person, or you can **camp** for just £2. The farm lies about 200m to the north of the Coast to Coast route.

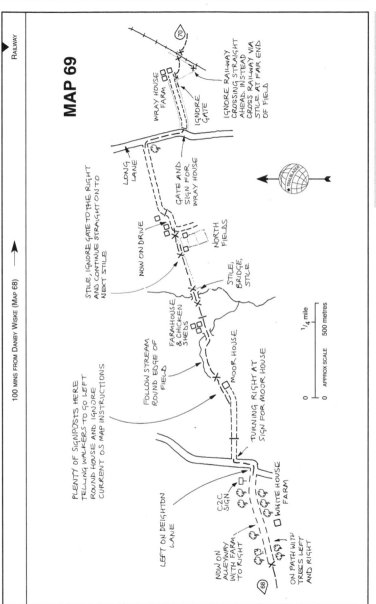

100 MINS FROM DANBY WISKE (MAP 68) →

RAILWAY →

MAP 69

PLENTY OF SIGNPOSTS HERE
TELLING WALKERS TO GO LEFT
ROUND HOUSE AND IGNORE
CURRENT OS MAP INSTRUCTIONS

STILE, IGNORE GATE TO THE RIGHT
AND CONTINUE STRAIGHT ONTO
NEXT STILE

NOW ON DRIVE

LONG LANE

WRAY HOUSE FARM

IGNORE GATE

GATE AND SIGN FOR WRAY HOUSE

IGNORE RAILWAY CROSSING STRAIGHT
AHEAD. INSTEAD CROSS RAILWAY VIA
STILE AT FAR END OF FIELD

70

NORTH FIELDS

STILE, BRIDGE, STILE

FOLLOW STREAM
ROUND EDGE OF FIELD

FARMHOUSE & CHICKEN SHEDS

MOOR HOUSE

TURNING RIGHT AT
SIGN FOR MOOR HOUSE

0   APPROX SCALE   500 metres
0   ¼ mile

LEFT ON DEIGHTON LANE

C2C SIGN

WHITE HOUSE FARM

NOW ON ALLEYWAY WITH FARM
TO RIGHT

ON PATH WITH
TREES LEFT AND RIGHT

68

ROUTE GUIDE AND MAPS

20 MINS FROM RAILWAY ——▶ HARLSEY GROVE FARM ▶ 80 MINS TO A19 (MAP 71) ——▶
(MAP 69)

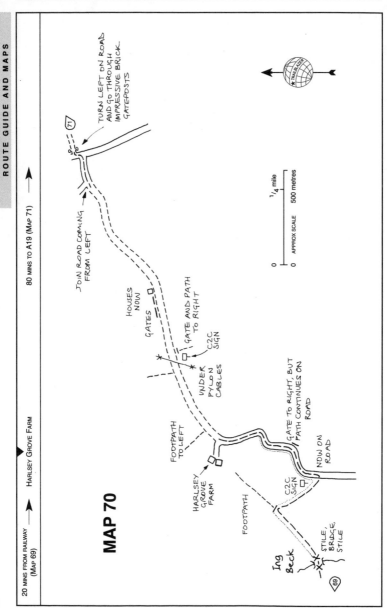

MAP 70

TRAILBLAZER

¹/₄ mile
0
0   APPROX SCALE   500 metres

TURN LEFT ON ROAD
AND GO THROUGH
IMPRESSIVE BRICK
GATEPOSTS

71

JOIN ROAD COMING
FROM LEFT

HOUSES
NOW

GATES

GATE AND PATH
TO RIGHT

C2C
SIGN

UNDER
PYLON
CABLES

FOOTPATH
TO LEFT

HARLSEY
GROVE
FARM

GATE TO RIGHT, BUT
PATH CONTINUES ON
ROAD

NOW ON
ROAD

C2C
SIGN

FOOTPATH

STILE,
BRIDGE,
STILE

Ing
Beck

69

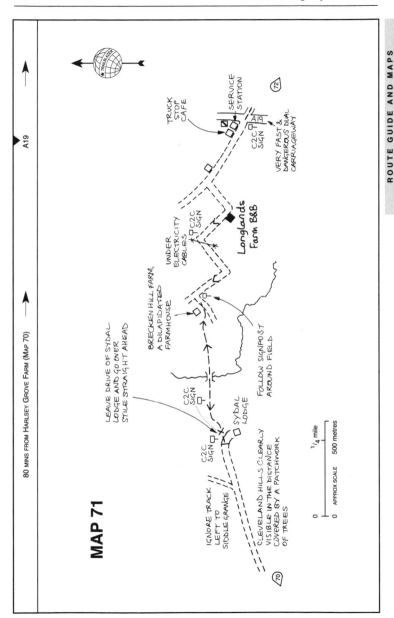

MAP 71

80 MINS FROM HARLSEY GROVE FARM (MAP 70) →

A19 ▶

IGNORE TRACK LEFT TO SIDDLE GRANGE

C2C SIGN

LEAVE DRIVE OF SYDAL LODGE AND GO OVER STILE STRAIGHT AHEAD

BRECKEN HILL FARM, A DILAPIDATED FARMHOUSE

UNDER ELECTRICITY CABLES

C2C SIGN

TRUCK STOP CAFE

SERVICE STATION

C2C SIGN

A19

72

VERY FAST & DANGEROUS DUAL CARRIAGEWAY

Longlands Farm B&B

FOLLOW SIGNPOST AROUND FIELD

C2C SIGN

SYDAL LODGE

CLEVELAND HILLS CLEARLY VISIBLE IN THE DISTANCE COVERED BY A PATCHWORK OF TREES

70

¼ mile

0   APPROX SCALE

0   500 metres

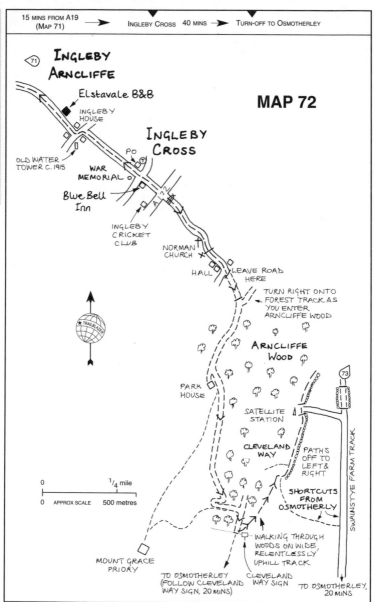

15 MINS FROM A19 (MAP 71) → INGLEBY CROSS 40 MINS → TURN-OFF TO OSMOTHERLEY

71 INGLEBY ARNCLIFFE

Elstavale B&B

INGLEBY HOUSE

INGLEBY CROSS

MAP 72

OLD WATER TOWER C.1915

PO

WAR MEMORIAL

Blue Bell Inn

INGLEBY CRICKET CLUB

NORMAN CHURCH

HALL

LEAVE ROAD HERE

TURN RIGHT ONTO FOREST TRACK AS YOU ENTER ARNCLIFFE WOOD

★ TRAILBLAZER

ARNCLIFFE WOOD

PARK HOUSE

SATELLITE STATION

CLEVELAND WAY

PATHS OFF TO LEFT & RIGHT

73

SWAINSTYE FARM TRACK

SHORTCUTS FROM OSMOTHERLY

0   ¼ mile
0   APPROX SCALE   500 metres

WALKING THROUGH WOODS ON WIDE RELENTLESSLY UPHILL TRACK

CLEVELAND WAY SIGN

MOUNT GRACE PRIORY

TO OSMOTHERLEY (FOLLOW CLEVELAND WAY SIGN, 20 MINS)

TO OSMOTHERLEY, 20 MINS

Opposite the white Oak Tree Farm, a rough track cuts across to White House Farm (Map 69) and on, across Deighton Lane and via a second farm track, to **Moor House**. Negotiating more farms (see Longlands Farm below), a rail track and a beck or two, you emerge at a **truck stop café** (Map 71) by the busy A19. Campers should note that the service station here is the only place, along with the Park House Adventure Centre (see below), on the route leading to the North York Moors where provisions can be bought. Crossing the highway with extreme care, you arrive, around 3¹/₂ to 4 hours after leaving Danby Wiske, at Ingleby Cross.

INGLEBY CROSS & INGLEBY ARNCLIFFE   MAP 72

Sandwiched between two busy 'A' roads, Ingleby Cross and its Siamese twin Ingleby Arncliffe are actually surprisingly peaceful places. Ingleby Cross – little more than the tail-end dangling from its larger neighbour – is named after the war memorial at its heart. Across the road is the **post office** (Mon & Thu 9am-12 noon, Tue 9am-1pm); to the south is a payphone and the Blue Bell Inn.

If you've walked from Danby Wiske and have time to kill, spend it visiting English Heritage's Mount Grace Priory, the best of the ruined abbeys on the Coast to Coast (see the box on p186).

Where to stay and eat

In **Ingleby Arncliffe**, *Elstavale* (☎ 01609 882302; 2D) is conveniently situated and offers B&B starting at £23. A few doors down *Ingleby House* (☎ 01609 882433; 1D/3T not en suite) charges £25. However, they may be closing so check before turning up.

The *Blue Bell Inn* (☎ 01609 882272; 🖳 www.the-blue-bell-inn.co.uk; 5D en

suite) in the centre of **Ingleby Cross** serves very good bar meals and has real ales and real fires. You can also **camp** in the field out the back for £3. B&B starts from £26. *Longlands Farm* (Map 71; ☎ 07767 775221 or 01609 882925, 1D/1T) also does informal B&B – both rooms are en suite and in a static caravan (with Sky TV); rates are £20 per person.

A mile further along the path, Park House (🖳 www.coast-to-coast.org.uk; 24 beds in sgl/twin/dorms), the North York Moors Adventure Centre, was a large place that tended to cater to groups, though not exclusively so, and offered camping in the paddock. The house was something of a spiritual centre for Coast to Coasters, with a shop selling trek memorabilia, maps and so forth. The owners also compiled one of the accommodation guides to the trail. However, Ewen Bennett was killed in December 2004 and the place is now closed.

Should you find that all accommodation has been booked in Ingleby Cross walk on to Osmotherley (see p189) for more options including the nearest youth hostel.

STAGE 11: INGLEBY CROSS TO BLAKEY RIDGE   MAPS 72-81

At **23 miles (37km, 8¹/₄hr)**, this is another stage that many walkers prefer to split into two. Unfortunately, there is no accommodation on the route that allows you to do this easily, thus placing you on the horns of a dilemma: split the walk in two, leaving the trail at **Clay Bank Top** to divert to one of the nearby villages such as Great Broughton to the north or Urra to the south? Or attempt the long march to Blakey Ridge in one go and to hell with the blisters? One argument in favour of the first option is that dividing the stage into two parts does, of course, allow for a more leisurely walk. On the next day, having returned to Clay Bank Top from your accommodation, you can then walk

(continued on p188)

❏ Mount Grace Priory

When a heritage site advertises itself by saying that it has one of the most remarkable medieval drainage systems in the country, you'd be forgiven for thinking that there's not much point in visiting. But you'd be wrong: the Priory of Mount Grace is the perfect place to potter about for an afternoon if you've taken the short hike from Danby Wiske in the morning and are wondering what to do with yourself for the rest of the day.

The best way to reach the priory is to continue on the Coast to Coast from Ingleby Cross, taking the right-hand fork just after the turn-off for Park House. (Those staying in Osmotherley should visit the priory on their way to the village. From the priory there is a path that leads up the hill to rejoin the Coast to Coast trail just before the turn-off to Osmotherley. See Map 72 p184 for details.)

The priory is open 10am-6pm daily and charges an **entrance fee** of £3.50/£2.60 adult/concessions; don't be tempted to duck out of paying, even though the path from the Coast to Coast trail brings you out at the gate at the back of the priory, while the ticket office is by the front. Look out for the pair of tame pheasants, by the way, which hang around the cottage by the back gate to greet visitors.

Mount Grace Priory was built by the **Carthusian** order, a very ascetic sect founded in 1084 by St Bruno, a canon of the Cathedral Church of Rheims. He established a religious community that settled at La Grande Chartreuse near Grenoble, from which we get the name Carthusian (and also the word for all Carthusian monasteries, which are known as charterhouses).

St Bruno and his followers saw the world as inherently wicked. For this reason they lived as hermits, so as not to be distracted by the temptations on offer. The monastic order that evolved from this community followed much the same principles. The prior was the only person in the monastery allowed access to the outside world, while each monk lived an essentially solitary existence, eating his meals alone and spending much of his life in his cell. The monk's day was fairly hard, rising at 5.45am and returning to bed only at 2.30am the next morning following a day spent mainly in prayer or contemplation.

Mount Grace Priory, founded in 1398, had 25 cells in total. We have two main people to thank for the preservation of the monastery. James Strangways bought the land from the government in 1540, immediately following the priory's dissolution on December 18, 1539, yet did not destroy the church as required by law at that time. Instead he let it stand as it was, intact save for the roof, possibly because his parents and grandparents had all been buried on the site. More than two centuries later, Sir Lowthian Bell bought the adjoining 17th-century house, in 1899, and during the course of his 30-year residency did some restoration to the priory, including the first attempt to rebuild cell number 8.

The priory today, though definitely a ruin, is an absorbing one, and one that clearly shows in its foundations the basic layout of the place. The restoration of **cell number 8** also makes clear that, for their time, these cells were remarkably comfortable, built on two floors with cabinets, a loom, a small bed, water closet and a small garden.

And the **drainage system**? Well with latrines fitted and clean water piped into every cell, the water supply and drainage system were indeed ahead of their time. Little of the system remains today save for the channels in which the water flowed all around the priory.

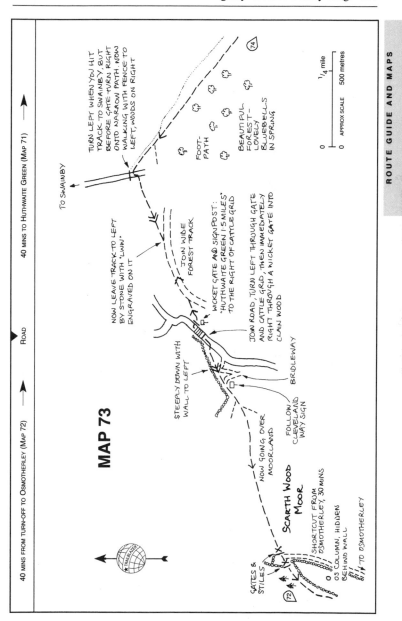

MAP 73

TO SWAINBY

TURN LEFT WHEN YOU HIT TRACK TO SWAINBY, BUT BEFORE GATE TURN RIGHT ONTO NARROW PATH NOW WALKING WITH FENCE TO LEFT, WOODS ON RIGHT

FOOT-PATH

BEAUTIFUL FOREST – LOVELY BLUEBELLS IN SPRING

NOW LEAVE TRACK TO LEFT BY STONE WITH 'LWN' ENGRAVED ON IT

JOIN WIDE FOREST TRACK

WICKET GATE AND SIGNPOST: "HUTHWAITE GREEN 1.5 MILES" TO THE RIGHT OF CATTLE GRID

JOIN ROAD, TURN LEFT THROUGH GATE AND CATTLE GRID, THEN IMMEDIATELY RIGHT THROUGH A WICKET GATE INTO CLAIN WOOD

STEEPLY DOWN WITH WALL TO LEFT

BRIDLEWAY

FOLLOW CLEVELAND WAY SIGN

SCARTH WOOD MOOR

NOW GOING OVER MOORLAND

SHORTCUT FROM OSMOTHERLEY, 30 MINS

OS COLUMN, HIDDEN BEHIND WALL

TO OSMOTHERLEY

GATES & STILES

0   ¼ mile

0   APPROX SCALE   500 metres

ROUTE GUIDE AND MAPS

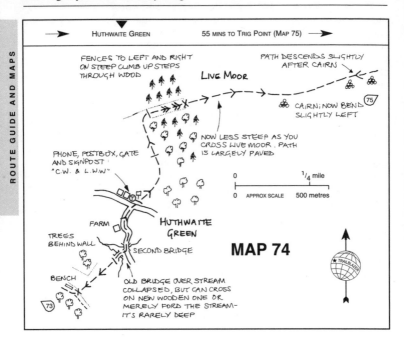

HUTHWAITE GREEN   55 MINS TO TRIG POINT (MAP 75) →

FENCES TO LEFT AND RIGHT
ON STEEP CLIMB UP STEPS
THROUGH WOOD

PATH DESCENDS SLIGHTLY
AFTER CAIRN

LIVE MOOR

CAIRN; NOW BEND
SLIGHTLY LEFT   75

NOW LESS STEEP AS YOU
CROSS LIVE MOOR. PATH
IS LARGELY PAVED

PHONE, POSTBOX, GATE
AND SIGNPOST
"C.W. & L.W.W"

0   1/4 mile

0   APPROX SCALE   500 metres

FARM

HUTHWAITE
GREEN

TREES
BEHIND WALL

SECOND BRIDGE

MAP 74

BENCH

73

OLD BRIDGE OVER STREAM
COLLAPSED, BUT CAN CROSS
ON NEW WOODEN ONE OR
MERELY FORD THE STREAM—
IT'S RARELY DEEP

★ TRAILBLAZER

(continued from p185) beyond Blakey Moor to Glaisdale and even further, so you needn't lose that much time overall. Providing you book your accommodation in advance, the B&Bs at Great Broughton, Urra and the other nearby villages are more than happy to pick you up at Clay Bank Top and deposit you back again the next morning. In my experience, most people seem to choose this alternative.

The second option also has its plus points, however. For one thing, though the first half of this walk is hard, the second half, when you are beginning to tire, is flat and straightforward once you have climbed up Urra Moor as you follow the course of a dismantled railway. And secondly, the destination, the Lion Inn at Blakey, is one of the more memorable places on the route, an atmospheric, isolated haven stranded on a windswept moor.

Thus our advice is as follows: if you are feeling fit and can get a room at Blakey Ridge (see p194; not easy because apart from the pub there is only one other B&B), grab it and attempt the 23 miles in one day. But if not, don't feel too upset, for the B&Bs near Clay Bank Top are fine.

One final thing: campers should note that there is camping at Urra and that the Lion Inn at Blakey Ridge also has a (very windy) campsite.

As for the walk itself, this stage takes us into the third national park on our route, the **Yorkshire Moors National Park**. Depending on the weather, this stage could be a joyful one as you skip merrily up and down the moors, stopping only to admire the iridescent plumage of the pheasant, sniff the gorse, gaze at the heather that turns the moor into a variegated sea of colour, or savour the views south to the idyllic valleys of Farndale or north to the industrial glories of Teeside. Or it could be a miserable, rain-soaked, shelterless trudge through the mud with all views obscured by an enveloping, bone-chilling white mist. Let's hope it's the former.

From Ingleby Cross the walk begins with a climb up past the **Norman church** (note the triple-decker pulpit and purple box pews) and on, above the village, to **Arncliffe Wood**, where the path takes a sharpish turn to the south.

Having passed the turn-off for Park House (see Map 72, p184), and the nearby junction with the path to Mount Grace Priory (see box p186), at the southernmost point of the wood a hairpin bend brings the path onto the Cleveland Way, which you'll follow for almost the entire way to Blakey Moor. (The Cleveland Way, incidentally, is well signposted, so orientation should not be a problem on this stage.) Those wishing to visit Osmotherley should turn off south here through the gate.

OSMOTHERLEY

Though a 30-minute walk off the Coast to Coast trail, Osmotherley is a delight and energetic walkers may want to visit even if they're not staying there. In the centre stands a **market cross** and a **barter table**, believed to be the same one from which John Wesley preached. Indeed, in Chapel Yard you can find what is believed to be the oldest practising **Methodist chapel**, constructed in 1754.

Another sight is **Thompson's**, a shop that has been in the same family since 1786 – and looks it! And finally there's the church, **St Peter's**, which is said to have been built on Saxon foundations.

The most distinctive thing about Osmotherley, however, is its beautiful stone terraced cottages, built for the workers who laboured at the flax mill, now *Osmotherley Youth Hostel* (☎ 0870 770 5982; osmotherley@yha.org.uk; 72 beds; £13.95) at the top end of the village. Just before it, *Cote Ghyll Caravan Park* (☎ 01609 883425; 🖳 www.coteghyll.com) has **camping** for £5.

In the village there is a **post office** inside the small **shop** (Mon-Fri 8.30am-5.30pm; Sat 8.30am-5pm; Sun 9am-5pm) while a little further down the hill, in the heart of the village, is **Osmotherley Walking Shop** (4 West End; ☎ 01609 883818) selling outdoor equipment.

Across the road, the *Queen Catherine* (7 West End; ☎ 01609 883209; 🖳 www.queencatherinehotel.co.uk; 2S/1D/2T all en suite) has the most popular bar in town, with live jazz every other Sunday and some great homemade meals. Rates are £25 per night. The pub is actually named after Henry VIII's wife, Catherine of Aragon, who is believed to have sheltered with monks at the Mount Grace Priory. It is, surprisingly, the only pub named after her in England. The pub is said to be haunted too. Back up the hill a little way is charming *Vane House* (11A North End; ☎ 01609 883448; 🖳 www.vanehouse.co.uk; 3D/4T/1F), with rooms from £30 per person (£40 single occupancy) in high season.

For **food**, the *Queen Catherine* has bar meals (12 noon-2.30pm and 6-9pm) including cod for £6.50 and steak for £10.95. The *Golden Lion* (☎ 01609 883526) is slightly more expensive with meals from around £9, while best of all there's the *Three Tuns* (☎ 01609 883301), also opposite the Green, a chic establishment with meals (12 noon-2.30pm, 5.30-9.30pm Mon-Sat, 12noon-8pm Sun), mainly game and seafood based. The tuna steak is £8.50 while the venison sausages are £8.25. For something lighter try *The Coffee Pot* (☎ 01609 883536), a pleasant little café just round the corner from the walking shop or, cheapest of all, *Osmotherley Fish and Chip Shop* (Wed 5.30-9pm; Thu 12 noon-2.30pm, 5.30-9pm; Fri-Sat 12 noon-3pm, 5-9.30pm).

To rejoin the trail, you needn't return to the junction with the Cleveland Way, but can take a short-cut up the long Swainstye Farm track (found on the left as you walk from the village towards Cote Ghyll camp-site), meeting up with the Cleveland and Coast to Coast paths at the top of Arncliffe Wood (see maps 72-73).

See pp43-5 for details of **bus services** to and from Osmotherley.

The route continues through Arncliffe Wood, over heather-clad **Scarth Wood Moor**, and joins the Lyke Wake Walk in bluebell-carpeted **Clain Wood** before joining the road to **Huthwaite Green**. There is nothing of interest to walkers in this hamlet save, perhaps, a payphone, but it is the gateway to a series of moors, a crossing of which now follows. The first is **Live Moor** (Map 74), reached via a steep climb, much of it on steps, beginning from the gate at the eastern end of Huthwaite. Note the first appearance of a number of stone

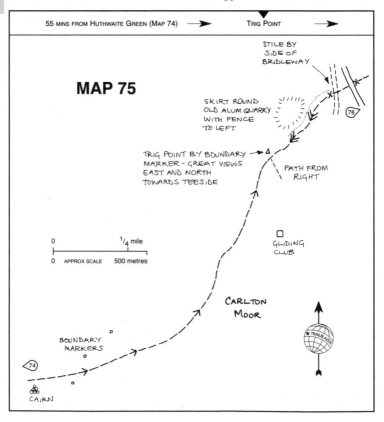

55 MINS FROM HUTHWAITE GREEN (MAP 74) ──▶   TRIG POINT ──▶

MAP 75

STILE BY SIDE OF BRIDLEWAY

SKIRT ROUND OLD ALUM QUARRY WITH FENCE TO LEFT

76

TRIG POINT BY BOUNDARY MARKER - GREAT VIEWS EAST AND NORTH TOWARDS TEESIDE

PATH FROM RIGHT

0   ¼ mile
0   APPROX SCALE   500 metres

GLIDING CLUB

CARLTON MOOR

★ TRAILBLAZER

BOUNDARY MARKERS

74

CAIRN

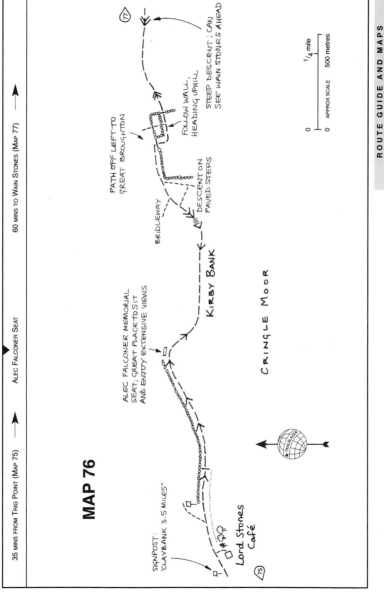

MAP 76

SIGNPOST:
"CLAYBANK 3.5 MILES"

Lord Stones Café

ALEC FALCONER MEMORIAL
SEAT; GREAT PLACE TO SIT
AND ENJOY EXTENSIVE VIEWS

PATH OFF LEFT TO
GREAT BROUGHTON

FOLLOW WALL,
HEADING UPHILL

STEEP DESCENT; CAN
SEE WAIN STONES AHEAD

BRIDLEWAY

DESCENT ON
PAVED STEPS

KIRBY BANK

CRINGLE MOOR

TRAILBLAZER

0   APPROX SCALE   ¼ mile
0   500 metres

boundary markers along the wayside. From here the path drops slightly to moor number two, **Carlton Moor** (Map 75), with its gliding club and runway. At the far end of the moor is a trig point and another boundary marker, from where the path drops steeply round a quarry to a road. Crossing this and its adjacent stile, look for *Lord Stones Café* (Map 76; ☎ 01642 778227, daily 9.30am-5pm) hiding next to a small tree plantation to your right. Half underground and tucked away, it's not the easiest café to find, though it is the only one on this stage – and a fine place too – and thus worth discovering, especially if you missed breakfast as they do big bacon butties for £2. They also have a secret garden where campers have been allowed to stay for free, and they would leave the toilet open for their use too! It's also the only place on this stretch where tap water is available.

From here another steep climb follows – this time up to **Cringle Moor** (Map 76), with the superbly situated **Alec Falconer Seat** at the top, from where one can relax and take in the views over the smokestacks of Teeside. Look closely and you can also make out the isolated peak of Roseberry Topping, as well as the monument to Captain Cook on Easby Moor.

Follow the bends south then east now (towards and then away from the summit of Cringle Moor), skirt the cliffs of **Kirby Bank**, then tackle the steep descent. The Wain Stones are clearly visible on top of the next moor, the gigantic boulders resembling cake decorations atop Hasty Bank (Map 77). From here, the path continues east to Clay Bank Top and the B1527 and, for those staying in one of the nearby villages, a possible rendezvous with your hosts. Those who are pressing on will doubtless be disappointed that the promise by the signpost of a café down the road at the picnic spot turns out to be an empty one.

URRA

Accommodation-wise, the nearest place to Clay Bank Top, the point where the B1527 meets the Coast to Coast path, is at Urra. It also happens to be the most recommended. *Maltkiln House* (☎ 01642 778216; 💻 www.maltkiln.co.uk; 1S/3D or T), lies less than a mile to the south on the road and charges from £19 to £25.

GREAT BROUGHTON

Great Broughton lies two miles to the north of the trail at Clay Bank Top. It boasts several pubs; the walker-friendly *Bay Horse* (☎ 01642 712319), on the High St, is a good choice for both bar meals and more formal two-and three-course meals in their restaurant. Food is served daily from 11.30am to 2pm and 6-9.30pm (12noon-9pm on Sunday).

As far as accommodation goes, almost all B&Bs without exception offer free lifts to and from Clay Bank Top. Of these, *Ingle Hill* (☎ 01642 712449; 3D/1F) has beautiful gardens and the rooms are en suite and all have TV. The tariff starts at £25. *Newlands House* (☎ 01642 712619; 1S/1D/1T) charges £25 en suite, £19 for the single with separate bathroom, and they put homemade cakes in the bedrooms for guests, while *Wainstone's Hotel* (☎ 01642 712268; 💻 www.wainstoneshotel.co.uk) on Great Broughton High St is a rather extravagant choice. The 24 en suite rooms are priced from £44.75 per person for a double or twin and a rather extortionate £72.50 for a single room.

See pp43-5 for details of bus services to and from Great Broughton.

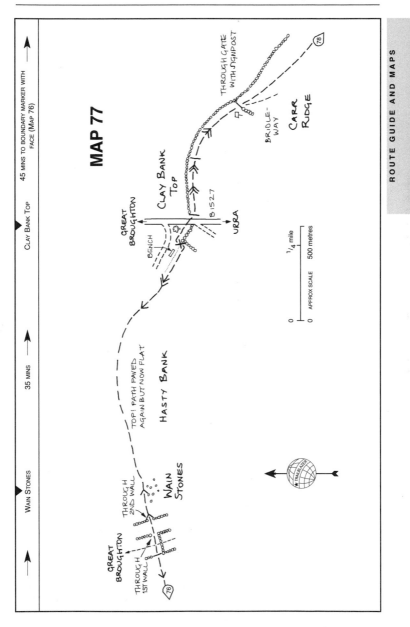

MAP 77

← WAIN STONES | 35 MINS → | ▶ CLAY BANK TOP | 45 MINS TO BOUNDARY MARKER WITH FACE (MAP 76) →

GREAT BROUGHTON

THROUGH 1ST WALL

THROUGH 2ND WALL

WAIN STONES

76

GREAT BROUGHTON

HASTY BANK

TOP! PATH PAVED AGAIN BUT NOW FLAT

GREAT BROUGHTON

CLAY BANK TOP

BENCH

B1527

URRA

THROUGH GATE WITH SIGNPOST

BRIDLE-WAY

CARR RIDGE

78

0 — ¼ mile
0 — 500 metres
APPROX SCALE

TIMBERLAND

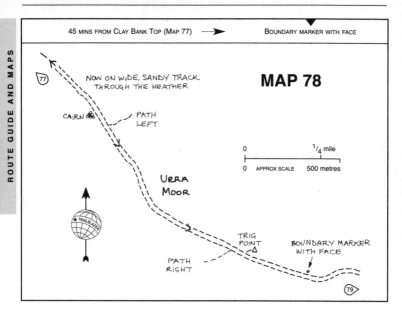

From Clay Bank Top the penultimate steep climb on the Coast to Coast follows, a tough-ish slog through farmland with the sound of cuckoos from the nearby wood mocking every step. After 20 minutes or so **Carr Ridge**, the top of **Urra Moor**, is reached, and thereafter the going is easy. Initially you follow a wide track over the moor past a **trig point** that lies a little way off the path to your left (Map 78). After then passing a boundary marker with a face clearly etched onto it, you arrive at a junction of paths. It is here that the Cleveland Way finally leaves us as, having passed round a couple of green barriers, you join the disused **Rosedale Ironstone Railway** (Map 79) that used to serve the nearby Rosedale iron mines that opened in 1856.

   Passing above the head of pretty Farndale, renowned for its daffodils in spring, the track loops south-east and then eastwards towards your destination, the isolated Lion Inn.

BLAKEY RIDGE   MAP 81

For everybody, be they walkers or drivers, Blakey Ridge *is* the *Lion Inn* (☎ 01751 417320; 🖳 www.lionblakey.co.uk; 1T/6D/3F). The inn is nothing much to look at on the outside. Indeed, it's rather disappointing for those expecting something more rustic. But inside, with its dark time-worn exposed beams and open fires, it looks like the 500 -year-old inn it claims to be. It's quite charming and with B&B from £18 per person for the twin, £25 for a double with shared bathroom or £31 for en suite (rising to £34 for the honeymoon suite with four-poster bed), exceptional value too. The **food**, served at the bar or in the restaurant (daily 12noon-10pm), *(continued on p198)*

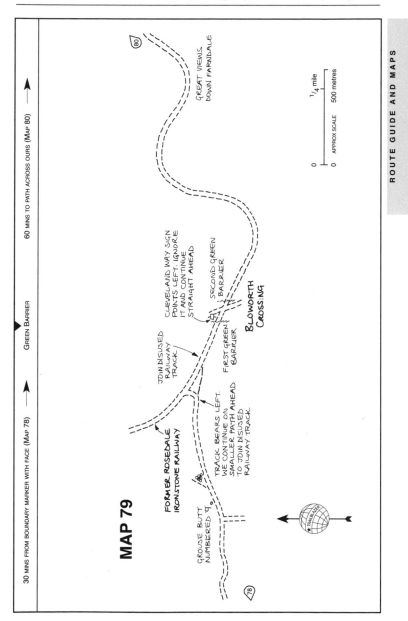

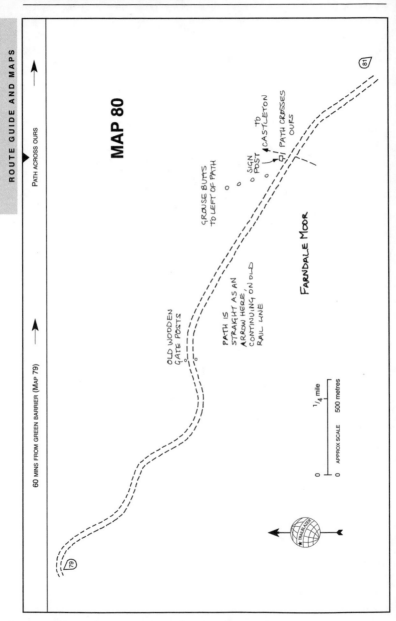

MAP 80

60 MINS FROM GREEN BARRIER (MAP 79) →

PATH ACROSS OURS ▶

79

OLD WOODEN GATE POSTS

PATH IS STRAIGHT AS AN ARROW HERE, CONTINUING ON OLD RAIL LINE

GROUSE BUTTS TO LEFT OF PATH

FARNDALE MOOR

SIGN POST

TO CASTLETON

PATH CROSSES OURS

81

¼ mile

0 ——— APPROX SCALE
0 ——— 500 metres

★ TRAILBLAZER

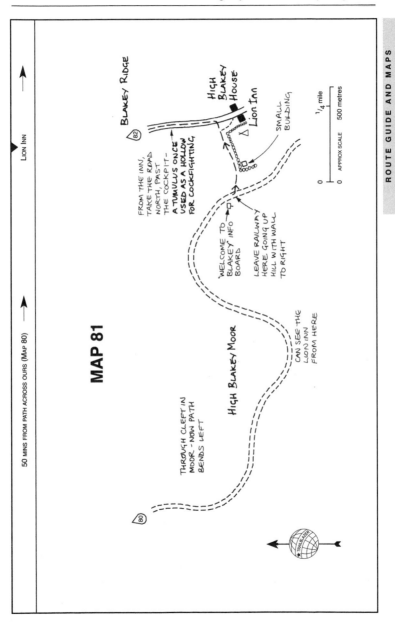

(continued from p194) is tailormade for walkers, being hearty and tasty. Most dishes, which include a sumptuous steak and Guinness pie, come in at about £7.50. **Camping** in the adjacent field costs £2.50 though be warned: there are no showers for campers and there's not much shelter from the wind up there either! Across the road from the inn is the very smart *High Blakey House* (☎ 01751 417186; 🖳 www.high-blakeyhouse.co.uk; 1S/1D/1T), one of the best positioned B&Bs on the whole route. Rates start at £26 per person.

STAGE 12: BLAKEY RIDGE TO GROSMONT   MAPS 81-87

Those of you who have decided to tackle the walk in reverse, from Robin Hood's Bay to St Bees, believing that the Lakes are the highlight and everything else will pale into comparison, are obviously not familiar with the River Esk. For many, particularly those who enjoy cosy English villages hidden amongst the finest, gentlest, most bucolic scenery this country has to offer, the **13¹/₂mile (21.5km, 4¹/₂hr)** stroll down the Esk Valley from Glaisdale to Grosmont is simply the best section of the walk. For charm, only the lakeland villages of Borrowdale, Grasmere and Patterdale come close to matching the extraordinary beauty of Egton Bridge and Grosmont. While of the places still to come, only Littlebeck village and its accompanying wood bears comparison.

As a final destination on this stage, either Egton Bridge or Grosmont will do. Glaisdale, too, for that matter, though if you do choose Glaisdale this stage will then be a very short one, and leave you with a lot to do on the final stage to Robin Hood's Bay.

But first you have to get to the valley, and that means getting down off the moors. The walk begins with a road-walk, following the tarmac north towards **Young Ralph Cross**, which just pokes its head over the horizon as you turn off right onto another road, this one signposted to Rosedale Abbey. Passing the stumpy white cross known as **Fat Betty** (off the path to the left), the official path then takes a quick short-cut, crossing a section of the moor to meet up with the wonderfully named Great Fryup Lane (Map 83). However, parts of this short-cut are extremely boggy – up to waist-deep, in my experience – and unless you want to end up like the dead sheep that occasionally litter this part of the moor it's probably safer to stick to the roads.

Leaving the road to pass **Trough House**, the path can clearly be made out continuing eastwards round the southern side of Great Fryup Dale. Some keen-eyed trekkers swear that they can see the **North Sea** from Trough House, though for most people that particular pleasure will have to wait until the end of **Glaisdale High Moor** where, rejoining the road, the sea is obvious at the far end of the valley.

After a mile of road-walking, Coast-to-Coasters then take the rough track along **Glaisdale Rigg** (Map 85) past various standing stones (and a particularly well-made **boundary marker** to the right of the path) and on down to a junction with a number of paths by a small tarn. Passing through farmland, the path descends to the houses of Glaisdale. *(continued on p204)*

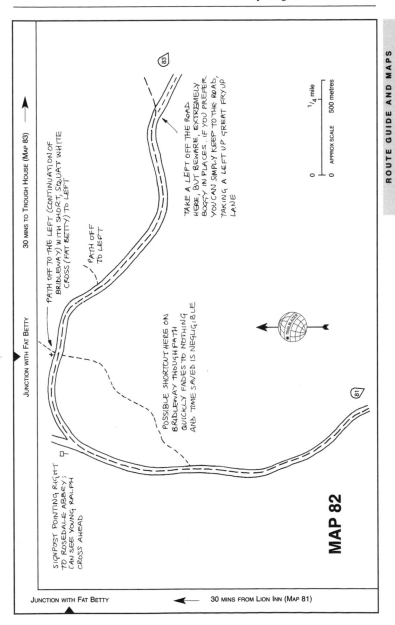

30 MINS to TROUGH HOUSE (MAP 83) →

JUNCTION WITH FAT BETTY

PATH OFF TO THE LEFT (CONTINUATION OF BRIDLEWAY) WITH SHORT, SQUAT WHITE CROSS (FAT BETTY) TO LEFT

PATH OFF TO LEFT

TAKE A LEFT OFF THE ROAD HERE, BUT BEWARE, EXTREMELY BOGGY IN PLACES. IF YOU PREFER YOU CAN SIMPLY KEEP TO THE ROAD, TAKING A LEFT UP GREAT FRYUP LANE

POSSIBLE SHORTCUT HERE ON BRIDLEWAY THOUGH PATH QUICKLY FADES TO NOTHING AND TIME SAVED IS NEGLIGIBLE

SIGNPOST POINTING RIGHT TO ROSEDALE ABBEY; CAN SEE YOUNG RALPH CROSS AHEAD

83

81

MAP 82

APPROX SCALE

0 ———— ¼ mile

0 ———— 500 metres

JUNCTION WITH FAT BETTY

← 30 MINS FROM LION INN (MAP 81)

ROUTE GUIDE AND MAPS

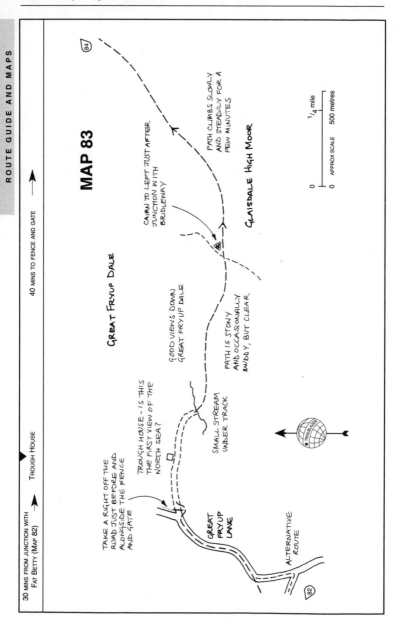

30 MINS FROM JUNCTION WITH FAT BETTY (MAP 82) → TROUGH HOUSE → 40 MINS TO FENCE AND GATE →

MAP 83

GREAT FRYUP DALE

TAKE A RIGHT OFF THE ROAD JUST BEFORE AND ALONGSIDE THE FENCE AND GATE

TROUGH HOUSE - IS THIS THE FIRST VIEW OF THE NORTH SEA?

GOOD VIEWS DOWN GREAT FRYUP DALE

GREAT FRYUP LANE

SMALL STREAM UNDER TRACK

ALTERNATIVE ROUTE

PATH IS STONY AND OCCASIONALLY MUDDY, BUT CLEAR

CAIRN TO LEFT JUST AFTER JUNCTION WITH BRIDLEWAY

PATH CLIMBS SLOWLY AND STEADILY FOR A FEW MINUTES

GLAISDALE HIGH MOOR

0 — — — — 1/4 mile
0 — — — — 500 metres
APPROX SCALE

84

82

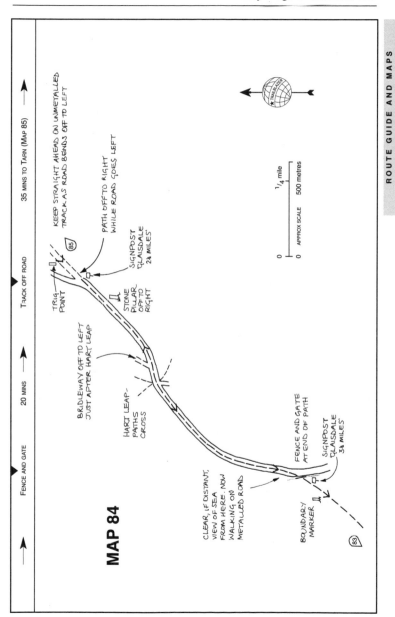

MAP 84

FENCE AND GATE — 20 MINS — TRACK OFF ROAD — 35 MINS TO TARN (MAP 85)

KEEP STRAIGHT AHEAD ON UNMETALLED TRACK AS ROAD BENDS OFF TO LEFT

PATH OFF TO RIGHT WHILE ROAD GOES LEFT

SIGNPOST 'GLAISDALE 2¾ MILES'

TRIG POINT

STONE PILLAR OFF TO RIGHT

85

BRIDLEWAY OFF TO LEFT JUST AFTER HART LEAP

HART LEAP - PATHS CROSS

CLEAR, IF DISTANT, VIEW OF SEA FROM HERE. NOW WALKING ON METALLED ROAD

FENCE AND GATE AT END OF PATH

SIGNPOST 'GLAISDALE 3¾ MILES'

BOUNDARY MARKER

83

APPROX SCALE ¼ mile 500 metres

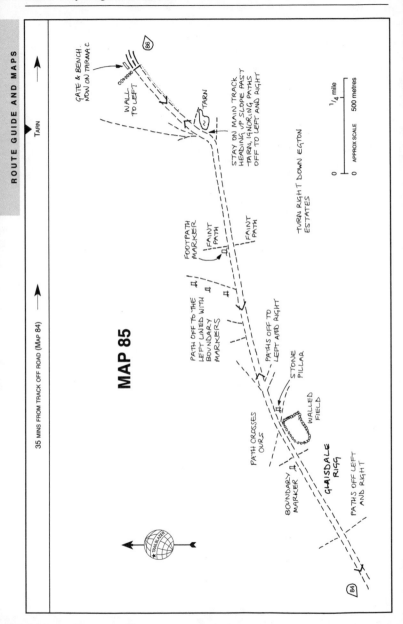

35 MINS FROM TRACK OFF ROAD (MAP 84)

TARN

MAP 85

GATE & BENCH.
NOW ON TARMAC

WALL
TO LEFT

86

TARN

STAY ON MAIN TRACK
HEADING UP SLOPE PAST
TARN, IGNORING PATHS
OFF TO LEFT AND RIGHT

TURN RIGHT DOWN EGTON
ESTATES

FOOTPATH
MARKER

FAINT
PATH

FAINT
PATH

PATH OFF TO THE
LEFT LINED WITH
BOUNDARY
MARKERS

PATHS OFF TO
LEFT AND RIGHT

STONE
PILLAR

WALLED
FIELD

PATH CROSSES
OURS

BOUNDARY
MARKER

GLAISDALE
RIGG

PATHS OFF LEFT
AND RIGHT

84

0   APPROX SCALE   ¹/₄ mile

0   500 metres

★ TRAILBLAZER

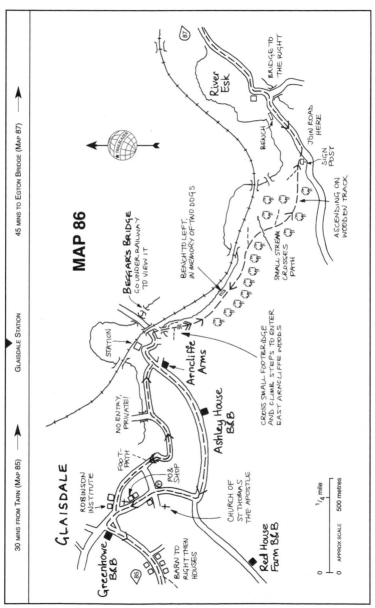

30 MINS FROM TARN (MAP 85) → GLAISDALE STATION ▶ 45 MINS TO EGTON BRIDGE (MAP 87) →

MAP 86

87

BRIDGE TO THE RIGHT

River Esk

TRAIL BLAZER

BEGGAR'S BRIDGE
GO UNDER RAILWAY TO VIEW IT

BENCH

JOIN ROAD HERE

SIGN POST

BENCH TO LEFT, IN MEMORY OF TWO DOGS

ASCENDING ON WOODEN TRACK

SMALL STREAM CROSSES PATH

STATION

Arncliffe Arms

CROSS SMALL FOOTBRIDGE AND CLIMB STEPS TO ENTER EAST ARNCLIFFE WOODS

NO ENTRY, PRIVATE!

GLAISDALE

Robinson Institute

FOOT-PATH

PO & SHOP

Ashley House B&B

CHURCH OF ST THOMAS THE APOSTLE

Greenhowe B&B

85

BARN TO RIGHT THEN HOUSES

Red House Farm B&B

0 — APPROX SCALE — ¼ mile
0 — 500 metres

GLAISDALE   MAP 86

The village of Glaisdale sprawls across its lofty perch overlooking the Esk Valley. The terraced houses that are a feature of the town were originally built to house the ironstone workers in the iron mines of the late 19th century. The **Robinson Institute** is a village hall that also acts as a small theatre.

The late 18th-century **Church of St Thomas the Apostle**, near the upper end of Glaisdale, is notable for its 16th-century wooden font cover and communion table. (Don't be fooled by the '1585' date stone in the side of the steps leading to the tower, for this is from an earlier chapel.) It also contains a picture of Thomas Ferris, the beggar made famous by Glaisdale's other main sight, the **Beggar's Bridge** at the other end of the village. In the 17th century, Ferris, a humble pauper, was courting the daughter of the wealthy local squire. In order to win her hand Ferris thought he needed to improve his standing in the community so with this in mind he struck upon a plan to set sail from Whitby and seek his fortune on the high seas. The night before he put this plan into action, however, Ferris went to visit his beloved who lived across the river. Unfortunately, the river happened to be swollen at the time due to heavy rain and Ferris' dreams of a romantic farewell were dashed. The story, however, does have a happy ending: Thomas returned from his adventures on the sea a wealthy man and married his sweetheart, and with some of his fortune made the Beggar's Bridge so that any other young lovers from the neighbourhood would not, in future, suffer the same torment as Ferris did that night.

As for facilities, the **shop** (Mon-Sat 7am-6pm, Sun 9am-2pm) is also home to the **post office** (Mon, Tue, Thu and Fri 8.30am-12.30pm, 1.30-5.30pm, Wed and Sat morning only).

Where to stay and eat

The first place you come to upon entering the village is *Greenhowe* (☎ 01947 897907; 1S/1D/1T en suite), a red-bricked house overlooking the village with B&B for £25. Down near the train station, *The Arncliffe Arms* (☎ 01947 897555; 2D/2T en suite) charges £28, or £33 for single occupancy. It also does food Mon-Sat 12 noon-2pm, 6-8pm; Sun 6-8pm. *Ashley House* (☎ 01947 897656; 2D/2S) is at the top of the hill above the Arncliffe Arms. B&B starts from £20 here. A quarter of a mile from the path is the award-winning 17th-century *Red House Farm* (☎ 01947 897242; 🖳 www.redhousefarm.com; 1S/3D/1F). Once a working farm and still the home of a number of farm animals, it is often cited as one of the best farm accommodations in the country – and with the farmhouse containing many of its original features it certainly is very, very beautiful. Dogs are welcome, but stabled. B&B is from £30 per person.

Transport (see also pp43-5)

Bus No 99 travels up and down the Esk Valley from Lealholm to Whitby 3-5 times a day, Mon-Sat.

Trains run between the same destinations via Glaisdale four times a day.

From Glaisdale, enter the woods near Beggar's Bridge and continue walking through this idyllic setting along the river until the path winds up to a road, where you should take a left down the hill and into Egton Bridge.

❏ **Important note – walking times**
Unless otherwise specified, **all times in this book refer only to the time spent walking**. You will need to add 20-30% to allow for rests, photography, checking the map, drinking water etc. When planning the day's hike count on 5-7 hours' actual walking.

EGTON BRIDGE   MAP 87

A strong competitor (and in many people's eyes, a clear winner) for the accolade of prettiest village on the Coast to Coast, Egton Bridge is a delight, a village of grand houses surrounding an uninhabited island sitting in the middle of the Esk. Everything about the place is charming, from the bridge itself – a 1990s' copy of the original 18th-century structure washed away in a flood in 1930 – to the stepping stones that lead across to the island and the gigantic mature trees that fringe the village.

The Catholic **St Hedda's Church**, too, is incredibly grand given the tiny size of the village. On the exterior are a series of friezes while inside, behind glass to the right of the altar, are the relics of Nicholas Postgate, a local Catholic priest and martyr hung, drawn and quartered for continuing to practise his faith in 1679.

Where to stay and eat

It would be a surprise if somewhere as gorgeous as Egton Bridge didn't have decent accommodation, and the village doesn't disappoint.

The ***Horseshoe Hotel*** (☎ 01947 895245, 2S/4D/2T), right on the walk at the start of the village, fulfils every expectation of a country inn, with an expansive beer garden, a variety of local ales and a snug interior. Meals are typically around the £7.50 mark and are served daily 12 noon-2pm and 7-9pm. B&B in the double/twin rooms with shared facilities is from £25, from £30 per person in the en suite rooms, and from £35 for a single room.

A little way to the west of the village ***Broom House*** (☎ 01947 895279; 🖳 www .egton-bridge.co.uk; 5D/1F) lies hidden behind its own orchard. A 19th-century farmhouse with plenty of exposed beams and other charming rural features; they charge £32-35 per night.

Above the station, the ***Postgate Inn*** (☎ 01947 895241; 🖳 www.postgateinn.co .uk; 2D/1F) is another top choice with food available throughout the day and B&B for £29.50 per person. To find it, head up the hill from the church.

Transport (see also pp43-5)

Four to five **trains** per day (Mon-Sat) travel in each direction between Whitby and Middlesbrough via Egton Bridge; a Sunday service (4/day) only operates between June and September. In addition, **bus** No 99 travels from Whitby up the Esk Valley to Glaisdale and Lealholm and back 3-5 times a day, Mon-Sat.

The next mile or so from Egton Bridge to Grosmont takes you past the impossibly elegant **Egton Manor** along an old toll road (the original toll charges are still written on a board hanging from **Toll Cottage**, halfway along). It's an easy walk now, taking you under the railway and along by the Esk to Grosmont.

GROSMONT   MAP 87

Tourists and trainspotters alike flock to Grosmont. The steam engines of the privately-run **North York Moors Railway** run for only 18 miles (29km) between here and Pickering, but it's quite a sight watching the trains huff and puff into action. If they seem a touch familiar it is because the railway is regularly used by film crews and in the past has featured in such films as *Brideshead Revisited* and, most famously, the first *Harry Potter* movie.

Rail buffs who still aren't sated can visit the nearby shop selling all manner of train-related stuff, including any number of model railways.

It's definitely worth waiting to see at least one train in motion before leaving Grosmont, and while you're waiting you can take the alleyway leading through a long train tunnel to the **sidings and loco sheds**, which offer a bit of an insight into what it takes to keep these trains on track.

The tunnel is, in fact, one of the oldest train tunnels in the world, one that used to serve George Stephenson's horse-drawn railway. It was during the digging of these tunnels that large amounts of ironstone were uncovered, leading to the start of the iron-stone mining industry in the Esk Valley.

As for the rest of Grosmont, it's a pleasant one-street village that boomed on the back of the ironstone industry and has most of the essentials a trekker needs: a **store**, **pub** (the Station Tavern, of course!), a **jazz café** (in the Grosmont Gallery; sand-wiches from £2.25; daily 11am-5.30pm), two **tearooms** (one on the station platform and one as part of the Hazelwood B&B), National Park information (inside the Railway Shop), and a few small and pleas-ant B&Bs. The **Co-op** (Mon-Sat 7.30am-5.30pm; Sun 9am-5.30pm) is one of the oldest community-run village shops in the country and is also home to the **post office** (Mon-Fri 9am-12noon). There's a church, too, with a boulder of Shap granite outside the west door, deposited here by a glacier back in the Ice Age.

Where to stay and eat

Priory Farm (☎ 01947 895324) sits at the very start of the village and offers **camping** for just £2 per person; for £2 more you can have a continental breakfast too or a packed lunch for £1.50. Use of the shower is £1.50 and there is a convenient 'camping room' a small room of the farmhouse, with a toilet and kettle, left open for campers. *Hazelwood* (☎ 01947 895292; 🖳 www .hazelwoodhouse.fsbusiness.co.uk; 1S/1D/

1T/1F; no pets) is a family-run place at the bottom of the village with a tearoom attached. B&B is just £25 here.

Grosmont House (☎ 01947 895539; 🖳 www.grosmonthouse.co.uk; 1S/2D/1T/ /1F) is a delightful place tucked away behind the Station Tavern, whose gardens have wonderful views over the railway. Rates start at £30, rising to £35 if staying in the en suite double or the en suite double with four-poster. The fresh lobster salad they serve here is said to be awesome.

The *Station Tavern* (☎ 01947 895060; food served Mon-Fri 7-8.45pm, Sat & Sun 12 noon-2.45pm, 7-8.45pm) serves pub grub on enormous plates. They also do B&B (1S/3D) from £25 to £30.

With advance notice some B&Bs pro-vide evening meals.

Transport (see also pp43-5)

The **steam train** (☎ 01751 472508, 🖳 www .northyorkshiremoorsrailway.com) to Pick-ering leaves Grosmont between four and eight times a day depending on the season. The journey takes an hour and ten minutes; an adult return costs £13, and a single £10.50, children are half price. Some of the trains are drawn by a diesel engine rather than a steam engine, so if you want that authentic chuff-chuff sound on your jour-ney check the timetable to see which serv-ices involve the steam engine.

Trains go to Whitby (5/day; 20 mins) and to Middlesbrough (4/day; 70 mins), Mon-Sat; Sunday 4/day June to Sep. **Bus** No 99 also travels to Whitby (3-5/day Mon-Sat; 15 mins) from the railway station.

STAGE 13: GROSMONT TO ROBIN HOOD'S BAY   MAPS 87-95

And so we come to the last stage. But don't be fooled into thinking this is a mere formality as the giant climb out of Grosmont will soon demonstrate. It's a long last leg, just under **15½ miles (25km, 6hr)** in total, with enough ups and downs to ensure that you arrive in Robin Hood's Bay suitably dishevelled. The scenery is largely similar to that which has gone before – namely moorland and, in an echo of the first leg, a few miles of cliff-top walking down the coast. The biggest and most pleasant surprise, however, is Little Beck Wood, a narrow belt of the most heavenly woodland in Yorkshire.

But first, there's the climb up to Sleights Moor, part of the intriguingly named Eskdaleside Cum Ugglebarnby. With views initially down to **Whitby**

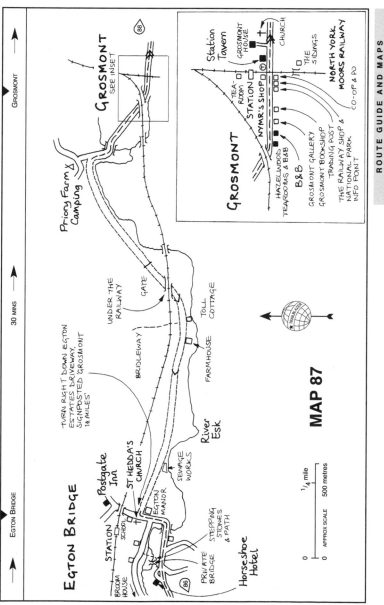

EGTON BRIDGE

30 MINS

GROSMONT

EGTON BRIDGE

Postgate Inn

Station

Broom House

School

St Hedda's Church

Egton Manor

86

Stepping Stones & Path

Private Bridge

Horseshoe Hotel

Sewage Works

River Esk

TURN RIGHT DOWN EGTON
ESTATES DRIVEWAY,
SIGNPOSTED 'GROSMONT
1½ MILES'

Bridleway

Under the Railway

Gate

Farmhouse

Toll Cottage

Priory Farm & Camping

GROSMONT
SEE INSET

88

MAP 87

0   ¼ mile
0   APPROX SCALE   500 metres

TRAILBLAZER

GROSMONT

Station Tavern

Grosmont House

Church

Station

NYMR's Shop

Tea-room

The Sidings

NORTH YORK
MOORS RAILWAY

CO-OP & PO

Hazelwood Tearooms & B&B

B&B

Grosmont Gallery

Grosmont Bookshop

The Railway Shop &
National Park
Info Point

Trading Post

Cathedral to your left, you pass the **High Bride Stones** – five ancient standing monoliths – to the right of the road. (Incidentally, the confusing jumble of the Low Bride Stones stand just below them on a terrace, to your right as you passed over the cattle grid.) Opposite the car park turn onto the path to the left (currently signposted to 'Littlebeck') and follow it down to the meeting with the A169. (Note the orientation of this path is different from that shown on the OS strip maps.) Turning right along the road, a gate opposite heralds the start of the path down through more heather to Littlebeck.

LITTLEBECK   MAP 89

Yet another tiny hamlet with a lengthy past, it's hard to imagine the picturesque rural idyll that is Littlebeck today was actually once the centre of the alum-mining industry in the 17th to 19th centuries. Alum, by the way, is used in dyeing as well as being added to leather to make it supple. One hundred tons of shale would be produced in order to extract one ton of alum, so it seems incredible that there aren't more scars in the surrounding land.

Littlebeck has one other minor claim to fame as the home of master woodcarver Thomas Whittaker (his house, now called Woodcarver's Cottage, is on the bend above Old Mill). Whittaker would 'sign' every piece of furniture he made with a gnome, in German folklore the oak tree's guardian. Above the cottage is Kelp House, where kelp, used in the processing of alum, was stored.

Fifteen minutes from the centre of the village is *Intake Farm* (☎ 01947 810273; 2D/1T/1F), where B&B is from £20 (£25 en suite); they also provide **camping** out the back for £4 and can do an evening meal (£12 for three courses) and a packed lunch (£3.50).

Pretty as Littlebeck is, it's nothing when compared to the incredible beauty that awaits in **Little Beck Wood**. This really is a stunning 65 acres of woodland, filled with oak trees, deer, badgers, foxes and birdlife galore. There are also a couple of man-made features to see on the way including, best of all, the **Hermitage** (see photo opposite this page), a boulder hollowed out to form a small cave. Above the entrance is etched the year 1790.

More delights await as the path from the Hermitage takes you to **Falling Foss** (Map 90), a 30m-high waterfall, and the abandoned **Midge Hall**. In front is a small wooden bridge which you should go over, and a second, larger bridge which you walk towards but not across, heading along the signposted path beside May Beck instead. This will eventually bring you to a car park at the southern extremity of the wood, from where you turn back north and walk along the road above the valley you've just walked through.

A traverse of two moors and a little road walking are all that now stand between you and the coast. Just before the coast the path passes through **Low Hawsker** (Map 92) and **High Hawsker** (Map 93).   (*continued on p215*)

(Opposite) Top: Walkers on Kirby Bank (see p192). **Bottom**: The Hermitage.

(Overleaf) Top left: A most welcome sight for weary walkers: Robin Hood's Bay (see p216). **Top right**: Cottages in the old town, Robin Hood's Bay. **Bottom**: The North York Moors Railway at Grosmont (see p205). (Photos © Jim Manthorpe).

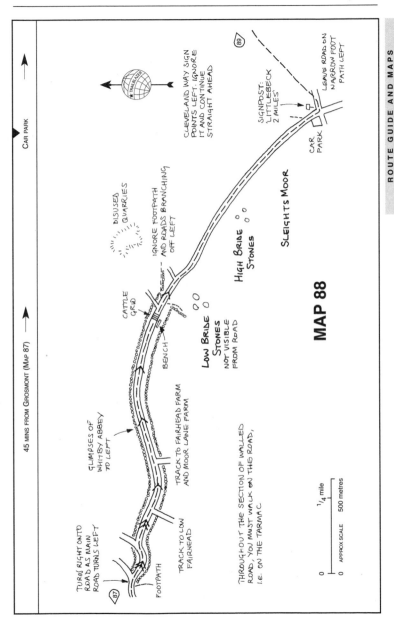

45 MINS FROM GROSMONT (MAP 87) →

CAR PARK

TURN RIGHT ONTO MAIN ROAD AS MAIN ROAD TURNS LEFT

FOOTPATH

TRACK TO LOW FAIRHEAD

GLIMPSES OF WHITBY ABBEY TO LEFT

TRACK TO FAIRHEAD FARM AND MOOR LANE FARM

THROUGHOUT THE SECTION OF WALLED ROAD, YOU MUST WALK ON THE ROAD, I.E. ON THE TARMAC.

BENCH

CATTLE GRID

DISUSED QUARRIES

IGNORE FOOTPATH AND ROADS BRANCHING OFF LEFT

LOW BRIDE STONES
NOT VISIBLE FROM ROAD

HIGH BRIDE STONES

MAP 88

SLEIGHTS MOOR

CLEVELAND WAY SIGN POINTS LEFT. IGNORE IT AND CONTINUE STRAIGHT AHEAD

89

SIGNPOST: LITTLEBECK 2 MILES'

CAR PARK

LEAVE ROAD ON NARROW FOOT PATH LEFT

0   ¼ mile
0   500 metres
APPROX SCALE

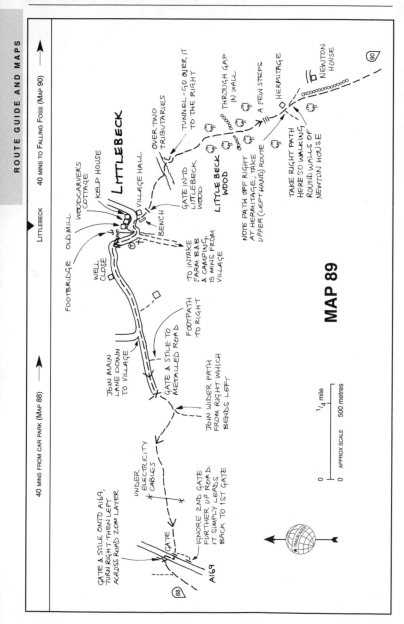

GATE & STILE ONTO A169, TURN RIGHT THEN LEFT ACROSS ROAD 20M LATER

UNDER ELECTRICITY CABLES

IGNORE 2ND GATE FURTHER UP ROAD, IT SIMPLY LEADS BACK TO 1ST GATE

GATE

A169

88

JOIN WIDER PATH FROM RIGHT WHICH BENDS LEFT

JOIN MAIN LANE DOWN TO VILLAGE

GATE & STILE TO METALLED ROAD

FOOTPATH TO RIGHT

FOOTBRIDGE

OLD MILL

WOODCARVER'S COTTAGE

KELP HOUSE

LITTLEBECK

WELL CLOSE

VILLAGE HALL

BENCH

GATE INTO LITTLEBECK WOOD

TO INTAKE FARM B&B & CAMPING, 15 MINS FROM VILLAGE

OVER TWO TRIBUTARIES

TUNNEL - GO OVER IT TO THE RIGHT

THROUGH GAP IN WALL

A FEW STEPS

LITTLE BECK WOOD

NOTE PATH OFF RIGHT AT HERMITAGE, TAKE UPPER (LEFT HAND) ROUTE

HERMITAGE

TAKE RIGHT PATH HERE SO WALKING ROUND WALLS OF NEWTON HOUSE

NEWTON HOUSE

90

MAP 89

¼ mile

APPROX SCALE

500 metres

TRAILBLAZER

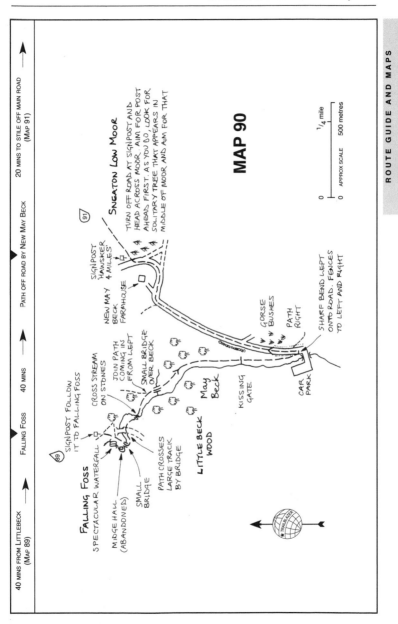

40 MINS FROM LITTLEBECK (MAP 89) — FALLING FOSS — 40 MINS — PATH OFF ROAD BY NEW MAY BECK — 20 MINS TO STILE OFF MAIN ROAD (MAP 91)

MAP 90

FALLING FOSS
SPECTACULAR WATERFALL

MIDGE HALL
(ABANDONED)

SMALL BRIDGE

PATH CROSSES LARGE TRACK BY BRIDGE

SIGNPOST FOLLOW IT TO FALLING FOSS

CROSS STREAM ON STONES

JOIN PATH COMING IN FROM LEFT

SMALL BRIDGE OVER BECK

LITTLE BECK WOOD

May Beck

KISSING GATE

NEW MAY BECK FARMHOUSE

SIGNPOST 'HAWSKER 4 MILES'

SNEATON LOW MOOR

TURN OFF ROAD AT SIGNPOST AND HEAD ACROSS MOOR. AIM FOR POST AHEAD FIRST. AS YOU DO, LOOK FOR SOLITARY TREE THAT APPEARS IN MIDDLE OF MOOR AND AIM FOR THAT

GORSE BUSHES

PATH RIGHT

SHARP BEND LEFT ONTO ROAD. FENCES TO LEFT AND RIGHT

CAR PARK

0 — ¼ mile
0 — 500 metres
APPROX SCALE

89

91

TRAIL BLAZER

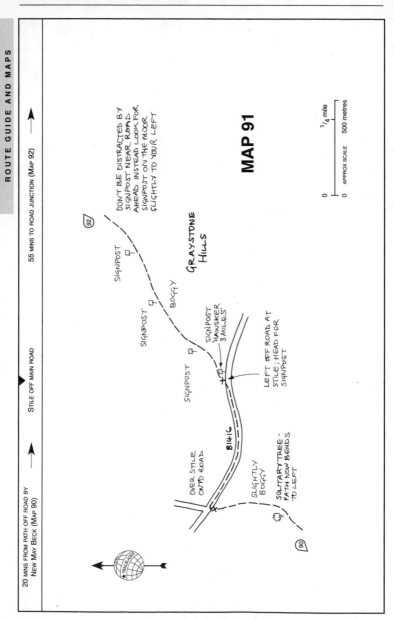

20 MINS FROM PATH OFF ROAD BY NEW MAY BECK (MAP 90)

STILE OFF MAIN ROAD

55 MINS TO ROAD JUNCTION (MAP 92)

MAP 91

SIGNPOST

SIGNPOST

SIGNPOST

SIGNPOST

BOGGY

DON'T BE DISTRACTED BY SIGNPOST NEAR ROAD AHEAD. INSTEAD LOOK FOR SIGNPOST ON THE MOOR SLIGHTLY TO YOUR LEFT

GRAYSTONE HILLS

SIGNPOST 'HAWSKER 3 MILES'

LEFT OFF ROAD AT STILE; HEAD FOR SIGNPOST

B1416

OVER STILE ONTO ROAD

SLIGHTLY BOGGY

SOLITARY TREE — PATH NOW BENDS TO LEFT

0   APPROX SCALE   500 metres

0   ¼ mile

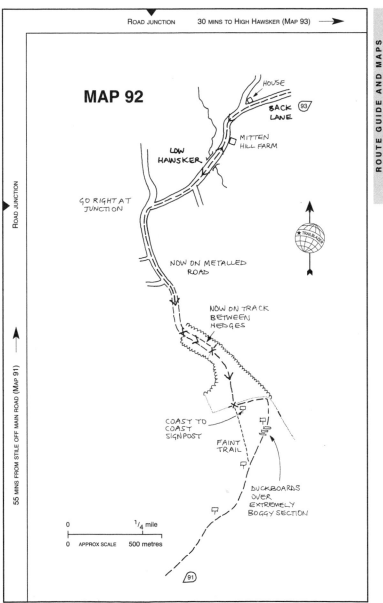

ROAD JUNCTION   30 MINS TO HIGH HAWSKER (MAP 93) ⟶

HOUSE

MAP 92

BACK LANE

93

MITTEN HILL FARM

LOW HAWSKER

GO RIGHT AT JUNCTION

★ TRAILBLAZER

NOW ON METALLED ROAD

NOW ON TRACK BETWEEN HEDGES

COAST TO COAST SIGNPOST

FAINT TRAIL

DUCKBOARDS OVER EXTREMELY BOGGY SECTION

ROAD JUNCTION

55 MINS FROM STILE OFF MAIN ROAD (MAP 91)

0   ¼ mile
0   APPROX SCALE   500 metres

91

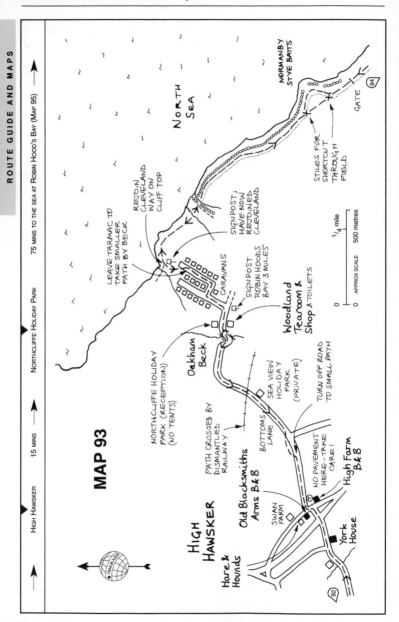

High Hawsker — 15 MINS — Northcliffe Holiday Park — 75 MINS TO THE SEA AT ROBIN HOOD'S BAY (MAP 95)

MAP 93

HIGH HAWSKER

Hare & Hounds

Old Blacksmiths Arms B&B

Swan Farm

York House

High Farm B&B

NO PAVEMENT HERE – TAKE CARE!

TURN OFF ROAD TO SMALL PATH

Sea View Holiday Park (Private)

Bottoms Lane

PATH CROSSED BY DISMANTLED RAILWAY

NORTHCLIFFE HOLIDAY PARK (RECEPTION) (NO TENTS)

Oakham Beck

Woodland Tearoom & Shop & Toilets

SIGNPOST ROBIN HOODS BAY 3 MILES

CARAVANS

SIGNPOST; HAVE NOW REJOINED CLEVELAND

LEAVE TARMAC TO TAKE SMALLER PATH BY BECK

REJOIN CLEVELAND WAY ON CLIFF TOP

NORTH SEA

NORMANBY STYE BATTS

STILES FOR SHORTCUT THROUGH FIELD

GATE

0   1/4 mile
0   500 metres
APPROX SCALE

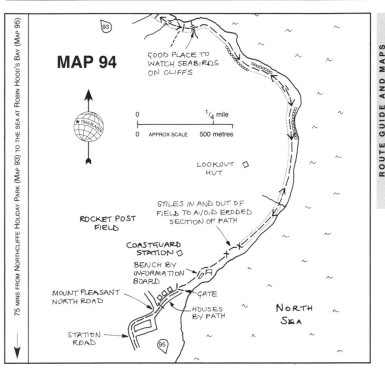

MAP 94

GOOD PLACE TO WATCH SEABIRDS ON CLIFFS

LOOKOUT HUT

STILES IN AND OUT OF FIELD TO AVOID ERODED SECTION OF PATH

ROCKET POST FIELD

COASTGUARD STATION

BENCH BY INFORMATION BOARD

MOUNT PLEASANT NORTH ROAD

GATE

HOUSES BY PATH

NORTH SEA

STATION ROAD

0 ... 1/4 mile
0 ... APPROX SCALE ... 500 metres

TRAILBLAZER

ROUTE GUIDE AND MAPS

(*continued from p208*) Those holding out for a cup of tea in Hawsker could call in at York House (see below), which claims that it serves tea to weary walkers, though most walkers choose to wait a while longer.

In Hawsker there's a pub, the ***Hare & Hounds*** (☎ 01947 880453), serving the likes of ploughmans £6.95 and sandwiches from £4.25 Mon-Sat except Wednesday 12 noon-2.30pm and 6-8.30pm; Sunday two lunch sittings at 12 noon and 1.30pm) – and a number of B&Bs including ***York House Hotel*** (☎ 01947 880314, 3D/3T) with B&B for £29 (£35 for a single) and the ***Old Blacksmiths Arms*** (☎ 01947 880800; 1S,1D, 2T), formerly the oldest pub in the village but now doing accommodation only, from £22.50. Finally, by the road junction is ***High Farm*** (☎ 01947 880907; 1T/2D) offering B&B for £21 per person. From Hawsker, your eastward progression continues down past Sea View and Northcliffe holiday parks (both private) and the ***Woodland Tearoom and Shop*** where you can get last-minute energy for the final stretch from their £4.55 pizzas.

And so you come to the final leg, a reunion with the Cleveland Way and a walk along the cliffs leading into Robin Hood's Bay. It's a straightforward though slightly wearying march, particularly if the wind is blowing in strongly off the North Sea. Though the beach at Robin Hood's Bay appears approximately half an hour before it is actually reached, the village itself, tucked away and sheltered by the headland, hides from trekkers until the very last moment. But soon enough, having passed a **coastguard station** and **Rocket Post Field** (Map 94), you join Mount Pleasant North Road at the top end of Robin Hood's Bay. Take a left at the end of the road here, and follow it down, down, down to the bay. Only one act remains to be done now: to dip your toes in the sea (or, as most people do, the puddles of seawater by the Bay Hotel).

And that's it. The walk is over. Congratulations: you've walked the width of England, a total of 191½ miles (307km), which is certainly something to tell the grandchildren. But there's still one question left unanswered: What are you going to do for an encore?

ROBIN HOOD'S BAY

Robin Hood's Bay is the perfect place to finish, a quaint, cosy little fishing (and, once upon a time, smuggling) village that is entirely in keeping with the picturesque theme of the walk. Though fishing has declined since its heyday in the 19th century, there has been a revival thanks to its crab grounds, said to be one of the best in the north. The bay can also boast the highest sea wall in Britain, 12m high.

The old town huddles around the slipway, row after row of terraced, stone cottages arranged haphazardly uphill from the bay with plenty of twisting interconnecting alleyways and paths to explore. Within there are a number of pubs to celebrate in – a few of them serving decent meals – and tearooms where you can wallow in cream teas to your heart's content. There are gift, souvenir and antique shops aplenty as well, and a **museum** (Tue-Sun, 9.30am-4.30pm; 50p entrance fee) with displays on life in the 18th century and an Albion exhibition.

And what is the connection with Robin Hood, you're probably wondering? Who knows? And after all the effort and energy you've expended over the past fortnight or so to get here – who honestly cares?

Services

There's no tourist office, though the official tourist information **website**, 🖳 www.robin-hoods-bay.co.uk, has plenty of useful information. There's no cashpoint either, though the **post office and general store** (Mon-Fri 9am-5.30pm, Sat 9am-12.30pm) will do cashback if you spend a minimum of £5.

Where to stay

At the very top of the village, *Hooks House Farm* (☎ 01947 880283; 🖳 www.hookshousefarm.co.uk) has a **campsite**; the charge per adult is £5.50. The *YHA hostel* (☎ 01947 880352; bogglehole@yha.org.uk; 80 beds; £12.50) is a picturesque former corn mill located in a ravine known as Boggle Hole, about a mile or so further south from the village and reachable either along the shore or the road inland.

Back in Robin Hood's Bay, at the top of the village is *Thackwood* (☎ 01947 880858; 🖳 www.thackwood.co.uk, 2D/1T en suite), the first B&B you see as the trail comes into town, which charges £30. This is followed by *North Cliff* (☎ 01947 880481; 🖳 www.north-cliff.co.uk; 3D all en suite) also on Mount Pleasant North Rd, a Victorian villa where every room comes with TV. Rates are from £25 per person.

On the same street is the *Manning Tree* (☎ 01947 881042; 🖳 www.manningtreebnb.co.uk; 1T/2D) with a similar standard of accommodation; rates also from £25.

On Mount Pleasant South Rd there is more of the same with the pick of the bunch either *Lee-side* (☎ 01947 881143; 1T/2D) or *Fernleigh* (☎ 01947 880523; 1S/1T/2D), almost next door to each other and both with B&B for £24-26. However, unusually, Fernleigh closes from July to September.

Ahead, on the road junction with Whitby Rd, is the *Grosvenor Hotel* (☎ 01947 880320) with B&B from £27.50, while around the corner, *The Villa* (☎ 01947 881043; 🖳 www.thevillarhb.co.uk; 2D/1T)

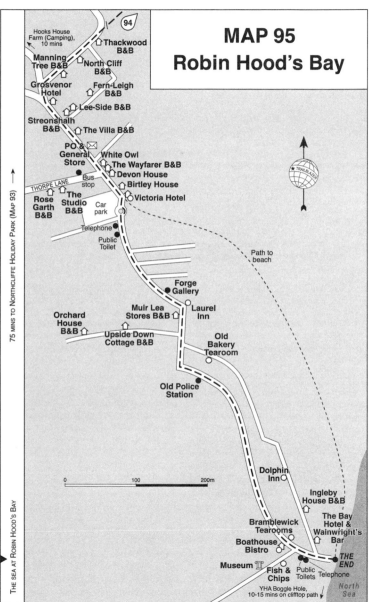

MAP 95
Robin Hood's Bay

94

Hooks House Farm (Camping), 10 mins

Thackwood B&B

Manning Tree B&B

North Cliff B&B

Grosvenor Hotel

Fern-Leigh B&B

Lee-Side B&B

Streonshalh B&B

The Villa B&B

PO & General Store

White Owl

The Wayfarer B&B

Devon House

Birtley House

Victoria Hotel

THORPE LANE

Bus stop

Rose Garth B&B

The Studio B&B

Car park

Telephone

Public Toilet

Path to beach

★ TRAILBLAZER

75 MINS TO NORTHCLIFFE HOLIDAY PARK (MAP 93)

Forge Gallery

Muir Lea Stores B&B

Laurel Inn

Orchard House B&B

Upside Down Cottage B&B

Old Bakery Tearoom

Old Police Station

0   100   200m

Dolphin Inn

Ingleby House B&B

The Bay Hotel & Wainwright's Bar

Bramblewick Tearooms

Boathouse Bistro

THE END

Museum

Fish & Chips

Public Toilets

Telephone

THE SEA AT ROBIN HOOD'S BAY

YHA Boggle Hole, 10-15 mins on clifftop path

North Sea

is another Victorian property, though one that has no en suite bedrooms – a deliberate decision to retain the period features of the property such as the cast-iron fireplaces and the servant bells. Rates are £40/30 sgl/dbl. Further down Station Rd, *White Owl Holiday Apartments* (☎ 01947 880879; 3D/1F) is a detached house divided into a series of apartments. B&B here starts at £26. Next door there are beds for £27.50 at *The Wayfarer* (☎ 01947 880240; 🖳 www .the-wayfarer.co.uk; 4D/1T).

Below, a whole string of B&Bs on Station Rd leads down towards the old village. They're all pretty similar. *Devon House* (☎ 01947 880197; 🖳 www.devon houserhb.freeserve.co.uk; 4D all en suite) is yet another Victorian house with en suite facilities and TVs in all the rooms; B&B starts at £30. *Birtley House* (☎ 01947 880566, 2S/3D/1T all en suite except for one single) is next with B&B from £26 to £29 per person. Below these comes the *Victoria Hotel* (☎ 01947 880205; 2S/8D, all en suite) where all rooms come with TV, hairdryer and radio alarm. Rates are £38, or £50 for single occupancy. Just off Station Rd, there are a couple of simple B&Bs on Thorpe Rd including *Rose Garth* (☎ 01947 880578, 1T/1D), charging £22.50, and *The Studio* (☎ 01947 880862, 1S/2D) with a similar rate.

In the **old village**, most of the accommodation has been given over to holiday apartments for those intending to stay for a week or more. One that hasn't is the B&B above the 300-year-old *Muir Lea Stores* (☎ 01947 880564; 1S/1D/1T), 1 The Bolts; there are no en suite facilities in the rooms

but there are TVs. Rates are from £25. Behind the stores, further along the alleyway known as The Bolts, is *Orchard House* (☎ 01947 880912; 2D/1T) with its own grounds and views over the countryside, charging from £29.50. Not far from the Dolphin Inn is the delightful *Ingleby House* (☎ 01947 880887, 1D) which has one beautifully decorated en suite double room for £45.

Finally, right by the sea is the *Bay Hotel* (☎ 01947 880278; 3D, 2 en suite), occupying the prime location in the village, with a great restaurant and a bar named after the author of the Coast to Coast. It sells various memorabilia of the walk. Rates start at £25 per person.

Other places to stay include: *The Boathouse Bistro* (☎ 01947 880099, 1S/4D/1T/1F all en suite), The Dock, charging from £30 per person (£40 single occupancy); *Upside Down Cottage* (☎ 01947 880564, 1S/1T/1D) from £25; and *Streonshalh* (☎ 01947 881065, 3D/2T all en suite), Mt Pleasant South, from £27.50.

Where to eat

There are plenty of good tea rooms to relax in should you arrive early and need to while away the afternoon. Near the seafront are *Bramblewick* and the *Boathouse Bistro* while further up the hill is the *Old Bakery*. The latter does excellent toasties for £2.75.

For evening dining, it's hard to look beyond *Wainwright's Bar* (12 noon-2.30pm, 6-9pm) at the Bay Hotel, or the *Victoria Hotel* (daily 12 noon-2pm, 6-9pm, no bar meals Sunday evening), both of which do some great bar meals for around

---

❏ **The rescue of** *The Visitor*

A small memorial just above the old village celebrates the heroic rescue of the brig *The Visitor* which ran aground off Robin Hood's Bay during a storm in 1881. With the village's small lifeboat unable to help in such rough seas, the villagers summoned help from Whitby. That night, the lifeboat from Whitby was dragged over the snow to Robin Hood's Bay, a distance of some 8 miles (13km). Sometimes the snowdrifts were up to 2m deep and it took 200 men to clear a path for the lifeboat. Yet having arrived at the bay it managed to launch safely and by some miracle all the crew of *The Visitor* were saved.

£5-7. The Victoria also has a proper restaurant overlooking the sea. Two other cosier pubs are the ***Dolphin Inn*** (12 noon-2pm, 6.30-8.30pm) and the ***Laurel Inn*** with the former also proving to be one of the best places for a celebratory drink in the evening with a good range of real ales and regular live music sessions. There's also a chippy (Mon, Wed 12 noon-3pm; Tue, Thu 12 noon-7pm; Fri, Sat 12 noon-8.30pm; Sun 12 noon-6.30pm) round by the museum.

Transport (see also pp43-5)
Buses No 93 travels between Whitby and Scarborough via Robin Hood's Bay (1-2/hour Mon-Sat, less frequently on Sunday); it takes 20 mins to Whitby and 40 mins to Scarborough. A single fare to Whitby is £2.30. In the other direction the No 93 goes to Middlesbrough (90 mins; 6-8/day Mon-Sat and 1-2/day on Sundays).

If you can't wait for the bus, call Bay **Taxis** on ☎ 01947 880603.

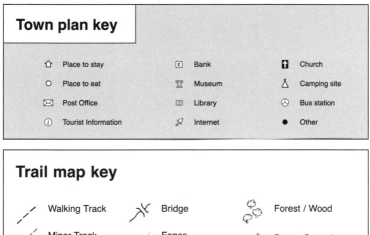

Town plan key

⌂ Place to stay	£ Bank	✞ Church
O Place to eat	⟐ Museum	Δ Camping site
⊠ Post Office	Library	☉ Bus station
ⓘ Tourist Information	Internet	● Other

Trail map key

Walking Track	Bridge	Forest / Wood
Minor Track	Fence	Boggy Ground
4WD Track	Stone Wall	Building
Road	Hedge	Accommodation
Steps	Water	Campsite
Slope	Sand	Church
Steep Slope	Stones	Public Toilet
Stile	Stream	Public Telephone
Gate	River	Bus Stop
		Map Continuation

INDEX

Page references in bold type refer to maps

TRAILBLAZER GUIDES – TITLE LIST

Adventure Cycle-Touring Handbook	1st edn May 2006
Adventure Motorcycling Handbook	5th edn out now
Australia by Rail	5th edn out now
Azerbaijan	3rd edn out now
The Blues Highway – New Orleans to Chicago	2nd edn out now
Coast to Coast (British Walking Guide)	2nd edn out now
Cornwall Coast Path (British Walking Guide)	2nd edn out now
Dolomites Trekking – AV1 & AV2	2nd edn out now
Good Honeymoon Guide	2nd edn out now

Inca Trail, Cusco & Machu Picchu	3rd edn out now
Indian Rail Handbook	1st edn late 2006
Hadrian's Wall Walk (British Walking Guide)	1st edn mid 2006
Japan by Rail	1st edn out now
Kilimanjaro – a trekking guide	2nd edn mid 2006
Mediterranean Handbook	1st edn out now
Nepal Mountaineering Guide	1st edn Sep 2006
New Zealand – The Great Walks	1st edn out now
North Downs Way (British Walking Guide)	1st edn mid 2006
Norway's Arctic Highway	1st edn out now

Offa's Dyke Path (British Walking Guide)	1st edn out now
Pembrokeshire Coast Path (British Walking Guide)	1st edn out now
Pennine Way (British Walking Guide)	1st edn out now
The Ridgeway (British Walking Guide)	1st edn mid 2006
Siberian BAM Guide – rail, rivers & road	2nd edn out now
The Silk Roads – a route and planning guide	1st end out now
Sahara Overland – a route and planning guide	2nd edn out now
Sahara Abenteuerhandbuch (German edition)	1st edn out now

Scottish Highlands – The Hillwalking Guide	1st edn out now
South Downs Way (British Walking Guide)	1st edn out now
South-East Asia – The Graphic Guide	1st edn out now
Tibet Overland – mountain biking & jeep touring	1st edn out now
Trans-Canada Rail Guide	3rd edn out now
Trans-Siberian Handbook	7th edn mid 2006
Trekking in the Annapurna Region	4th edn out now
Trekking in the Everest Region	4th edn out now
Trekking in Corsica	1st edn out now

Trekking in Ladakh	3rd edn out now
Trekking in the Moroccan Atlas	2nd edn mid 2006
Trekking in the Pyrenees	3rd edn out now
Tuva and Southern Siberia	1st edn late 2006
West Highland Way (British Walking Guide)	2nd edn out now

For more information about Trailblazer, for where to find your nearest
stockist, for guidebook updates or for credit card mail order sales visit:

www.trailblazer-guides.com

TRAILBLAZER'S LONG-DISTANCE PATH (LDP) WALKING GUIDE SERIES

We've applied to destinations which are closer to home Trailblazer's proven formula for publishing definitive route guides for adventurous travellers. Britain's network of long-distance trails enables the walker to explore some of the finest landscapes in the country's best walking areas and they are an obvious starting point for this series. These are guides that are user-friendly, practical, informative and environmentally sensitive.

● **Unique mapping features** In many walking guidebooks the reader has to read a route description then try to relate it to the map. Our guides are much easier to use because walking directions, tricky junctions, places to stay and eat, points of interest and walking times are all written onto the maps themselves in the places to which they apply. With their uncluttered clarity, these are not general-purpose maps but fully-edited maps **drawn by walkers for walkers**.

● **Largest-scale walking maps** At a scale of just under 1:20,000 (8cm or 3⅛ inches to one mile) the maps in these guides are bigger than even the most detailed British walking maps currently available in the shops.

● **Not just a trail guide – includes where to stay, where to eat and public transport** Our guidebooks are a complete guide, not just a trail guide. They include: what to see, where to stay, where to eat: pubs, hotels, B&B, camping, bunkhouses, hostels. There is detailed public transport information for all access points to each trail so there are itineraries for all walkers, both for hiking the route in its entirety and for day walks.

West Highland Way Charlie Loram   **Available now**
2nd edition, 192pp, 53 maps, 10 town plans, 40 colour photos
ISBN 1 873756 90 9, £9.99, Can$22.95, US$17.95

Pennine Way Ed de la Billière & Keith Carter   **Available now**
1st edition, 256pp, 135 maps & town plans, 40 colour photos
ISBN 1 873756 57 7, £9.99, Can$22.95, US$16.95

Coast to Coast Henry Stedman   **Available now**
2nd edition, 224pp, 108 maps & town plans, 40 colour photos
ISBN 1 873756 92 5, £9.99, Can$22.95, US$17.95

Pembrokeshire Coast Path Jim Manthorpe   **Available now**
1st edition, 208pp, 96 maps & town plans, 40 colour photos
ISBN 1 873756 56 9, £9.99, Can$22.95, US$16.95

Offa's Dyke Path Keith Carter   **Available now**
1st edition, 208pp, 88 maps & town plans, 40 colour photos
ISBN 1 873756 59 3, £9.99, Can$22.95, US$16.95

Cornwall Coast Path Edith Schofield   **AvailableMay 2006**
2nd edition, 224pp, 112 maps & town plans, 40 colour photos
ISBN 1 873756 93 3, £9.99, Can$22.95, US$17.95

South Downs Way Jim Manthorpe   **Available now**
1st edition, 192pp, 60 maps & town plans, 40 colour photos
ISBN 1 873756 71 2, £9.99, Can$22.95, US$16.95

Hadrian's Wall Path (available May 2006)
North Downs Way (available June 2006)
The Ridgeway (available July 2006)

'The same attention to detail that distinguishes its other guides has been brought to bear here'. **The Sunday Times**

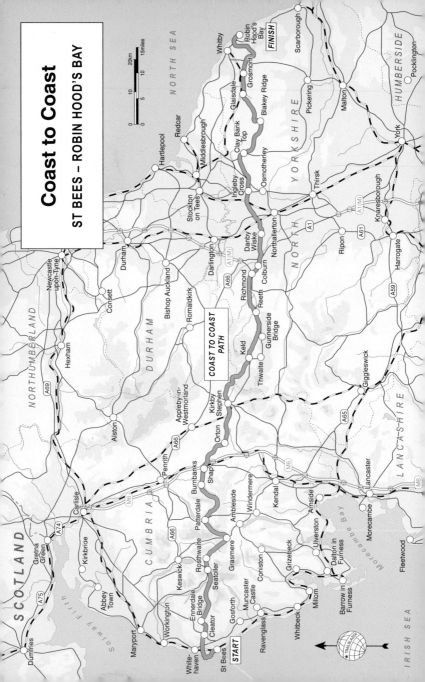